Copyright © 2021 All rights reserved worldwide. Published in the United States.

Disclaimer: The information contained in this book is based on the experience and research of the author. It is not intended as a substitute for consulting with your physician or other health-care provider. Any attempt to diagnose and treat an illness should be done under the direction of a health-care professional. The publisher and author are not responsible for any adverse effects or consequences resulting from the use of any of the suggestions, preparations, or procedures discussed in this book.

Some of the recipes in this book include raw eggs, meat, or fish. When these foods are consumed raw, there is always the risk that bacteria, which is killed by proper cooking, may be present. For this reason, when se1ving these foods raw, always buy certified salmonella -free eggs and the freshest n1eat and fish available fron1a reliable grocer, storing them in the refrigerator until they are se1ved. Because of the health risks associated with the consumption of bacteria that can be present in raw eggs, meat, and fish, these foods should not be consumed by infants, small children, pregnant women, the elderly, or any persons who may be immunocompromised. The author and publisher expressly disclaim responsibility for any adverse effects that may result from the use or application of the recipes and information contained in this book.

CONTENTS

INTRODUCTION 6
ABOUT THE BLACKSTONE FLAT TOP GRIDDLE 6
HOW TO USE THE BLACKSTONE FLAT TOP GRIDDLE 9
  10 Minute Quick-Start! 11
PRO TIPS 13
GRIDDLE & GRILL RECIPES 16

Cream Filling For Crepes 16	Cranberry Brussel Sprouts With Pistachios & Parmesan 29
Airfryer Oreos 16	Ham Fried Rice 29
Black Bean Triangle Bites 16	Sweet And Spicy Mexican Chicken 30
Cheesesteak Pasta 17	Bacon Cheese Burger Dogs 30
Tacos Borrachos 17	Bacon Cheese Burger With Coriander Pickled Red Onions & Smoky Mayo 30
Beer Braised Bratwurst 18	Margarita 31
Carne Asada Fajitas 18	Oklahoma Fried Onion Burgers 31
Thai Kai Chicken Sliders 19	Elevated Avocado Toast 32
Thai Style Beef Souvlaki With Peanut Sauce ...19	Stuffed French Toast 32
Patty Melt 19	Turkey Party Pita Pockets 32
Tequila Chicken Skewers 20	Honey Garlic Chicken Skewers 33
Chicken Caesar Salad 20	Butter Bathed Filet And Lobster Surf & Turf ... 33
Betty Springs Chicken 21	Air Fryer Homemade Sweet And Savory Tortilla Chips 34
Muffuletta Panini 21	Betty's Shrimp Fried Rice 34
Bettys Buffalo Chicken Cheesesteaks 22	Mini Beef Wellingtons 35
Lemon Blueberry Pancakes 22	Chicken Sausage & Vegetable Stir Fry ... 35
Blue Cheese Burgers 23	Cashew Chicken Stir Fry 36
Zucchini Pizza Bites 23	Crepes 36
Griddled Peaches 23	Corn Crab & Cheddar Fritters 37
Steak Frites 2-ways 23	Funnel Cake Swirls 37
Garlic Shrimp With Ponzu Rice 24	Buffalo Ranch Chicken Flatbread 37
Juicy Lucy Bacon Burger 24	Butte Montana Style Beef & Pork Pasty 38
Betty's Thyme Wings 25	Griddled Banana Bread With Cream Cheese Glaze And Candied Bacon 39
Betty's Bigger Better Crab Bahms 25	Chicken Stir Fry Noodles 39
Sausage Gravy Breakfast Totchos 26	Pancetta Green Beans With Shitakes And Cranberries 40
Pickle Brined Chicken Sandwich 26	Bonzai Pipeline Tacos 40
Tomatillos Avocado Salsa Fresca 27	Mediterranean Pork Kabobs 40
New York Style Pizza Dough (fast Rise) ...27	Gochujang Sticky Steak Bites 41
Airfryer Sausage Pancake Muffins 27	
Chicken Cordon Bleu 27	
Pizza Cheesesteak 28	
Hawaiian Chicken Skewers 28	

S'mores Mini Pies 41	Airfryer Mini Spinach And Cheese Quiche 59
Fajitas 41	Buttermilk Syrup 59
Brussels Sprouts With Dried Cranberries 42	Classic Margherita Pizza 60
Grilled Vegetable Italian Quinoa Bowl 42	Mini Chicken Pot Pies 60
Street Tacos With Pineapple Pickled Jalapeno Peppers 43	Air Fryer Spinach, Feta, And Sun-dried Tomato Stuffed Chicken 60
Sausage And Sage Thanksgiving Stuffing 43	Steamed Ranch Carrots 61
Fried Green Tomatoes 44	Sweet Dessert Sandwich 61
Bacon, Egg, And Cheese Pancake Sliders 44	Rosemary Garlic Potatoes 61
Griddled Pineapple And Ice Cream 44	Slammin' Cajun Salmon 62
Nate's Favorite Breakfast Sammich 45	Airy Fryer Breakfast Biscuit Bombs 62
Bacon Fried Corn 3.0 45	Thanksgiving Turkey Breast 63
Shrimp Lejon With Thousand Island Dressing 46	Bbq Chicken Stir-fry 63
Frito Bandito 46	Quick Collards 64
Bbq Chicken Bacon Pizza 46	Betty's Italian Cutlets 64
Korean Fire Chicken Lettuce Wraps 47	Griddled Chicken Street Tacos 65
Octopus 47	Jamaican Jerk Seasoning 65
Caramelized Grilled Pineapple 47	Betty's Bite Sized Chinese Meatballs 66
How To Make Crepes 48	Pulled Pork Breakfast Tacos 66
Maple Glazed Green Beans 48	Cj's Rooty Tooty Fresh And Fruity Breakfast 66
Chicken Bruschetta 48	Thanksgiving Leftovers Grilled Cheese Sandwich 67
Spicy Griddle Pineapple Margarita 49	Onchos 68
Mango Tango Turkey Burger 49	Apple Stuffed French Toast With Bourbon Caramel Sauce 68
Crab Cakes With Grapefruit Salad 50	Huckleberry Pancakes 68
Tumeric Cauliflower 50	Marinated Balsamic Pork Chops 69
Spinach Omelette 51	California-style Salmon Tacos 69
Grilled Shrimp & Arugula Salad 51	Griddled Grapefruit Shandy 70
Amaretto Brioche French Toast With Chocolate Syrup 52	Salmon Street Taco 70
Cheese Chicken Sandwiches 52	Loaded Italian Pork Sandwiches 70
Chicken Parmesan Ranch Sandwich 52	Tequila Party Cake 71
Buffalo Chicken Fritters 53	Blackstone Betty's Blackstone Airfryer Cannolis 71
Salmon With Honey Soy Glaze 53	Buttermilk Pancakes 72
Cranberry Jalapeño Sausage Stuffing 54	Sweet & Spicy Parmesan Pickle Chips 72
Beer Battered Fish & Chips 54	Chili Lime Chicken Fajitas 72
Ricotta Lemon Griddle Cakes 54	Flank Steak With Chimichurri Sauce 73
Portobello Mushrooms 55	Twice Cooked Griddle Baked Potatoes 73
Ultimate Breakfast Platter 55	Bacon Wrapped Beer Battered Deep Fried Pickles ... 74
Ramen Burger 55	Amish Onion Patties 74
Philly Cheesesteak 56	Corn Fritters 75
Bbq Reuben Pork Sandwich 56	Tamari Ponzu Salmon With Sweet Chili Broccoli And Potato Crisps 75
Bacon Blue Cherry Brussels 57	New York Style Pizza Dough (cold Rise) 76
Strawberries And Cream Pancakes 57	Airfryer Biscuits And Maple Sausage Gravy 76
Crispy Steak Bites 58	Greek Tzatziki Sauce 76
Crunchy Crab Melts 58	Crispy Smashed Potatoes With Bacon And Cilantro 77
Marinated Flat Iron Steak 59	

Recipe	Page
Pepperoni Pizza	77
Olive Oil Flatbread	77
Thai Sweet Chili Chicken Pizza	78
Griddle Girl Air Fryer Apple Fries	78
Chicken Piccata Pasta	78
Chorizo Breakfast Hash	79
Griddle Chili Dogs	79
Mexican Breakfast Molletes	80
Pork Cutlets	80
Gouda Ale Sliders	81
Pancake Kabobs	81
Buffalo Blue Cheese Chicken Balls	82
Crispy Cod	82
Ground Turkey Taco Stir Fry	82
Blt Hot Dogs With The Blackstone Air Fryer Combo	83
Garlic Soy Pork Chops	83
Cherries Jubilee	84
Shrimp Scampi	84
Breakfast Sausage & Egg Baskets	85
Savory Candied Sweet Potatoes	85
Wild Caught Jumbo Scallops With Shredded Sprouts & Prosciutto	86
Croque Madame	86
Greek Turkey Burger	87
Fall Harvest French Toast	87
Tomato Salad	87
S'mores Pancakes	88
Pickle Chic Sandwiches	88
Caribbean Jerk Vegetables	89
Bacon Pancakes With Strawberry Whiskey Syrup And Whipped Cream	89
Green Chile Chicken Quesadilla	90
Bacon Chicken Party Dip	90
Hawaiian Meat Marinade And Sauce For Chicken Or Pork	91
Cinnamon Apple	91
Fluffy Protein Pancakes	91
Peanut Butter & Banana Crepes	92
The Lippy Spritz Cocktail	92
Buttermilk Bathed Rosemary Chicken Thighs	92
Betty's Ricotta Doughnuts	92
Sweet Potato Pizza	93
Reversed Sear Ribeye With Smoked Garlic, Zucchini, And Squash	93
Garlic Parmesan Zucchini	94
Betty's Burrata Sandwiches	94
Corn Bread Thanksgiving Stuffing	95
Mongolian Chicken Lettuce Wraps	95
Air Fryer Stuffed French Toast	95
Johnny Cakes With Bourbon Salted Caramel Sauce	96
Whiskey-honey Salmon With Cajun Stir Fried Rice	96
Crispy Salmon Belly Salad With Honey Soy Glazed Shiitakes And Arugula	97
Pasta Primavera	97
Halloween Buffalo Chicken "pumpkins"	98
Easy Cinnamon Roll Bites	98
Crispy Asian Broccoli	98
Blackstone Airfryer Pork Egg Rolls	99
Chocolate Greek Yogurt Pancakes	99
Sautéed Garlic Green Beans	99
Air Fryer Buffalo Cauliflower	100
Pita Bread / Flat Bread	100
Teriyaki Beef Kabobs	100
Sweet Spicy Bang Bang Shrimp	101
Jalapeno Cheese Crisps	101
Chicken Enchiladas	102
Griddled Frozen Pina Colada	102
Boston Cream Pie Pancakes	103
Parmesan Crisp Bruschetta	103
Greek Gyros (pork Or Chicken)	103
Ginger & Soy Glazed Salmon With Asian Green Beans	104
The Better Mac	105
Lamb Lollipops With Mint Chimichurri	106
Bacon Fried Rice With Spicy Mayo	106
Airfryer Strawberry Hand Pies	107
3 Simple Burger Sauces	107
Chicken Steak & Vegetable Hibachi	107
Easy 5 Ingredient Air Fried Calzones	108
Loaded Bloody Marys	108
Bacon Popcorn	109
Zucchini & Squash	109
Marinated Cauliflower Steaks And Veggies	110
Bananas Foster	110
Italian Sausage And Cheese	111
Scrapple And Eggs Breakfast Flatbread	111
Steakhouse Classic	112
Salmon Tacos With Avocado & Corn Salsa	112
Maple Sausage Sweet Potato Hash	113
Steak, Arugula, Pear & Balsamic Flatbread	113
Pomegranate Soy Glazed Lamb Chops	114

Griddle Girl Air Fryer Cinnamon Apple Pie Cups . 114
Pesto-ranch Chicken Artichoke Flatbread 115
Jambalaya 115
Zucchini Fritters 116
Pineapple And Pork French Toast 116
Onion Mushroom Bbq Swiss Burger 117
Air Fried Beef Tacos 117
Thai Chicken Quesadillas 118
Shiitake And Asparagus Risotto With Seared Salmon 118
Sweetbabytots 119
Airfryer Blackberry Scones 119
Enchiladas 119
Buffalo-sriracha Ranch Chicken Sandwich 120
Margherita Grilled Cheese 120
Betty's Upside Down Pizza 121
Bruschetta Crostini 121
Pineapple Chicken And Adobo Crunchwraps 122
Peach Bourbon Cocktail 122
Crispy Sweet Potato Cubes With Cinnamon 123
Chili-mojo Steak Kebabs 123
Griddle Girl Breakfast Pancake Tacos 123
Sesame Seared Ahi Tuna 124
Mini Ham And Cheddar Quiche Cups 124
Elotte 125
Cheese Steak Egg Rolls 125
Pineapple Chicken Quesadillas 126
Hot Honey Tequila Lime Slaw 126
Sweet Potato & Black Bean Burritos 126
Seared Ahi Tuna 127
Croque Monsieur 127
Cheesechicken Sandwiches 128
Healthy Pineapple Chicken 128
Lamb Tacos 128
Marinated Lamb Chops 129
Seared Garlic Ribeye With Carrots, Asparagus, And Gremolata 129

Arugula And Prosciutto Pizza With Balsamic Reduction 130
Bacon Jalapeño Corn Fritters 130
Pastrami Cheese Burger With Smack Sauce 130
Garlicky Sesame Teriyaki Yaki Soba Noodles 131
Bacon Cheeseburger Quesadillas 131
Crispy Buffalo Cauliflower 132
Salmon Potato And Brussel Sprout Boats 132
Marinated Caprese Chicken 133
Country Western Burger 133
Jalapeño Popper Quesadilla 133
Crabby Melts 134
Hot Italian Sausage Rigatoni In Red Sauce 134
Cheese Sausage Stuffing Balls 135
Bacon Fried Corn 2.0 135
Bbq Chicken Cheesesteaks 136
Lo-country Broil 136
Taco Salad 137
Funfetti Pancakes 137
Marinated Steak Tips 137
Grilled Corn Salad 138
Mozzarella En Carrozza 138
Bourbon Berry Lemonade 138
Bacon Jalapeño Popper Burger 139
Family-style Mussels With Red Sauce 139
Zesty Chicken Caesar Sticks 140
Grilled Chicken And Roasted Red Pepper Sandwiches With Fontina Cheese 140
Garlic Parmesan Potatoes 141
Caribbean Jerk Chicken 141
Pesto Ranch Chicken Sandwich 142
Shiitake Cranberry Green Beans 142
Hawaiian Mac Salad 142
New Mexico Breakfast Quesadillas 143
Pretzel Sliders 143

RECIPE INDEX 145

INTRODUCTION
ABOUT THE BLACKSTONE FLAT TOP GRIDDLE

What Does it Do?

The Blackstone Flat Top Griddle provides 720 inches of professional grade griddle for your back yard or really anywhere you go. Now, you can make professional quality meals and get the same results professional chefs achieve every time you cook. Make eggs, pancakes, quesadillas, grilled cheese, steak, potatoes, teppanyaki style foods and more. The Blackstone Flat Top Griddle is designed to produce perfectly even and adjustable heat over four different cooking zones, so you can always have the exact temperature you need at a moment's notice.

The Blackstone Flat Top Griddle is made with professional grade materials and provides professional quality heat in the form of 60,000 BTU of cooking power with four independent cooking zones. This means you can carefully control everything you cook with individual controls for each zone. Eggs don't cook properly at the same temperature as a steak, and the Blackstone Griddle allows you to cook both, perfectly, at the same time.

Are you an avid camper? Do you love to tailgate before the big game? Do you like to cook at friends' houses? Well, the Blackstone Griddle allows you maximum flexibility by letting you take your griddle wherever you need to go. With minimal effort you can remove the flat top, safely fold and stow the legs, and remove the propane tank. Best of all, the griddle comes with industrial grade casters so you can roll the griddle wherever it needs to go.

Because it's built from industrial grade materials, your Blackstone Griddle will be a versatile appliance for many years to come. The frame of the griddle is built with super durable powder coated steel. The burners are made from restaurant grade stainless steel and are guaranteed to produce perfectly even and powerful heat for years to come. Once you've spent some time with your Blackstone Griddle you might even consider getting rid of your more conventional gas or charcoal grills.

Say goodbye to dirty charcoal and matches forever. Charcoal is dirty, expensive, and harmful to your health, so why are you still using it? The Blackstone Griddle uses a standard refillable propane tank which attaches to the griddle with ease. And thanks to the simple push button ignitor, starting your griddle is as easy as pushing a button.

Who is it Good For?

Because the Blackstone Griddle is large enough to cook all the parts of a complete meal at the same time, it is perfect for families who love perfectly prepared backyard favorites like burgers, steaks, and veggies, but it's also perfect for families who love to make big breakfasts. Prepare eggs, bacon, hashbrowns, and pancakes for everyone at the same time.

Do you love to cook big meals on the go? The Blackstone Griddle is perfect for camping and tailgating because of how easy it is to transport and set up. Pack it up for your next camping trip and set it up when you want to make an amazing outdoor meal. The Griddle is also perfect for anyone who loves making fresh grilled food for a professional tailgate party. Since the Griddle easily fits in the trunk of a car, you can take it with you to the game and set it up in minutes. Impress the whole parking lot with the amazing food you make for your fellow fans.

Who is it NOT Good For?

Everyone loves food cooked in the open air, but if you don't have a large enough outdoor space in which to use the Griddle, this may not be for you. A good rule of thumb is that you can use the griddle anywhere you would use a conventional gas or charcoal grill.

A Few Cautions

Because the Blackstone Griddle uses an external propane tank, you will want to exercise caution while connecting and disconnecting the tank. Always make sure all connection points are clean and free of debris. When attaching the hose to the tank, make sure the valve is completely tight before allowing gas to flow to the griddle.

The Blackstone Griddle's cold rolled steel flat top produces amazing results, but because it gets very hot, you should make sure children are always supervised when near the griddle.

What Are its Health Benefits?

Charcoal grilling has been the standard for many years, but it carries a whole host of risks. First of all, charcoal fires increase the risk of fires in your yard. That's pretty bad, but did you know that cooking with charcoal also increases your risk of cancer? The combination of charcoal, lighter fluid, and dripping fats causes a variety of compounds that are considered carcinogenic. And you're not just breathing these chemicals when you cook. They're actually coating your food! Charcoal grills also contribute to air pollution by releasing large amounts of carbon monoxide and carbon dioxide into the atmosphere. The Blackstone Griddle, on the other hand, uses no charcoal and is much safer to use.

A Brief History of Grilling

You may not be surprised to hear that grilling food is a pretty old technique. In fact, it goes back over a half a million years. Early humans found that meat cooked over fire was actually more nutritious than raw meat. The reason? Bioavailability. In short, cooking meat changes the structure of proteins and fats allowing them to be more efficiently digested and absorbed by the body. Until the 1940s grilling was mostly something that people did around campfires, but after World War II and the expansion of suburbs, the popularity of backyard grilling skyrocketed. By the 1950s the back yard BBQ was a staple of family entertaining, and it remains this way today.

Better Than Conventional Grills?

Since the invention of the burger, the debate has raged over whether a grill or a flat top griddle does the best job. While it's true that grills offer burgers a smokier flavor, does that really result in a better burger? After years of research burger experts reached the conclusion that the flat top griddle is actually superior to the grill for one simple reason: It allows the burger to cook in its own juices rather that have all of those juices fall through the grate and into the fire. The end result is a more evenly cooked, juicier, more flavorful burger.

Modern Gas Griddles

When most people think of griddles they either picture a small counter top griddle that you plug in, or a giant flat top that sits in the kitchen of a diner. Because the griddle is so perfect for cooking such a wide variety of foods, the invention of the modern gas griddle makes perfect sense. By marrying the idea of a propane grill with the cooking surface of a griddle, you get an appliance that is both versatile and portable.

HOW TO USE THE BLACKSTONE FLAT TOP GRIDDLE

Setting up the Griddle

Once you have removed the Blackstone Griddle from its packaging, be sure to consult the user manual to ensure you have all of the included parts and fasteners.

Follow the step-by-step instructions to assemble the griddle, and makes sure to place it on a level surface so that it cannot roll.

Once you have fully assembled the griddle, you can use the valve hose to attach a canister of propane.

Learning the controls

The Blackstone Griddle has easy to use controls that will have you cooking in no time.

1. Ignition button: The battery controlled ignition button lights your griddle. Simply press, hold, and the left most burner will light.
2. Left Burner Knob: Turn clockwise to control the heat on the left burner.
3. Left-Center Burner Knob: Turn clockwise to increase the heat on the left-center burner.
4. Right-Center Burner Knob: Turn clockwise to increase the heat on the right-center burner.
5. Right Burner Knob: Turn clockwise to increase the heat on the right burner.

The grilling process

Thanks to the Blackstone Griddle you can make almost anything with amazing results. Because the griddle has four independent zones, you are free to cook different foods at different temperatures at the same time. Unlike conventional grills, this gives you far greater flexibility with one appliance.

Since the Blackstone Griddle features a heavy cold rolled steel cooking surface, you will need to wait a few minutes for the burners to properly heat the surface. To prevent your food from sticking, you should take the time to season your griddle before use. We'll cover the seasoning process in the Pro Tips section. Once you have finished cooking, turn the burners off one by one, and be sure to turn off the valve on the propane tank.

Workarounds

The Blackstone Griddle features an easy to use ignition system, but if you find that the ignition burner is not lighting there are several possible causes. First, check to see if the battery in the ignitor has enough power. If that is not the problem, make sure you have enough gas in the tank. Another problem may be a clogged burner or gas jet. Because food or other debris can fall into the burners, they may become clogged over time. If this is the case, remove the cooking surface and use a damp sponge to clean out the burners or gas jets.

Some users have noticed that the grease drain can allow grease to drip out of the trough and down the leg of the grill, which can cause grease to pool on the ground. In order to combat this, make sure the grease trough and the catch can are properly aligned. Misalignment can cause leaks. Also, make sure to monitor the grease level so that it does not overflow or overwhelm the grease drain. Be mindful of bits of food that may fall into the grease trough as these may also cause the grease drain to become clogged.

If you find that food sticks to the surface of the griddle, there are several causes with simple solutions. First, you may not have properly seasoned the griddle. Because the griddle does not come pre-seasoned you should be sure to do this before using. Your food may also stick because you are adding it to the griddle too soon. Since the heavy cooking surface needs a little time to heat up, make sure that it is at the proper temperature before adding food. You can do this by touching a corner or small piece of food to the griddle. If it immediately sticks, wait another few minutes. Another common cause of food sticking to the griddle, is not giving it enough time to cook. Great chefs know that you shouldn't be in a hurry to flip your food. This is because most foods undergo a chemical reaction called the Maillard reaction which creates a charred layer on the food by raising it to a certain temperature. This reaction is also responsible for what is commonly known as a "sear." Giving your food enough time to sear before flipping will ensure it does not stick.

10 Minute Quick-Start!

The goal of "10 Minute Quick-Start" is to walk you through making your first meal so you "learn by doing" in under 10 minutes. Once you've had a chance to get familiar with how your griddle works, you can begin experimenting with all different types of foods.

Let's get started!

Your First Breakfast

Overview.

Since your Blackstone Griddle has four individual temperature zones you can cook a complete breakfast all at once. This is perfect for camping or for a festive weekend breakfast for the whole family. We're going to start with classic steak and eggs with a side of fried potatoes. This amazing breakfast is sure to excite the entire family.

Collect These Ingredients:

8 large eggs
4 tablespoons vegetable oil
2 russet potatoes, sliced
1/2 yellow onion, finely chopped
1/2 green pepper, diced
2 12 oz. sirloin steaks, about 1 inch thick
Salt and black pepper

Collect These Tools:

Tablespoon
Paring knife
Instant read thermometer
Spatula

Follow These Steps:

1. Light your Blackstone Griddle, and set the right two burners to high and the left two burners to medium heat.
2. Slice the potatoes and vegetables and season with a pinch of salt and pepper. Season the steaks, generously, with salt and pepper.
3. Place the potatoes on the griddle and allow them to cook for approximately five minutes. Then add the onions and green peppers.
4. When the right side of the grill is hot, add the steaks and cook about three minutes per side.
5. When the steaks are nearly finished, Crack your eggs directly onto the griddle surface on the left side. The Blackstone Griddle gives you plenty of room to cook everything at once. Flip the eggs, or leave them sunny side up.
6. Use the spatula to remove the eggs from the grill and distribute among four plates. Remove the potatoes and vegetables and divide them.
7. Remove the steaks and allow them to rest for a few minutes before cutting them in half and adding to the plates with the eggs and potatoes. Make sure to turn the burners off when you're finished and turn off the gas valve.
8. And that's it! you've just made your first complete breakfast on the Blackstone Griddle.

Congratulations!

You now have a perfectly cooked breakfast for the whole family, and you have learned the basics of how to use the Blackstone Griddle!

PRO TIPS

Season the Cooking Surface
Like most high quality cooking appliances, the cold rolled steel cooking surface of your Blackstone Griddle needs to be properly seasoned to ensure optimal cooking results. So you may be asking, "what is seasoning?" Before non-stick coatings existed, there was only one way to make sure food didn't stick to the cooking surface. By creating a layer of burnt on oil, you will not only achieve a perfect non-stick surface, you will also protect the cooking surface from scratches and oxidation. Let's get started. First, use soap and water to thoroughly wash the cooking surface. Use a cloth to dry the surface. Next, apply a small amount of oil to the cooking surface. The best oils to use are those with a high smoke point like vegetable or canola. Use a paper towel to spread the oil evenly across the cooking surface. Turn on all four burners and set the temperature to 275°F. Wait until the oil begins to smoke and the surface begins to darken. Once it is smoking, turn off the burners and allow the griddle to cool. Repeat this process two to three more times until the entire surface is evenly dark. Now your griddle is naturally non-stick and protected from damage and rust.

Keep your Griddle Working from Season to Season
Because you are most likely going to keep your griddle outside, you will need to make sure to do a few things before you store it and before you use it again after being stored. Before you store, make sure to disconnect the gas tank and store away from the griddle with a cap on the valve. You can also purchase a cover for the griddle to keep out insects and dust. When you are ready to start using your griddle again, make sure to check the burner area for spider webs. Webs are flammable and can cause flare ups if you do not clean them out before cooking. Check the level in your gas tank to make sure you have enough fuel to start cooking. Once the tank is attached and you are ready to cook, it's a good idea to perform a new season on the cooking surface. Simply follow the instructions above and your griddle will be good as new.

The Best Way to Clean Your Griddle
After each use you will want to clean your griddle, but your griddle should not be cleaned like regular pots and pans. Since you want to build up a nice coating of seasoning to protect your griddle and get the best possible results, you need to make sure not to use things like dish soap to clean the cooking surface. Most detergents have a grease cutting ingredient and this will eat right through your layer of seasoning. The best way to clean your griddle is the way the pros do in restaurants: with a griddle scraper and hot water. You can purchase a griddle scraper which is designed to get rid of any bits of food left behind without sacrificing the seasoning layer you've achieved. To remove things like fat or sauces, a wash with very hot water will dissolve most things, which you can then scrape away. While you don't have to season your grill after every cleaning, continuous seasoning will ensure that your griddle stays dark and shiny.

Invest in the Proper Tools

Since the Blackstone Griddle is a professional grade piece of equipment, you should have professional grade cooking tools to get the most out of it. While you may have an array of spatulas in the kitchen, to get the best out of your griddle, we recommend buying two long metal spatulas. These spatulas are not only durable, they allow you to transport and flip a large amount of food at the same time. They are also thin and flexible so you can scoop up things like a whole hashbrown without dropping anything. Also recommended are at least one pair of long handled metal tongs which will allow you to reach anywhere on the griddle without worrying about getting burned.

Try Different Cooking Fats

Unlike a traditional grill which allows any cooking fat to fall onto the coals or gas jets, the Blackstone Griddle keeps your cooking fat right where you want it: on your food! Because of this, you can experiment with different flavors of cooking fat to optimize your results. Different oils impart different flavors, but they also work differently from each other. Olive oil imparts a robust and sometimes spicy black pepper flavor that gives an extra richness to food. The problem with olive oil, however, is that is has a pretty low smoke point, which means that over a certain temperature, the oil will start to taste burned. Use olive oil for foods you are cooking at lower to medium temperature, but avoid it for foods cooked over high heat. If you're looking for oil for high heat cooking, try canola or regular vegetable oil. They will allow you to cook to high heats without that unpleasant burnt taste. And of course, butter packs more flavor than almost anything, but it also has a tendency to burn; so use butter for low heat cooking or for foods you plan to cook quickly.

The Ultimate Burger

For centuries, mankind has quested after the perfect burger. Since its invention, burger chefs have argued about the best way to grind it; the best way to form the patties; and of course… the best way to cook it. Some say you have to use fancy waygu beef imported from Japan, some say the best method is high heat over charcoal. Well, we're going to put the debate to rest once and for all. The first key to the best burger you've ever had is fat content. If you go to your local supermarket you usually have a choice between 20 percent fat or 10 percent fat. For the perfect burger, this will not do. The perfect burger has between 25 and 30 percent fat, and the best way to achieve this is to grind it yourself using a combination of chuck and short rib. If you don't feel like doing this at home, talk to your local butcher and tell them that you need ground beef with a higher fat content. Also, but sure to always use freshly ground beef. The longer it's sitting in packaging the more compressed it's getting, and compressed beef is the enemy of the perfect burger.

Once you have the right beef, form it into loose balls about 1/3 of a pound. Don't work it too much, and don't press it together, as you want the balls to just barely hold together. Light your griddle and turn the burners to medium heat. You might think that burgers cook best at high heat, but this is wrong. You want to give your burgers time to let their fat render and develop a nice flavorful sear. If you cook too fast you'll end up with overcooked burgers that are chewy inside. Drizzle a little vegetable oil on the griddle and place the ball on the griddle. Using a grill weight, press down to "smash" the burger as flat as you'd like. Don't reshape it, just let it press onto the griddle and sprinkle with salt. Use your thumb to make an indentation in the center of the burger so that it stays flat. When the first side has developed a nice sear, flip, season with salt and cook for an equal amount of time. This way your burger will have the time to render it's fat and reabsorb it as it cooks. When you've reached the temperature you prefer, remove it from the griddle and allow it to rest for five minutes. Top it however you'd like and enjoy what will be the best burger you've ever had.

GRIDDLE & GRILL RECIPES

Cream Filling For Crepes

Servings:x
Cooking Time:x

Ingredients:
- 32 oz. of Yogurt (Lemon or Vanilla flavor)
- 16 oz. Cool Whip
- Small box of Vanilla Instant Pudding powder
- 12oz of Vanilla Yogurt (Two small containers)
- 8oz Cool Whip (one small container)
- 3-4 TBLS Vanilla Instant Pudding Powder

Directions:
1. Combine yogurt and pudding powder.
2. Fold in Cool Whip.
3. Refrigerate mixture to let the pudding set up.
4. Spread on half of a cooked crepe, add fruit of your choice, and finish with fresh squeezed lemon.

Airfryer Oreos

Servings:4
Cooking Time:15 Min

Ingredients:
- 1 Can of crescent rolls
- 8 Oreos
- 1/8 Cup Powdered Sugar (For Sprinkling)
- Cooking Spray

Directions:
1. Place an Oreo in the middle of each crescent triangle. Wrap it around the cookie making sure its fully covered, and there are no bubbles.
2. Preheat air fryer to medium.
3. Spray cooking spray on air fryer trays, and place 4 cookies in each tray.
4. Cook for 6-7 minutes or until golden brown, then flip and cook another 3 mins.

Black Bean Triangle Bites

Servings:4
Cooking Time:x

Ingredients:
- 1 package wonton wrappers
- 1 can black beans or 2 cups cooked black beans
- ¾ cup corn
- ½ cup minced onion
- 1 tablespoon minced garlic
- 1 tablespoon cumin
- 1 tablespoon chili powder
- Pinch of cinnamon
- 1 egg

Directions:
1. Over low heat, sauté the minced onion and garlic in about 2 tablespoons of oil on the griddle until translucent.
2. Add the cumin, chili powder, and cinnamon to the onion mixture and cook for 2 minutes to allow the flavors to bloom. Add the corn and cook for an additional 2 minutes, stirring frequently to blend the flavors.
3. Set aside to cool in a medium sized mixing bowl.
4. If using canned beans, rinse the beans and drain, removing as much liquid as possible.
5. Combine the beans with the corn and onion mixture.
6. Make an egg wash by whisking together the egg with 1 tablespoon cold water.
7. Assemble the bites by laying a wonton wrapper on a dry work surface.
8. Arrange the wrapper with a point at the top. This will make for easier assembly.
9. Use a pastry brush or even your finger to paint a light coating of egg wash on the left and right side of the wrapper. Start at one of the corners and cover the outer ½ inch of the wrapper with egg wash on the top half of the wrapper. Repeat with the other corner.
10. Place a heaping tablespoon of filling on the bottom third of the wrapper above the lower point.
11. Fold from the bottom up making a triangle. Make sure no filling touches the outermost ½ inch of the triangle.

12. Use your finger to completely seal the top and bottom of the wrapper together. Optionally, you can also crimp the edges of the wrapper for a decorative seal.
13. Pre-heat the air fryer to 400F.
14. Lightly skim-coat both sides of the triangles in oil to promote browning.
15. Air fry for 8-10 minutes or until golden brown and warm throughout flipping at least once.
16. Serve warm.

Cheesesteak Pasta

Servings:4-6
Cooking Time:30 Min

Ingredients:
- 1 lb pasta, cooked reserving 1 cup pasta water
- 1 lb ground beef, (sub shaved ribeye or sirloin)
- 2 green bell peppers, diced
- 1 large sweet onion, diced
- mushrooms, sliced
- ¼ lb provolone cheese, deli sliced or grated
- ¼ lb American cheese, deli sliced or grated
- ¼ c worcestershire sauce
- 4 fresh garlic cloves, chopped
- Blackstone Cheese Steak Seasoning
- 1 tbsp oil
- 1 tbsp butter

Directions:
1. Boil 1 lb of pasta, drain reserving 1 cup of pasta water.
2. While the pasta is boiling, sauté onions, mushrooms and peppers in oil and butter over medium heat on your Blackstone. Cook until tender.
3. On a separate heat zone cook your beef until cooked through, chopping ground beef or separating shaved beef.
4. Combine cooked beef and vegetables together. After mixing together add half of the cheese to melt through.
5. Add pasta to the meat mixture and toss to mix.
6. Add remaining cheese, pasta water and season with Blackstone cheese steak seasoning. Toss together and plate!

Tacos Borrachos

Servings:4
Cooking Time:185 Min

Ingredients:
- 12 Oz. of Blond Beer
- 2 Lb. of Sirloin Steak
- 1 Bunch Cilantro (Finely Chopped)
- 1/4 White Onion (Finely Chopped)
- 1/4 Tablespoon of Black Pepper
- 4 Garlic Cloves (Chopped in Big Chunks)
- 1/4 Cup of Vegetable Oil
- 24 Tortillas (Small, Taquito Tortillas)
- Salt (To Taste)
- 1 Plastic Bag

Directions:
1. Season the sirloin steaks with salt and black pepper, making sure that you rub the salt and pepper well into the steaks
2. Slice the steak into small pieces
3. In a plastic bag, place the steak pieces, onions, garlic, and cilantro. Mix all ingredients together.
4. Once all ingredients are mixed, add little by little the content of the bottle of beer (cold or room temperature) into the plastic bag.
5. Take the air out of the plastic bag and let the meat marinade in the refrigerator between 2 and 4 hours
6. When the meat is ready, drain the beer and place the meat on a plate
7. Pre-heat the Blackstone griddle at medium heat for five minutes. Then, add vegetable oil to the surface and let it get to temperature for thirty seconds. Add your previously marinated steak to the Blackstone griddle.
8. Cook the steak for about three minutes or until the steak is thoroughly cooked, and place in a bowl
9. Spread all remaining steak juices in the griddle, and place the tortillas on top until the tortillas are cooked (the tortillas change color slightly and they become malleable), turning the tortillas from time to time.
10. To make the tacos, place one tortilla on top of the other (two tortillas together). With a spoon place the steak on top of the tortillas and garnish with white finely chopped onion and cilantro . You can also add your favorite salsa as well.

Beer Braised Bratwurst

Servings: 1
Cooking Time: 10 Min

Ingredients:
- 10 Bratwursts
- 2 Bottles of Beer (any Lager or Ale will work)
- 2 Large Onions
- 2 Green Peppers
- 2 Red Peppers
- 1 Stick of Butter
- 10 Bratwurst Buns
- Stone Ground Mustard (or Spicy Brown)
- Kosher Salt
- Fresh Ground Black
- 1 Teaspoon of Garlic powder

Directions:
1. Preheat your griddle to medium-high heat.
2. Place a tin tray or a 9x13″ cake pan on the griddle top (make sure it is does not have a non-stick coating on it).
3. Pour the beer into the tray and add Kosher salt, black pepper, and garlic powder to the beer.
4. Slice the onions and peppers and add them to the beer as well.
5. Bring braising liquid to a low simmer for about 5 minutes.
6. Add all the bratwurst to the braising liquid and simmer for about 5 minutes, turning them once.
7. Move the bratwurst to the griddle top and cook until each side is golden brown. Move the onions and peppers to the griddle at the same time as the bratwurst and cook them until they start to brown as well.
8. Serve the bratwurst on a toasted bratwurst bun topped with the onion and peppers and stone ground mustard.

Carne Asada Fajitas

Servings: 4
Cooking Time: 70 Min

Ingredients:
- 1, 1 lb. outside skirt steak
- 3 limes
- 1 orange
- 2 teaspoons ground cumin
- 2 teaspoons chili powder
- ½ teaspoons smoked paprika
- 1 red bell pepper, julienne
- 1 green bell pepper, julienne
- 1 sweet yellow onion, julienne
- 3 red jalapeno peppers
- 1 tablespoon honey
- 1/4 cup red wine vinegar
- Blackstone Tequila Lime Seasoning
- ½ cup sour cream
- 1 bunch cilantro
- Flour tortillas
- Salt & pepper
- Olive oil

Directions:
1. In a large resealable plastic bag, add the skirt steak, lime juice, ½ of the orange juice, cumin, chili powder, smoked paprika with a pinch of salt and pepper, and a bit of olive oil. Seal the bag and toss the steak to evenly coat. Let marinate for 1 hour.
2. Slice the jalapeno and place into a small mixing bowl. Add the red wine vinegar and honey with a pinch of salt and pepper and mix. Allow to sit for 30 minutes.
3. Pre-heat your griddle to medium-high heat. Add a bit of olive oil and the bell peppers and onions. Add a bit of Blackstone Tequila Lime Seasoning over the top and toss to evenly season. Cook for 3-4 minutes then slides to the cooler side of your griddle.
4. Turn your griddle to High Heat. Take the skirt steak out of the marinade and cook on high heat for 2-3 minutes per side. When the steak is 50% finished, add the sliced orange half to caramelize.
5. In a small mixing bowl, add the sour cream and a few tablespoons of the jalapeno honey liquid. Add a few shakes of Blackstone Tequila Lime Seasoning and mix evenly.
6. Once the steak is cooked to the desired doneness, remove it from the griddle and let rest for a few minutes. Slice the skirt steak against the grain into thin strips.

Thai Kai Chicken Sliders

Servings:1
Cooking Time:10 Min

Ingredients:
- 3 Lb. of Ground Chicken
- 2 Cup of Shredded Carrots
- 1/2 Cup of Chopped Green Onion
- 4-5 Cloves of Minced Garlic
- 1 Cup of Chili Galic Sauce
- 1-1¼ Cups of Diced Red Cabbage
- 1/2 Cup of Mayonnaise
- 1/4 Cup of Sweet Thai Chili Sauce
- 1 Teaspoon of Granulated Garlic
- Chopped Cilantro
- Sea Salt or Pink Himalayan Salt
- Green Leaf Lettuce
- Sweet Hawaiian Rolls
- Ice-Cream Scoop with Lever

Directions:
1. Place 3 lbs of ground chicken in a large bowl. Add shredded carrots, chopped green onion, minced garlic, chili garlic sauce, and some Himalayan Pink Salt. Mix everything together thoroughly.
2. For the Southeast Asian slaw, start with your diced red cabbage in a bowl. Add Mayonnaise, Sweet Thai Chili Sauce, small handfuls of cilantro, and 1 tsp of granulated garlic. Mix everything together to a consistency of a thick coleslaw.
3. Preheat griddle on high, add some olive oil. Use a Ice-cream scoop with lever to place scoops of chicken on griddle. Flip once the bottom is blackened. Once the outside of the patties are seared, turn the griddle to medium-low so the outside won't burn but the middle will continue to cook. Once the patties are finished, place them on Sweet Hawaiian Rolls. Add some Green Leaf Lettuce, and the South East Asian Slaw. Enjoy!

Thai Style Beef Souvlaki With Peanut Sauce

Servings:4
Cooking Time:15 Min

Ingredients:
- 1 lb. 80/20 Ground Beef
- 2 tablespoons Tamari or Soy Sauce
- 3 tablespoons chopped green onion
- 2 teaspoons ground ginger
- 2 teaspoons garlic powder
- Wooden Skewers
- 1/3 cup creamy peanut butter
- 3 tablespoons Thai Chili Sauce
- 2 tablespoons Ponzu
- 1 tablespoon sesame oil
- 2 tablespoons Tamari
- 2 tablespoon, sliced green onion (for garnish)
- 1/4 cup chopped cashews (for garnish)

Directions:
1. In a large mixing bowl, add all of the souvlaki ingredients and gently incorporate evenly. Loosely pack the meat mixture onto the skewers. They should hold together a little softer than a meatball.
2. Heat your Blackstone to medium-high heat and add a bit of olive oil. Cook the Souvlaki for 2 minutes per side until fully cooked.
3. In a small mixing bowl, add all of the sauce ingredients and mix evenly. Use a bit of water to thin it out if you would like.
4. To plate, place the Souvlaki onto a platter and drizzle the sauce over the tops of each. Garnish with the sliced green onions & chopped cashews and serve.

Patty Melt

Servings:1
Cooking Time:10 Min

Ingredients:
- 1 1/2 Lb. of Ground Beef
- 2 Large Yellow Onions
- 12 Slices Rye Bread
- 12 Slices Swiss Cheese (or use half Cheddar Cheese)
- 2 Tablespoons of Dijon Mustard
- 1 Tablespoon of Worcestershire Sauce
- Butter
- Olive Oil
- Salt & Pepper to taste

Directions:

1. Divide meat into 1/4 lb. patties. Use something heavy or the bottom of a pot to smash the patties between parchment paper to about 1/4" thick.
2. Turn the griddle on to medium low heat
3. Slice onions. Put a tablespoon of butter on the griddle with a tablespoon of olive oil. Add all of the onion slices to the griddle and season with salt and pepper.
4. Sauté the onions until they get soft, then add the Dijon mustard and Worcestershire Sauce to the onion and let cook a few more minutes until combined.
5. Transfer the onions to a bowl.
6. Turn the griddle up to medium high and add the burger patties. Season liberally with salt and pepper. Cook until done, then set aside while you assemble the sandwiches.
7. Lay out all the bread slices. Add a slice of cheese, the burger patty, some caramelized onions and top with another slice of cheese. Butter the top and bottom of each sandwich.
8. Turn the griddle down to medium low again and add the sandwiches to the griddle. Cook until both sides are browned and serve.

Tequila Chicken Skewers

Servings:4
Cooking Time:5 Min

Ingredients:
- 3 Boneless and Skinless Chicken Breast, cut into 1/2 inch cubes
- 1 Teaspoon of Garlic Powder
- 1 Teaspoon of Cumin
- 1 Teaspoon of Chili Powder
- 2 Tablespoons of Olive Oil
- The juice of 2 Limes
- 1/4 Cup of Orange Juice
- 1/4 Cup of Tequila
- 1/4 Cup of Fresh Cilantro
- 2 Red Chilies, Sliced Thin
- Salt and Pepper
- Wooden Skewers
- 3/4 Cup of Sour Cream
- The juice of 1 Lime
- 1 Teaspoon of Garlic Powder
- 1 Teaspoon of Chili Powder
- 1 Tablespoon of Tequila

Directions:
1. In a large resealable plastic bag, add the chicken, garlic powder, cumin, chili powder, olive oil, the juice of 2 limes, orange juice, tequila, and a pinch of salt and pepper. Seal the bag and toss the ingredients to evenly coat. Refrigerate for 1 hour to marinate the chicken.
2. In a small bowl, add all of the sauce ingredients and mix to evenly combine. Chill and reserve for later.
3. Remove the chicken from the marinade and build your skewers. For appetizer portions, use 2-3 cubes chicken per skewer, for large portions use more chicken per skewer.
4. With your Blackstone set to medium-high heat, add a bit of olive oil and cook the skewers for 2-3 minutes per side. Turn the skewers often and cook fully. Add a bit more lime juice at the end for a pop of sweetness.
5. To plate, add the skewers to a serving platter and drizzle the sauce over the top. Garnish with the fresh cilantro and sliced red chili's.

Chicken Caesar Salad

Servings:2
Cooking Time:35 Min

Ingredients:
- 1 Romaine Lettuce Head (Large)
- 1 Lb. of Chicken Breasts (Boneless and Skinless)
- 4 Bacon Slices (Thickly Cut)
- Salt and Pepper or Rub (of your choice)
- Olive Oil
- 1 Cup of Croutons
- 1 Cup of Parm Reggiano (Shaved)
- 1 Avocado (Ripe)
- 1/2 Lemon (Juiced)
- 2 Tablespoons of Olive Oil
- 2 Teaspoons of Anchovy Paste
- 2 Tablespoons of Parmesan Cheese (Finely Grated)
- 1/2 Teaspoon of Dijon Mustard
- 1 Garlic Clove

Directions:

1. To make the dressing, combine all the ingredients in a food processor. Blend on high for approximately 30 seconds. Take a rubber spatula, scrape down sides and pulse until dressing is creamy. Set aside.
2. Now you'll cook the meats. Preheat griddle to high heat and coat it with oil.
3. Coat chicken with olive oil and season with salt and pepper or your preferred choice of seasoning.
4. Place chicken breast on griddle and cook until finished. Remove and let rest.
5. Place thickly cut bacon on griddle and cook until finished. Remove and set aside.
6. Turn burners down to medium heat.
7. Lightly oil the head of romaine and season with salt and pepper. Place the head of romaine on the griddle. Rotate it to get a nice char on each side.
8. Slice or cube the chicken and chop the bacon.
9. Place cooked head of romaine on a plate. Arrange chicken around the romaine. Top with avocado caesar dressing, crumbled bacon, parmesan reggiano, and croutons.

Betty Springs Chicken

Servings:4
Cooking Time:20 Min

Ingredients:
- 4 Chicken Breast
- 1 c Mayonnaise (Dukes preferred)
- 8 slices Bacon
- 16 oz Mushrooms, sliced
- 8 oz Cheddar Cheese, shredded
- 4 tbsp Dijon Mustard
- 2 tbsp + 2 tsp Blackstone Seasoning, Whiskey Burger or Chicken and Herb
- 2 tbsp Butter, unsalted
- dried Parsley, garnish

Directions:
1. Trim chicken and lightly pound using the palm of your hand too thin out the thicker end of the chicken breast so that it is even. A thinner chicken breast will cut down the cook time and ensure even cooking.
2. Mix mayo and 2 tbsp Blackstone Seasoning. Whiskey Burger or Chicken and Herb are favorites for this dish. Coat chicken breast with mayo mixture using a bowl or a food storage bag to massage chicken to coat evenly.
3. Turn Blackstone griddle on low heat on one side and add bacon to cook. Remove onto paper towels until ready to use.
4. Meanwhile, on the other side using medium heat add 2 tbsp butter to melt and toss mushrooms in butter. Season with 2 tsp Blackstone seasoning. Tossing mushrooms to cook evenly. Slide mushrooms into some of the bacon fat to add flavor. Remove when cooked through or set aside on low-off heat.
5. Add chicken breast to medium heat and allow to cook 4-5 minutes or until golden brown.
6. Flip chicken, and spread 1 tbsp dijon mustard over each chicken breast. Top with cooked mushrooms, bacon, and a handful of freshly shredded cheddar cheese.
7. Dome to cook through and melt cheese, 4-5 minutes.
8. Remove chicken, plate, garnish with dried parsley.
9. Serve and enjoy!

Muffuletta Panini

Servings:4
Cooking Time:15 Min

Ingredients:
- 3/4 Cup of Giardiniera
- 1/4 Cup of Chopped Kalamata Olives
- 1/4 Cup of Chopped Capers
- 1/4 Cup of Chopped Roasted Red Pepper
- 3/4 Lb. of Sliced Mortadella
- 3/4 Lb. of Capicola
- 3/4 Lb. of Salami
- 12 Slices Provolone
- 1/3 Cup of Sweet Pepper Relish
- 4 Round Sandwich Rolls
- Olive Oil

Directions:
1. Add the Giardiniera, kalamata olives, capers and red pepper to a large mixing bowl. Mix evenly and reserve for later.

2. Heat your Blackstone Griddle to medium heat and add a bit of olive oil. Toast the cut side of the sandwich rolls.

3. Add a couple of tablespoons of the giardiniera mix to the bottom bun of each roll. Add 2 slices of provolone and then a couple of slices of each of the sliced meats. Add a tablespoon or so of the pepper relish and then 2 more slices of cheese over the top.

4. Add the top bun and place back on the Blackstone. Using an XL Griddle Press or bacon weight, press the sandwiches and cook for 2-3 minutes. Flip and press. Cook another 3-4 minutes.

5. Slice and serve hot.

Bettys Buffalo Chicken Cheesesteaks

Servings:2
Cooking Time:20 Min

Ingredients:
- 2 large Chicken Breast
- 1/2 c Wing Sauce, Sweet Baby Rays Mild preferred
- 1/4 cup Ranch Dressing
- 1 tsp Garlic Powder
- 1 tsp Dried Parsley
- Salt and Pepper to taste
- 1 tbsp Oil
- 1/4 lb good quality deli thin sliced American Cheese, Cooper sharp preferred
- 2 foot long Italian Hoagie rolls

Directions:
1. Chop raw chicken into small pieces. This can be done ahead of time and stored in the refrigerator until ready to cook.
2. Preheat Blackstone griddle to medium high heat. Drizzle with oil. Add chicken and toss to cook 3-4 minutes or until cooked through.
3. Lower heat to medium. Season with salt, pepper, garlic, and parsley.
4. Add hot sauce, toss to coat evenly, adding more if needed.
5. Mix in ranch or blue cheese dressing.
6. Add about 6 slices of cheese mixing to melt cheese throughout the chicken.
7. Lower heat to medium low. Divide chicken into two piles, place a couple extra slices of cheese on top of each pile of chicken, and place rolls on top of the cheese for 30-60 seconds.
8. Place one hand on top of the roll using the other hand to slide a long Blackstone spatula under the sandwich and flip.
9. Plate and enjoy!

Lemon Blueberry Pancakes

Servings:4
Cooking Time:20 Min

Ingredients:
- 1 Cup of All-purpose Flour
- 1 Teaspoon of Salt
- 1 Tablespoon of Baking Powder
- 3 Tablespoons of Sugar
- 1 Cup of Evaporated Milk
- 3-4 Tablespoons of Lemon Juice (Juice of 1 whole Lemon)
- 1 Egg
- 1 Tablespoon of Vanilla
- 2 Tablespoons of Butter
- 1 Cup of Blueberry
- Zest from 1 Lemon

Directions:
1. Preheat Blackstone Griddle to medium low.
2. In a large bowl, whisk together flour, salt, baking powder, and sugar.
3. Meanwhile, squeeze lemon juice into another bowl. Add lemon zest (if desired) and evaporated milk. Let mixture sit for 2 minutes, then add the egg, vanilla, and melted butter. Whisk gently until batter is moist with small to medium lumps.
4. Combine wet mixture and dry mixture. Slowly stir in blueberries.
5. Test the griddle by sprinkling a few drops of water on the surface. Water droplets should scatter and sizzle.
6. Brush griddle top with a little melted butter.
7. Pour ¼ cup of batter onto the griddle.

8. Cook until the surface of the pancake fills with small bubbles. Flip pancake and continue cooking until the other size has browned.
9. Serve warm and enjoy with your favorite toppings.

Blue Cheese Burgers

Servings:6
Cooking Time:12 Min

Ingredients:
- 2 Lb. of Ground Beef
- 1 Cup of Blue Cheese
- Salt & Pepper to Taste
- 1/2 Cup of Melted Butter
- 1 Large Red Onion, sliced
- Lettuce
- Tomato Slices

Directions:
1. Preheat Blackstone Griddle to medium-high heat.
2. Mix 1/2 of the blue cheese into the hamburger.
3. Make six 1/3 pound burger patties. Season each side with salt and pepper.
4. Brush Blackstone griddle with a coat of butter. Spread onions onto the butter and cook until softened.
5. Place patties onto the melted butter and cook for 3-4 minutes per side.
6. When burgers are almost done, toast the buns on the griddle until they are golden brown.
7. When the burgers are done, remove them from the griddle and place on the toasted buns and bed of lettuce. Then top the burger with the onions, more crumbled blue cheese, and tomatoes.

Zucchini Pizza Bites

Servings:6
Cooking Time:15 Min

Ingredients:
- Zucchini
- Rao's Marinara Sauce
- Pepperonis
- Shredded Mozzarella

Directions:
1. Slice Zucchini in ¼" pieces.
2. Top with marinara sauce, then pepperoni and finish with a sprinkle of cheese.
3. Set Air Fryer to high heat and coat with cooking spray.
4. Put zucchini bites into air fryer tray and cook for 5-7 mins or until the tops are toasted.
5. Remove and serve immediately.

Griddled Peaches

Servings:8
Cooking Time:10 Min

Ingredients:
- 4 Fresh Peaches (halved and pitted)
- 2 Teaspoons of Honey
- 1 Teaspoon of Cinnamon
- 2 Cups of Vanilla Ice Cream

Directions:
1. Heat your griddle to medium-high heat and cover with a small amount of melted butter.
2. Cut your peaches into halves and remove the pit.
3. Drizzle honey on the cut half of each peach - approximately 1/2 tsp per peach half.
4. Sprinkle cinnamon on the cut half of each peach - approximately 1/8 tsp per peach half.
5. Place on hot griddle - cut half down.
6. Cook approximately 8 minutes (rotating every 2 minutes) or until honey starts to caramelize on the cut half of the peach.
7. Remove from griddle and place in bowl.
8. Top with a 1/4 cup scoop of vanilla ice cream and serve.

Steak Frites 2-ways

Servings:4
Cooking Time:20 Min

Ingredients:
- 4 NY Strip steaks
- 1 bag frozen French fries
- Salt and pepper
- Olive oil
- 1 bunch flat leaf parsley
- 1 bunch cilantro

- The juice of 2 limes
- 2 teaspoons minced garlic
- 1 teaspoon red pepper flakes
- Olive oil
- Salt and pepper
- 1 shallot, minced
- 2 garlic cloves minced
- A few sprigs fresh thyme
- 3 tablespoons Dijon mustard
- 2 tablespoons capers
- ¼ cup heavy cream
- Olive oil
- Salt and pepper

Directions:
1. Pre-heat the griddle to medium high heat.
2. Pre-heat the Air Fryer to medium-high heat then add the frozen fries and cook for 7-10 minutes.
3. Season the steaks with salt and pepper on both sides. Add a drizzle of olive oil to the griddle and sear the steaks for 3-4 minutes per side.
4. Using a sauté pan on the griddle top, add a drizzle of olive oil, shallots, garlic, and fresh thyme. Cook for 2-3 minutes stirring often. Add the mustard, capers, and cream with a pinch of salt and pepper. Stir to evenly combine.
5. In a mixing bowl, add all of the "Chimi-Style" ingredients and mix to evenly combine.
6. Once the steaks are cooked to the desired doneness, add some of the fries to your serving plate and then add the steak over the top. Garnish with one or both sauces and serve hot.
7. Enjoy!

Garlic Shrimp With Ponzu Rice

Servings:1
Cooking Time:10 Min

Ingredients:
- 1 Tablespoon of Olive Oil
- 2 Tablespoons of Butter
- 4 Garlic Cloves, Minced
- 12 Oz. of Shrimp
- 1 Pinch of Salt
- 1 Tablespoon of Freshly Squeezed Lemon Juice
- 3 Dashes Cayenne Pepper
- Chopped Parsley
- 2 Cups of Cooked rice
- 1 Teaspoon of Sesame Oil
- 2 Teaspoons of Soy Sauce
- 1 Tablespoon of Ponzu Sauce

Directions:
1. Turn griddle to medium heat and add the olive oil and butter.
2. Add the garlic and sautÃ© until aromatic.
3. Add the shrimp and stir to combine well.
4. Add the salt and lemon juice, then move the shrimp around to coat it all evenly.
5. Top the shrimp with the cayenne pepper and parsley.
6. Move the shrimp to the side and add the rice to the griddle.
7. Add the sesame oil, soy sauce, and ponzu to the rice. Toss the rice to coat in the sauce. Add chopped parsley and toss some more.
8. Plate the rice first, then top with the shrimp. Sprinkle a little more fresh chopped parsley on top and serve immediately.

Juicy Lucy Bacon Burger

Servings:4
Cooking Time:12 Min

Ingredients:
- 2.5 Lb. of 80/20 Ground Beef
- 4 Pieces of Bacon
- 4 Slices of Cheddar Cheese
- Lettuce
- Tomato
- 4 Hamburger Buns
- Salt and Pepper
- 1/4 Cup of Ketchup
- 1/4 Cup of Mustard
- 1/4 Cup of Mayonnaise
- 1 Tablespoon of Dill Relish

Directions:
1. The trick to making burger magic is having a screaming hot surface to get the perfect sear and crust

on your beef. Pre-heat your Blackstone Griddle to medium-high before cooking to get the best crust!

2. Cook 4 pieces of bacon. Once finished remove from the griddle on drain on a paper towel.

3. On a separate plate, form 8-10 oz. of ground beef into two thin patties. On the first patty, place a slice of cheddar cheese broken up and a slice of bacon split up. Get the second thinly formed patty and seal the two patties. Salt and pepper both sides.

4. Remove most of the bacon fat, and cook burger for 3-4 minutes. Flip the patty, add water, and cover with a basting dome. Cook to desired doneness.

5. Toast buns. Chop up the lettuce and the tomato slices on your cutting board.

6. Flip the buns and remove from the griddle. To plate, add special sauce, lettuce, burger, tomato slices, and more sauce. Best served while still hot.

Betty's Thyme Wings

Servings:2-3
Cooking Time:30 Min

Ingredients:

- 2 lb fresh chicken wings (about 10)
- ¼ cup Extra light tasting olive oil
- 2 tbsp thyme, dried
- 2 tsp coarse salt
- 1 tsp black pepper
- 2 tsp garlic powder
- 2 tsp onion powder

Directions:

1. Cut wings into portions, drums, and drumettes.

2. Pat wings dry with and place in-between paper towels on a baking sheet and let sit in the refrigerator overnight uncovered.

3. Remove wings from the refrigerator and rub them with extra light tasting olive oil. Season wings with salt, pepper, garlic and onion powder, thyme tossing to coat evenly.

4. Allow wings to sit out on the kitchen counter in a mixing bowl at room temp for 30-60 minutes before cooking.

5. Preheat Blackstone griddle to medium-low heat and add wings. Turn wings every few minutes to cook through. Wings should take about 15-20 minutes.

6. Turn heat to high towards the end to crisp the skin to your liking towards the end.

7. Enjoy

Betty's Bigger Better Crab Bahms

Servings:8
Cooking Time:35 Min

Ingredients:

- 2 lbs jumbo lump crab meat
- 1 cup panko bread crumbs
- 1-1.5 sticks of salted butter
- 3/4 cup mayonnaise, Dukes preferred
- 1.5 tbsp white vinegar
- 1 tbsp old bay seasoning
- Flat leaf parsley for garnish
- Cocktail and or tartar sauce

Directions:

1. Mix old bay seasoning with mayonnaise. Carefully add the crab meat and panko without breaking up the meat.

2. Using your hands, carefully form 8 individual dinner size crab bahms (or mini appetizer sized balls) place in refrigerator on a baking tray for 20 minutes.

3. Turn Blackstone's airfryer between medium and high heat to preheat. Line the Airfryers with parchment paper.

4. Melt the butter and the vinegar together, carefully place crab bahms onto the lined trays in the airfryer and pour a spoonful of melted butter/vinegar mixture over the crab bahms right before cooking.

5. Cook for 10 minutes, checking halfway through. Turn heat up to high and let cook about 5 more minutes or until golden brown.

6. Remove airfryer drawers and allow to cool a few minutes before carefully removing crab bahms from trays.

7. Garnish with parsley, lemon and a sprinkle of old bay. Serve with tarter sauce and cocktail sauce. Enjoy!

Sausage Gravy Breakfast Totchos

Servings: 4-6
Cooking Time: 30 Min

Ingredients:
- 1 lb ground sausage, (any flavor works)
- 4 tbsp butter, unsalted
- 4 tbsp all purpose flour
- 1 cup milk
- 1 cup half and half
- 1/4 tsp black pepper
- 1/4 tsp salt
- 1/4 tsp garlic powder
- 1/4 tsp onion powder
- 1/4 tsp sage
- 1/4 paprika
- 1 package frozen tater tots
- eggs
- 1 block of cheddar cheese, shredded

Directions:
1. Cook ground sausage, using your Blackstone scraper chop up the sausage into small pieces saving all the sausage grease.
2. In a deep skillet on high heat add the butter to melt, whisk in the flour until golden brown and fragrant, about 1-2 minutes.
3. Add the milk and half and half continue to whisk until it begins to thicken.
4. Add the sausage and the reserved grease from the sausage along with all the dry seasonings. Note if using a flavored sausage, or spicy sausage then dry seasonings are not needed.
5. Cook frozen tots on griddle starting on low heat to thaw, adjust heat to medium and drizzle with a light coating of vegetable oil sliding your spatula under the tots to help them roll without breaking to cook on each side evenly until crispy.
6. While tots are finishing up cooking, cook as many eggs as desired. Assemble a serving platter with tots, cheese, sausage gravy and eggs. Enjoy!

Pickle Brined Chicken Sandwich

Servings: 4
Cooking Time: x

Ingredients:
- 4 boneless skinless chicken thighs
- 1 cup pickle juice
- 1 egg
- 2 tablespoons oil
- 2 cups panko breadcrumbs
- 8 pickle slices
- 1 can Jumbo biscuits
- Mayonnaise (optional)

Directions:
1. Trim any extra fat from chicken thighs and discard. If necessary, lightly pound chicken thighs to lower any high spots and make the cutlet an even thickness.
2. Marinade chicken thighs in pickle juice 12-48 hours. Discard the pickle juice when marinade is complete.
3. Preheat air fryer to medium high for 10 minutes.
4. Cook canned or frozen jumbo biscuits in the air fryer based on manufacturers directions. NOTE: Because the air fryer will cook quicker than a normal oven, be sure to check the biscuits at half the time the manufacturer recommends. Typically, the air fryer will cook 25% quicker than a normal oven, so plan accordingly and monitor the biscuits frequently.
5. When done, set biscuits aside and allow them to cool.
6. Whisk egg and oil until well combined.
7. Pat chicken thighs dry with a paper towel. Dredge chicken one piece at a time in egg mixture and then panko breadcrumbs to coat completely.
8. Place breaded chicken in the air fryer and cook for 20-25 minutes or until internal temperature is above 165F and the exterior is browned.
9. Place chicken thigh cutlet on a fresh biscuit. Top with mayonnaise (if desired) and pickles.

Tomatillos Avocado Salsa Fresca

Servings:x
Cooking Time:x

Ingredients:
- 5 Tomatillos Quartered
- 1 Large Avocado
- 4-5 Fresh Garlic Cloves, whole
- 1/2 - 1 Whole Jalapeno
- Juice of One Large Lime
- 1/2 White Onion, finely chopped
- 1 Bunch of Cilantro, finely chopped
- 1/4 Cup of Water
- Salt to Taste

Directions:
1. Blend together tomatillos, avocado, garlic cloves, jalapeno, and water until smooth. Pour into a large mixing bowl.
2. Mix in finely chopped cilantro and white onion.
3. Add salt to taste. Add more water if needed; salsa should be on the thinner side.

New York Style Pizza Dough (fast Rise)

Servings:1
Cooking Time:10 Min

Ingredients:
- 4 Cups of Bread Flour
- 1 and 1/2 Cups of Warm Water
- 1 Teaspoon of Isntant Dry Yeast
- 4 Teaspoons of Sugar
- 2 Teaspoons of Salt
- 4 Teaspoons of Olive Oil

Directions:
1. Add water, flour, yeast, sugar and salt together in a large bowl. Don't add the oil yet. You want the flour to hydrate first before adding oil.
2. Mix the dough until most of the flour is incorporated.
3. Add the oil and knead your dough for 5-10 minutes.
4. Cover dough and let it rest for 10-15 minutes.
5. Divide the dough into 3 pieces and round into balls. Wipe the dough balls with oil or cooking spray.
6. Cover dough balls and let rise for about an hour.

Airfryer Sausage Pancake Muffins

Servings:4
Cooking Time:20 Min

Ingredients:
- 2 Cups Pancake Mix
- 1 ½ Cups Water
- 1 tsp Vanilla
- 1 Package Jimmy Dean Maple Sausage
- Syrup
- Cooking Spray

Directions:
1. In a mixing bowl, combine pancake mix, water, and vanilla to make the pancake batter. Set to the side.
2. Heat Air Fryer to medium. Spray trays with cooking spray.
3. Roll sausage into 1" balls, and place in the air fryer. Cook for 5-6 minutes.
4. Remove sausage balls and place on a paper towel.
5. Spray silicone muffin cups with cooking spray, and add 1 tablespoon pancake batter into the bottom. Add 1 meat ball to each cup, and cover with another 1-2 tablespoons of batter.
6. Add muffin cups to air fryer and cook for 8-10 minutes or until the tops are golden brown.
7. Remove the muffins from the cups, place on a plate, and drizzle with syrup.
8. Enjoy!

Chicken Cordon Bleu

Servings:x
Cooking Time:x

Ingredients:
- 1 half boneless skinless chicken breast
- 1 slice deli ham (honey, maple, or Black Forest work best)
- 1 slice Swiss cheese
- 1 cup bread crumbs

- 1 cup oil
- Salt and Pepper
- Toothpicks

Directions:
1. Pre-heat your air fryer to 400F.
2. Butterfly the chicken by slicing through the middle of the breast with the knife horizontal to your cutting board. Be careful to not cut all the way through the chicken. You should get close to the edge but not entirely slice through.
3. Season the inside or cut side of the chicken with salt and pepper.
4. Place the cheese onto the ham and fold the ham around the cheese so it fits inside of the chicken.
5. Fold the chicken over the ham and secure the seams with 2-3 toothpicks.
6. Dredge the chicken bundle first into the oil, and then into the breadcrumbs, making sure the chicken is evenly coated. Repeat on any thinly covered spots if necessary.
7. Place the chicken breast into the air fryer and cook for 12-14 minutes until the chicken breast reaches an internal temperature of 165F.
8. Remove from the air fryer and remove all toothpicks.
9. Serve warm

Pizza Cheesesteak

Servings:4
Cooking Time:20 Min

Ingredients:
- 2, 8 oz. Ribeye steaks
- Blackstone Steakhouse Seasoning
- 4 Roma Tomatoes, sliced
- 1 tablespoon chopped fresh Oregano
- 1 tablespoon chopped fresh Basil
- 8 slices Mozzarella Cheese
- 8 large slices Pepperoni
- 2 foot long Italian Hoagie rolls
- 1 cup Rao's Pizza Sauce
- Olive oil

Directions:
1. Heat your griddle to high heat. Add a bit of olive oil to the steaks and then add as much Blackstone Steakhouse seasoning as you like. Cook the steaks over high heat for 2 minutes per side and then remove from the heat and cut into small bite-sized pieces.
2. Reduce the heat to medium-low and add the steak pieces back to the griddle arranged into 2 lines the same shape as the hoagie rolls. .
3. Add 4 slices of tomato over the top of each pile of meat, then a few pinches of basil and oregano, add a few slices of peperoni and then the mozzarella over the top. Cover with a dome and melt the cheese for 2 minutes.
4. While the cheese is melting, toast the cut side of the hoagies in a bit of olive oil and then add some of the pizza sauce to both of the cut sides.
5. To plate, remove the dome and using 2 spatulas, add the meat and melty cheese to the hoagie roll, slice and serve hot.
6. Enjoy

Hawaiian Chicken Skewers

Servings:x
Cooking Time:x

Ingredients:
- 1 Package Chicken Tenders, around 2-2 1/2 LBS, Cut into Bite Size Pieces
- 1 Red Onion, Chopped into Bite Size Pieces
- 1 Handful Fresh Cilantro, chopped
- Kabob Sticks
- 1 Tablespoon of Olive Oil
- 1/4 Cup of Low Sodium Soy Sauce
- 3/4 Cup of Pineapple Juice, from can of pineapple
- 1/4 Cup of Brown Sugar, packed
- 1/4 Cup of Ketchup
- 3 Garlic Cloves, grated
- 1/2 Teaspoon of Ground Ginger
- Sea Salt and Fresh Black Pepper, to taste
- 20 Oz. of Can Pineapple Chunks in 100% Pineapple Juice (can substitute for fresh pineapple)
- 1/2 Cup of Brown Sugar

Directions:
1. Soak kabob sticks in water for at least 20 minutes. Marinate the chicken in a freezer bag for at least 2 hours to overnight. Marinate your pineapple 30 minutes to 2 hours.

2. Assemble your skewers with chicken, pineapple, and red onions in a deep container or dish. You want to reserve some, not all, of the marinade in there from assembling to use while cooking!

3. Heat your Blackstone to medium-high heat and add your skewers, lining them up across the griddle.

4. Cook for 3 minutes and drizzle a little extra marinade across the skewers. The steam will help cook the chicken and keep it moist.

5. Cook 1 additional minute. Turn griddle to medium-low heat and flip skewers cooking 3 more minutes or until chicken is cooked.

6. Remove skewers and let rest 5 minutes. Garnish with sea salt and cilantro.

Cranberry Brussel Sprouts With Pistachios & Parmesan

Servings:x
Cooking Time:x

Ingredients:
- 1-1/2 Lb. of Shaved Brussels Sprouts
- Avocado Oil
- 1/2 Yellow Onion, sliced
- Salt & Pepper for Seasoning (about 1/2 teaspoon each)
- 1/2 Cup of Dried Cranberries
- 1/2 Cup of Pistachios (roasted & shelled)
- 1/4 Cup of Red Wine Vinegar (drizzle over the whole dish)
- 1/2 Cup of Parmesan Cheese (grated or shaved ribbons)

Directions:
1. Preheat the Blackstone to medium high. Note: Do not leave the griddle alone or preheat for too long, as this could warp the griddle top.
2. Add avocado oil to the griddle. Add sliced onion and Brussels sprouts. Drizzle a little more avocado oil on top.
3. Spread Brussels sprouts out so they are easier to season. Season liberally with salt and pepper.
4. Toss until well mixed, then add some water and cover with a basting dome.
5. Let steam for a couple minutes, then toss them and add more water to steam if they're not done. It shouldn't take more than 5 minutes total.
6. Once they're cooked through, take off the dome and let them sit on the hot griddle to get a good char.
7. Remove the Brussels sprouts from the griddle and put them in a bowl. Add the dried cranberries, pistachios, red wine vinegar, and Parmesan cheese. Toss all together.
8. Garnish with Parmesan ribbons.

Ham Fried Rice

Servings:1
Cooking Time:10 Min

Ingredients:
- 4 Cups of Cooked Rice
- 1 Lb. of Diced Ham
- 1 Onion
- 4-6 Garlic cloves, Minced
- 1 Tablespoon of Minced Fresh Ginger (or 1 tsp Ground Ginger)
- 1/4 Teaspoon of Ground Black Pepper
- One 12 Oz. of Bag of Frozen Peas and Carrots
- 1 Tablespoon of Butter
- 3 Eggs
- 4 Green Onions, Diced
- 3 Tablespoons of Soy Sauce
- Juice from 1 Lemon

Directions:
1. Preheat your griddle to medium high heat.
2. Put some oil on the griddle.
3. Start sautéing the onion and cook until onions start to get soft. Add garlic, ginger, and black pepper. Cook until fragrant.
4. Next to the onions, add a little more oil and add the frozen peas and carrots and the diced ham to the griddle.
5. Add the cooked rice on top of the onion, garlic, and ginger mix. Toss to combine.
6. When the peas, carrots, and diced ham are heated through, combine with the rice. Mix everything thoroughly.

7. Melt the butter on the griddle and add the 3 eggs. Scramble until fully cooked, then incorporate into the rice mixture.
8. Add soy sauce, green onions, and lemon juice to the rice. Toss to combine. Add more soy sauce to taste.
9. Remove from griddle and serve warm.

Sweet And Spicy Mexican Chicken

Servings:8
Cooking Time:25 Min

Ingredients:
- 3.5 Oz. of Achiote Paste
- 1 Orange (Fresh)
- 1/2 Red Onion (Cut in Quarters)
- 2 Oz. of White Vinegar
- 2 Lb. of Chicken Legs
- 2 Lb. of Chicken Thighs
- 1/4 Stick of Butter

Directions:
1. Place the achiote paste in a medium-size bowl. Add juice from a fresh orange, vinegar and mix all ingredients until completely diluted - no chunks.
2. In another bowl, place a plastic bag. Add the chicken legs and half of the achiote mix. Then, rotate the bag until legs are covered entirely by the mix. Add half of the onions, then close the bag and make sure to remove its air.
3. Repeat the plastic bag process for the chicken thighs.
4. Preheat the griddle at medium level for 5 minutes. Add butter, and spread it on the surface. Put the chicken legs and thighs and cook turning pieces around from time to time. Cooking takes about 15 minutes at 176 degrees.

Bacon Cheese Burger Dogs

Servings:4
Cooking Time:10 Min

Ingredients:
- 3/4 Lb. of 80/20 Ground Beef
- 4 Pieces of Bacon
- 4 Pieces of American Cheese
- 1/3 Cup of Yellow Onion, Diced
- 4 Hot Dog Buns
- Salt and Pepper
- Ketchup and Mustard (optional)

Directions:
1. Heat your Blackstone to medium heat and cook the bacon until well done, about 5-6 minutes. Once the bacon is finished, remove from the griddle and drain on a paper towel.
2. Lay out a sheet of plastic wrap on your cutting board and place 1/4 of the ground beef in the center. Using your fingers, flatten out the ground beef into a rectangle slightly longer than your hot dog buns. Season with salt and pepper and lay 1 piece of bacon in the middle. Cut the cheese in half and lay over the bacon. Add a bit of diced onion.
3. Using the plastic wrap, roll the ground beef around the bacon and cheese to form a "link". It should look like a sausage or a hot dog. Be sure to pinch the edges and seal the gaps for a tight burger dog. Season with a bit more salt and pepper.
4. Cook the burger dogs in the bacon grease for 2-3 minutes per side, or until cooked to desired doneness.
5. To plate, add the burger dogs to the buns and add any condiment you like.

Bacon Cheese Burger With Coriander Pickled Red Onions & Smoky Mayo

Servings:4
Cooking Time:15 Min

Ingredients:
- 1 ½ pounds 80/20 ground beef
- 8 pieces thick cut applewood smoked bacon
- 1 large red onion, thinly sliced
- 1/3 cup red wine vinegar
- 1 tablespoon ground coriander
- ¼ cup mayonnaise
- ¼ cup sour cream
- 1 tablespoon smoked paprika
- 1 teaspoon ground chipotle
- The juice of 1 lime

- 1 cup shredded lettuce
- 4 slices cheddar cheese
- 4 seeded hamburger buns
- Salt and pepper
- Olive oil

Directions:
1. In a small mixing bowl, add the onions, red wine vinegar a little drizzle of olive oil, ground coriander and a pinch of salt and pepper. Mix evenly and set aside to marinate for later.
2. Heat your griddle to medium heat and cook the bacon well done and crisp. Once its finished, drain on some paper towel.
3. Form the ground beef into 4 equal patties and season both sides with salt & pepper. Cook in the bacon fate for 3-4 minutes per side or until desired doneness.
4. In a small mixing bowl, add the mayo and sour cream with the smoked paprika, chipotle, lime juice and a pinch of salt and pepper. Mix to evenly incorporate.
5. Slice the bacon to fit on top of the burger. Once the burgers are finished, add a few pieces of bacon and then top with a slice of cheese. Cover with a dome to melt.
6. Lightly toast the buns and add some of the sauce to the bottom bun.
7. Add some lettuce to the bottom bun and then the burger, add some of the pickled onions over the top and then the top bun. Serve hot.

Margarita

Servings:4
Cooking Time:15 Min

Ingredients:
- 4 Oz. of Tequila
- 4 Oz. of Triple Sec
- 12 Limes, Cut in Half
- 4 Oz. of Simple Syrup (Equal parts sugar and water)
- Sprite OR Lime Soda

Directions:
1. Set your griddle to high heat. Slice 12 limes in half and dry off with a paper towel. On one side of your griddle, add a very thin layer of vegetable oil and place the limes cut side down and cook for 5 - 6 minutes, or until the limes are caramelized and golden.
2. In a plastic container add equal parts water and sugar to make your simple syrup. Seal the container and shake until sugar is dissolved.
3. To make your cocktail, in a cocktail shaker add ice, 4 - 5 griddled limes squeezed, 2 ounces of tequila, 2 ounces of triple sec, 2 ounces of simple syrup and shake well. In a margarita glass rub the rim with a lime wedge and salt the rim. Then add ice and pour your cocktail ingredients over the ice. Add a splash of lime soda and garnish with a lime wedge.

Oklahoma Fried Onion Burgers

Servings:4
Cooking Time:5 Min

Ingredients:
- 1/2 Lb. of 80/20 Ground Beef
- 1 Vidalia Onion (sliced paper thin)
- 4 Slices American Cheese
- 1/4 Cup of Dill Pickle Chips
- Salt

Directions:
1. Pre-heat your Blackstone to high heat.
2. Make 2 oz. loosely packed meatballs with the ground beef and place on the hot griddle. Add a pinch of salt over each and using your flat spatula, smash them very thin.
3. Add 2-3 ounces of thinly sliced onion over each patty.
4. Cook for 60-90 seconds and flip so that the onion's are under the patty. Add 1 slice of American cheese to each patty and then place the top bun over the cheese and then the bottom bun on top of the top bun. Cook for another 60 seconds.
5. To plate, remove the bottom bun from the top, using your spatula, lift the burger with top bun and add to the bottom bun.
6. Serve hot with a few dill pickle chips.

Elevated Avocado Toast

Servings:x
Cooking Time:x

Ingredients:
- Whole Grain Bread
- Ripe Avacado
- Eggs
- Tajin Seasoning
- Cotija Cheese
- Grape Tomatoes, cut in halves
- Green Tabasco (optional)

Directions:
1. Heat Blackstone to low heat and put bread on to start toasting.
2. Add small amount of butter or oil to cook eggs in if desired.
3. Crack one egg per toast and add salt and pepper to eggs.
4. Cut avocado in half and slice thinly. Spread across toast & season with salt, pepper, and Tajin seasoning.
5. Add grape tomato halves.
6. Add over easy egg on top of the avocado.
7. Sprinkle with Cotija cheese and extra Tajin seasoning. If desired, top with green Tabasco sauce.

Stuffed French Toast

Servings:4
Cooking Time:20 Min

Ingredients:
- 8 Oz. of Cream Cheese, Softened
- 2/3 Cup of Powdered Sugar
- 2 Teaspoons of Almond Extract
- 2 Tablespoons of Milk
- 2 Cups of Raspberries
- 1/4 Cup of Slivered Almonds
- 12-16 Slices Stale French Bread
- 4 Eggs
- 1 Cup of Half and Half

Directions:
1. In a large bowl, mix the cream cheese, powdered sugar, almond extract, and milk. Add milk a tablespoon at a time to reach desired consistency.
2. Lay slices of bread out in pairs and spread mixture evenly on all of them. On one side of each pair put raspberries and almonds.
3. Fold the pieces of bread together to form a sandwich.
4. In another bowl whisk together eggs, half and half, and a pinch of salt.
5. Preheat the griddle to medium heat.
6. Soak both sides of each sandwich in the egg mixture and set aside to rest.
7. Melt butter on the griddle and place each stuffed French toast on the griddle and cook until each side is browned and cooked through.
8. Remove from heat, dust with powdered sugar, top with any remaining raspberries and almonds, and maple syrup.

Turkey Party Pita Pockets

Servings:8
Cooking Time:25 Min

Ingredients:
- 2 Lb. of Ground Turkey
- 1 Cup of Cheddar Cheese, Shredded
- 1 Teaspoon of Onion Powder
- 1 Teaspoon of Paprika
- 1 Teaspoon of Cumin
- 1 Tablespoon of Chili Powder
- 1/2 Teaspoon of Pink Sea Salt
- 3-4 Garlic Cloves, Grated
- 1/2 Cup of Green Onions, Sliced
- 4 Rounds Pita Bread, Cut in Halves

Directions:
1. In a large mixing bowl, combine all ingredients.
2. Roll out meatballs (makes about 26) and slightly press down to flatten some for even cooking on the griddle.
3. Turn your Blackstone on medium to medium-high heat and drizzle a light coating of olive oil.
4. Cook Turkey balls/patties on each side for about 5 minutes per side using, your dome midway for about 1-2 minutes to help cook through.
5. If desired, place your pita pockets onto hot griddle to slightly heat/toast.
6. Add your favorite toppings like cheese, tomatoes, guacamole, fresh salsa fresca, sour cream, lettuce, jalapenos and cilantro.

Honey Garlic Chicken Skewers

Servings:4
Cooking Time:30 Min

Ingredients:
- 2 Tablespoons of Vegetable oil
- 2 Tablespoons of Sesame oil
- 3 Garlic Cloves, Minced
- 1/3 Cup of Soy Sauce
- 1/3 Cup of Honey
- 4 Chicken Breasts, Chopped into Bite-Sized Pieces
- 2 Red Bell Peppers, Chopped into Chunks
- 1 Onion, Peeled and Sliced into Chunks
- 2 Tablespoons of Sesame Seeds
- 2 Tablespoons of Fresh Cilantro, Roughly Chopped

Directions:
1. Mix together all marinade ingredients in a sealable plastic gallon bag.
2. Add chicken to marinade, seal in bag, and knead bag to coat thoroughly. Let sit in refrigerator 1-8 hours, turning occasionally.
3. Soak wooden skewers for 30 minutes to prevent burning; metal skewers require no pre-cook treatment.
4. Heat your griddle to medium-high heat.
5. Alternate threading chicken, pepper, and onion onto your skewer. Continue until the entire skewer is full and all your skewers have been used.
6. Coat griddle surface with 1 Tbsp extra virgin olive oil.
7. Place skewers on griddle and turn every 2-3 minutes for 8-10 minutes until chicken is cooked (no longer pink in the middle or internal temperature reaches 165 degrees).
8. Plate your skewers on a platter and sprinkle with sesame seeds and cilantro.

Butter Bathed Filet And Lobster Surf & Turf

Servings:4
Cooking Time:20 Min

Ingredients:
- 4, 6-8 oz. Filet Mignon
- 4 Lobster Tails
- 2 stick of Unsalted Butter
- A few sprigs of Fresh Rosemary
- A few sprigs of Fresh Thyme
- 2 cloves Fresh Garlic, rough chop
- 1 Lemon
- A handful of Asparagus
- 2 pints Mushrooms
- Blackstone Steakhouse Seasoning
- Olive Oil

Directions:
1. Pre-heat the Blackstone Air Fryer to medium-high heat.
2. To prep the lobster, using shears, cut the top of the shell through the middle all the way to the tail leaving the last rib connected. Squeeze the shell so that the bottom section cracks and releases. While keeping the meat connected at the end of the tail, pull the lobster meat out and over the top of the cut shell. Using a sharp knife, make shallow cuts to create a "cross hatch" pattern on the surface of the lobster meat.
3. Heat one side of your griddle to medium and add a small sauce pot. Add the butter, herbs and garlic and melt.
4. Heat the other side of your griddle to high heat and add a drizzle of olive oil.
5. Season your steaks with Blackstone Steakhouse seasoning generously on all sides and cook on high heat for 2-3 minutes per side.
6. Add a bit of the melted butter over the tops of each lobster tail and season with Blackstone Steakhouse Seasoning. Place into the Air Fryer and cook for 6-7 minutes
7. Once the steaks are seared on both sides, submerge them in the herb butter. Be sure to coat on all sides then return to the griddle for another minute per side. Remove from the griddle and let rest them for a few minutes.
8. Add the asparagus and mushrooms to the griddle with a few shakes of Blackstone Steakhouse seasoning over the top. Add a bit of the herb butter and cook for 4-5 minutes.
9. To plate, add the steak to one side and a lobster tail to the other. Add the vegetables in the middle and drizzle a bit more butter over both the steak and the lobster.
10. Enjoy!

Air Fryer Homemade Sweet And Savory Tortilla Chips

Servings:x
Cooking Time:x

Ingredients:
- 5 small flour tortillas
- 1 stick of butter
- 1 cup of sugar
- 2 tablespoons of cinnamon
- Cooking spray
- 5 small corn tortillas
- 1 stick of butter
- 1 teaspoon Chili Powder
- 1 teaspoon Garlic Powder
- 1 teaspoon Smoked Paprika
- 1 teaspoon Onion Powder
- Pinch of Salt/Pepper
- Cooking spray
- 4 oz cream cheese
- 1/4 cup powder sugar
- 1/2 teaspoon cinnamon

Directions:
1. Cut flour tortillas in triangles.
2. In a microwave safe bowl, melt butter for 45 seconds. In a separate bowl, combine cinnamon and sugar.
3. On a cutting board lay out as many flour tortillas that you can fit and brush over both sides with butter. Then, using a spoon, sprinkle with cinnamon and sugar.
4. Preheat Air-Fryer to medium.
5. Spray Air-Fryer trays with cooking spray, and place tortillas in the tray.
6. Cook the tortillas for 5-6 minutes, or until golden brown. Carefully, flip the tortillas and cook another 3 minutes.
7. Before beginning the second batch of savory tortillas, wash the trays, and respray with cooking spray.
8. Cut corn tortillas in triangles.
9. In a microwave safe bowl melt butter for 45 seconds. In a separate bowl, combine all of the spices.
10. Lay out the triangle cut tortillas on a large cutting board and brush both sides with butter. Sprinkle with spices.
11. Cook the tortillas for 5-6 minutes, or until golden brown. Carefully, flip the tortillas and cook another 3 minutes.
12. In a bowl, mix softened cream cheese, powdered sugar, and cinnamon

Betty's Shrimp Fried Rice

Servings:4
Cooking Time:40 Min

Ingredients:
- 4 cup White Rice
- 1 lb Shrimp, wild caught
- 3-4 Eggs
- 1 cup fresh Snow Peas, cut into thirds
- 1 large Onion, chopped (white or yellow)
- 3 Garlic cloves, minced
- 1 bunch Green Onions, sliced separated green/whites
- Wok or stir fry oil
- 2 tbsp Butter, unsalted
- Low Sodium Soy Sauce
- 1 tbsp Rice Wine Vinegar (toasted sesame)
- Sesame Oil
- Toasted Sesame Seeds
- ½ cup Mayo, Kewpie preferred
- ¼-½ cup Sriracha (depending on level of heat)
- 1.5 tbsp Sesame Oil

Directions:
1. Cook rice (in a rice cooker preferred) with 1 tsp each low sodium and regular soy sauce. Spread rice on a baking sheet to cook then place in the fridge uncovered overnight until ready to cook or at least 4 hours to dry out.
2. On medium to medium high heat add a drizzle of wok oil (about 1 tbsp) and spread out over the Blackstone and add the eggs. Break the yolks and lightly scramble eggs to cook about 1 minute then slide them to the side on low to no heat.
3. Add another drizzle of wok oil and add the chopped onions, snow peas, garlic and sliced white onions to cook 3-4 minutes, constantly tossing vegetables with two spatulas. Then slide vegetables to the low or off side with the eggs.

4. Add a drizzle of wok oil and 1 tbsp butter to melt together then add the shrimp. Tossing to cook. If shrimp are large cut shrimp to bite sized pieces as they cook, about 3-4 minutes. Slide them to the side as well.
5. Drizzle some wok oil 1 tbsp of butter and add the rice. Using a scraper and spatula toss rice to coat in oil and butter break apart any clumps of rice.

Mini Beef Wellingtons

Servings:4
Cooking Time:x

Ingredients:
- 1 pound ground beef
- 1 packet onion soup mix
- 1 teaspoon Worcestershire sauce
- 1 tablespoon Dijon mustard
- 1 egg
- 1 packet puff pastry sheets
- 1 egg + 1 tablespoon water

Directions:
1. Mix together ground beef, onion soup mix, Worcestershire sauce, Dijon mustard, and egg in a large bowl. Place in a refrigerator covered for 1 hour or up to 24 hours to allow the flavors to come together.
2. Preheat your griddle to medium.
3. Divide the ground beef mix into about 8 portions, 2 oz each.
4. Roll the portions into balls and place on the griddle. Using a spatula and parchment paper, lightly press down on the meatballs to flatten both the top and bottom slightly into a disc almost as tall as it is wide.
5. Cook the ground beef for 2 minutes per side. Using tongs, sear the sides of the meatballs slightly. You can also rotate the meat along the side of your griddle to sear the sides.
6. Place on a cooling rack and allow them to cool in the refrigerator.
7. To assemble, follow the directions on the puff pastry box, allowing it to come to a malleable state. Usually 30 minutes at room temperature and the dough is thawed just enough to cut and fold.
8. The key to the magic of puff pastry is keeping it very cold so do your best to work quickly and if your kitchen is warm, keep completed portions in the refrigerator.
9. Cut the puff pastry into 4-inch squares or at least twice the size of the width of the meatball.
10. Place the meatball in the center of the puff pastry square. Join all 4 corners of the puff pastry together on the top of the meatball, sealing to close and adhere them to one another.
11. Seal any additional puff pastry around the meatball by crimping it together tightly using your fingers. Try to make a tightly sealed pastry shell around the meatball.
12. Preheat your air fryer to 400F or the recommended temperature on the puff pastry box.
13. Mix together the egg and water to form an egg wash. Paint the egg wash on the top, bottom, and all sides of the pastry. This will promote browning in the air fryer.
14. Keep the mini Wellingtons cold until cooking.
15. Place a piece of parchment paper in the bottom of the air fryer basket. In batches, air fry the mini beef Wellingtons for 16-18 minutes or until the internal temperature is at least 140F and the pastry has puffed and is golden brown flipping once.

Chicken Sausage & Vegetable Stir Fry

Servings:6
Cooking Time:30 Min

Ingredients:
- 3 Tablespoons of Olive Oil
- 5 Chicken Sausage Links (precooked), sliced
- 2 Garlic Cloves, minced
- 1 Red Onion, cut into large chunks
- 1 Zucchini, sliced
- 1 Yellow Squash, sliced
- 1 Red Bell Pepper, cut into chunks
- 1 Yellow Bell Pepper, cut into chunks
- 1 Green Bell Pepper, cut into chunks
- 1 Cup of Sugar Snap Peas
- 1/2 Teaspoon of Italian Seasoning
- 1/2 Teaspoon of Crushed Red Pepper Flakes
- 1/2 Teaspoon of Garlic Salt
- Sea Salt and Black Pepper, to taste

Directions:
1. In a large bowl, combine all vegetables, olive oil, and seasonings (everything except the chicken sausage). Stir to coat vegetables evenly with oil and seasonings.
2. Heat your griddle to medium-high heat and cover with a thin layer of olive oil.
3. Add vegetables to hot griddle and cook approximately 10 minutes, stirring occasionally.
4. Add chicken sausage and stir to combine. Cook an additional 5 minutes until vegetables are tender and sausage is heated.

Cashew Chicken Stir Fry

Servings:6
Cooking Time:22 Min

Ingredients:
- 1 1/2 Tablespoons of Olive Oil
- 1 1/2 Lb. of Boneless, Skinless, Chicken Breasts. Cut into bite-size pieces
- Salt and Pepper, to taste
- 4 Cloves Garlic, minced
- 3 Cups of Broccoli Florets
- 1 Red Bell Pepper, thinly sliced
- 1 Yellow Bell Pepper, thinly sliced
- 1 Cup of Sugar Snap Peas
- 1 Cup of Shredded Carrots
- 1/2 Cup of Cashews (preferably unsalted or low sodium)
- 5 Green Onions, sliced
- 6 Tablespoons of Reduced-Sodium Soy Sauce
- 4 Tablespoons of Natural Peanut Butter
- 3 Tablespoons of Honey
- 1 1/2 Teaspoons of Sesame Oil
- 1/3 Teaspoon of Ground Ginger
- 3 Tablespoons of Water

Directions:
1. Heat your griddle to medium-high heat and cover with a thin coat of olive oil.
2. Season the chicken with salt and pepper, then add the chicken and cashews to the griddle (I like to add the cashews at the same time as the chicken so that they get nice and crispy - but you can add them in at the end if you prefer). Cook for 4-5 minutes stirring occasionally, then add the garlic and cook for about 30 seconds more (the chicken will not be fully cooked yet - that's okay!)
3. Add in all the vegetables and saute for 5-7 minutes (or until all the vegetables are tender and the chicken is fully cooked to 165 degrees internal temperature).
4. In a medium bowl, mix together all the ingredients for the homemade sauce and drizzle over the chicken and vegetables.
5. Mix everything together and keep over the griddle until everything is heated through.
6. Serve or portion into meal prep containers.

Crepes

Servings:1
Cooking Time:10 Min

Ingredients:
- 2 Large Eggs
- 3/4 Cup of Milk
- 1/2 Cup of Water
- 1 Cup of Flour
- 2 Tablespoons of Melted butter
- 4 Large Eggs
- 1 1/2 Cups of Milk
- 1 Cup of Water
- 2 Cups of Flour
- 4 Tablespoons of Melted butter
- 8 Large Eggs
- 3 Cups of Milk
- 2 Cups of Water
- 4 Cups of Flour
- 8 Tablespoons of Melted butter

Directions:
1. Whisk eggs. Whisk in milk and water.
2. Whisk in flour a little at a time.
3. Add melted butter last and mix until everything is combined.
4. Set griddle to medium low heat and spread a light layer of oil evenly over the surface.
5. Once up to temp, use a ladle to pour batter onto the griddle and use a crepe spreader (found in our crepe kit) to spread the batter out into a large circle.
6. Cook until the edges start to lift from the griddle surface then flip them over.

Corn Crab & Cheddar Fritters

Servings:4
Cooking Time:x

Ingredients:
- 1/4 Cup of Onion, minced
- 1/2 Cup of Cooked Corn (cut off the cob)
- 1 1/2 Cup of Lump Blue Crab
- 2 Eggs
- 1 Tablespoon of Fresh Parsley, chopped
- 1/3 Cup of Milk
- 1 Cup of Cheddar Cheese, shredded
- Vegetable Oil for Frying
- 3/4 Cup of Flour
- 2 Teaspoons of Baking Powder
- 2 Teaspoons of Old Bay Seasoning
- 3 Tablespoons of Mayonnaise
- Fresh Lemon Juice (about 1/2 of a lemon)
- 1 Teaspoon of Garlic Powder
- 2 Teaspoons of Old Bay Seasoning
- 1 Tablespoon of Chopped Fresh Parsley

Directions:
1. Gently mix together wet ingredients in a mixing bowl. In a separate bowl, mix together dry ingredients, then slowly add them to the wet ingredients until combined well. Refrigerate mixture 2-4 hours before cooking.
2. With your griddle on medium low heat, drizzle vegetable oil and add a spoonful of mixture. Gently press down to create a round patty for even cooking.
3. Let cook until golden brown and then flip and cook the other side.
4. Cook for about 4-5 minutes per side, adding vegetable oil with a squirt bottle around fritters as needed for even shallow frying.
5. Drain fritters on paper towels. Serve with lemon crab aioli.

Funnel Cake Swirls

Servings:1
Cooking Time:10 Min

Ingredients:
- 2 Eggs
- 1 Cup of 2% Milk
- 1 Cup of Water
- 1/2 Teaspoon of Vanilla, or a Different Baking Flavor Extract by McCormick
- 3 Cups of All-Purpose Flour
- 1/4 Cup of Sugar
- 3 Teaspoons of Baking Powder
- 1/4 Teaspoon of Salt
- Vegetable Oil for Frying
- Confectioner (Powdered) Sugar

Directions:
1. Whisk dry ingredients in a bowl and set aside.
2. Whisk wet ingredients in a bowl until combined, slowly whisk in dry ingredients until there are no lumps left.
3. Fill your Blackstone pancake batter dispenser (found in our breakfast kit).
4. Heat the Blackstone griddle to medium-medium/low heat.
5. Add your oil to the griddle and dispense your batter, using a swirling motion onto the oil.
6. Let cake swirls cook 1-1 ½ minutes per side in oil until golden brown, adding extra oil as needed. (A squirt bottle for oil makes this process easy!)
7. Remove cake swirls from the griddle once cooked and top with confectioner's sugar.

Buffalo Ranch Chicken Flatbread

Servings:2
Cooking Time:20 Min

Ingredients:
- Flatbread
- Chicken Cutlets
- Red Onion
- Grated mozzarella
- Buffalo Sauce
- Ranch dressing
- Blue Cheese Crumbles
- Salt
- Pepper
- Blackstone All Purpose Seasoning

- Olive Oil
- Cooling rack

Directions:

1. Let's start by preheating your Blackstone to medium - medium high. While that's heating let's season our chicken cutlets. On both sides lightly coat with olive oil and season with salt, pepper, and Blackstone all-purpose seasoning.
2. Place the chicken on the griddle to cook for about 3-4 minutes, flip and cook an additional 3-4 minutes until the chicken is fully cooked.
3. While the chicken is cooking you can slice up some red onion. You should only need about 1/4 of the onion sliced.
4. When the chicken is done remove it and allow it to rest for 2-3 minutes. While the chicken is resting add a slight amount of olive oil to your griddle top, spread evenly with a spatula, and place your flatbread on the griddle too lightly brown. This should take 3-4 minutes on each side.
5. Once you have a light toasting on each side place your cooling rack on the griddle, turn the heat to high, place the flatbread on the cooling rack above the hight heat zone, cover with your basting dome and allow to toast an additional 3-4 minutes or until the bottom is browned and toasted. Leaving the flatbread on the cooling rack add you chicken, red onion, a desired drizzle of buffalo sauce and ranch dressing, top with mozzarella, blue cheese crumbles, and another drizzle of buffalo sauce and ranch dressing.
6. Spray some water around your cooling rack and cover with your basting dome to melt the cheese. This should take 2-3 minutes or until the cheese is melted. Remove from the cooling rack, slice, and enjoy!

Butte Montana Style Beef & Pork Pasty

Servings:4
Cooking Time:x

Ingredients:

- 16 oz top sirloin, cubed
- 2 cups cooked cubed potato
- 1 tablespoon garlic salt
- 1 tablespoon pepper
- 1 tablespoon Dijon mustard (optional)
- 2 tablespoons oil
- 1 package of 2 pie crust rolls
- 1 egg + 1 tablespoon water

Directions:

1. Trim any excess fat or gristle from top sirloin. If not already cubed, cut the beef into cubes the same size of your potato or about the size of Yahtzee dice.
2. In a large bowl, season the beef with the garlic salt, pepper, mustard, and oil. Toss to combine. Allow to rest in the refrigerator for 30 minutes or up to overnight.
3. Preheat your griddle to medium high.
4. Preheat air fryer to 350F.
5. Sear the beef on the griddle, stirring frequently for 3-5 minutes or until a crust has developed on the majority of the cubes. The cubes should be slightly pink in the middle or cooked to a minimum of 140F. Set aside and allow the cubes to cool.
6. Once cooled, fold them in with the potato cubes.
7. Unroll the piecrust and lay flat on your work surface.
8. Add half of the beef and potato mixture to the left side of the piecrust in a half moon shape. Repeat with the other half of the mixture leaving a 1-inch gap in the middle and around all sides.
9. Lay the other sheet of piecrust over the top of the crust and beef mixture. Press the piecrust first down the middle to adhere and separate into two halves. Press the edges of the crust around the perimeter to adhere together.
10. At this point you should have two separate pockets sealed shut. Cut down the middle of the piecrust and separate the two pockets. Using your fingers, make rough crimps around the edges to adhere.
11. Mix the egg with 1 tablespoon of water to make egg wash. Paint the egg wash over the top and sides of the pasty to promote browning. Place the pasty on a piece of parchment paper that will fit inside the airfryer.
12. Cook the pasty in the air fryer for 15 minutes or until the crust is golden brown and the interior is piping hot.

Griddled Banana Bread With Cream Cheese Glaze And Candied Bacon

Servings: 3-4
Cooking Time: 15 Min

Ingredients:
- 1 loaf Banana Bread
- ½ tbsp Butter per slice of bread for frying
- 6-8 slices Bacon
- 1 tbsp real Maple Syrup
- 1 tbsp Sriracha
- Blackstone sweet Maple seasoning
- Candied Walnuts, optional
- 4 oz Whipped Cream Cheese
- 1 1/2 cups Powdered Sugar
- 1 teaspoon Vanilla Extract
- 2 tablespoons Milk (adjusted as needed)

Directions:
1. Turn Blackstone airfryer on to preheat to 400. Slice bacon strips in half and brush lightly with maple syrup and sriracha on both sides. Dust with Blackstone sweet maple seasoning on both sides. Arrange bacon on parchment paper lined airfryer racks and place in the airfryer for 8-10 minutes checking occasionally. Remove when finished and allow to cool on a cooling rack, bacon will harden as it cools.
2. Preheat griddle to medium low-low heat. Slice banana bread in 1-2 inch slices. Swirl a little butter around the griddle before adding slices of bread to slowly fry up about 2-3 minutes per side. Removing when toasted on each side and warmed through.
3. In a bowl, using a fork or a whisk, mix cream cheese, powdered sugar and vanilla together slowly adding in milk until smooth and thin enough to drizzle glaze.
4. Serve banana bread topped with cream cheese glaze and candied bacon strips on top or crumble bacon to sprinkle on top.

Chicken Stir Fry Noodles

Servings: 1
Cooking Time: 10 Min

Ingredients:
- 2 Lb. of Boneless Skinless Chicken Thighs (trimmed and cut into 1â pieces)
- 2 Packs of 6 Oz Chow Mein Noodles (could substitute spaghetti noodles)
- 4 Tablespoons of Vegetable oil
- 1 Tablespoon of Fresh Ginger (finely diced or grated)
- 2 Cloves Garlic (finely diced)
- 1 Head Broccoli (stems and florets chopped)
- 1-2 Tablespoons of Soy Sauce (more or less to taste)
- Fresh Ground Black Pepper
- 1 Teaspoon of Soy Sauce
- 1 Teaspoon of Sugar
- 1 Tablespoon of Corn Starch
- 1/2 Teaspoon of Backing Soda
- 1/2 Teaspoon of Salt
- 4 Tablespoons of Water
- 2 Cloves Garlic (finely diced)

Directions:
1. In a bowl, combine chicken and marinade ingredients. Cover and let chill for at least 20 minutes.
2. Prepare the noodles per the packet instructions, but reduce the cooking time a minute as the noodles will keep cooking on the griddle. Drain noodles and rinse under cold water to stop them from over cooking.
3. Preheat your griddle to medium high heat. Pour 2 tablespoons of oil on the griddle. Add the marinated chicken to the griddle in a single layer and allow it to brown. Pour a couple tablespoons of water around the chicken and cover with a basting dome.
4. Pour 2 tablespoons of oil on the other side of the griddle and cook the ginger and garlic until fragrant (30-45 seconds). Add the broccoli and toss with the ginger and garlic. Pour a couple tablespoons of water around the broccoli and cover with the basting dome for about 1 minute.
5. Add a couple tablespoons of water to the chicken as the sauce around it thickens.
6. Turn the heat on the griddle down to medium low. Combine the chicken, noodles, and vegetables. Toss everything together until they are evenly coated with the seasonings and warmed through. If the noodles are still a bit too hard, sprinkle water onto them as you toss.
7. Add soy sauce and black pepper to taste. Toss to combine and serve.

Pancetta Green Beans With Shitakes And Cranberries

Servings:4-6
Cooking Time:20 Min

Ingredients:
- 4 oz diced pancetta
- 2 cups sliced shitake mushrooms
- ½ pound fresh green beans, cleaned and trimmed
- 2-3 cloves fresh garlic, thinly sliced
- 1/3 cup dried cranberries
- 2 tablespoons unsalted butter
- 1 tablespoon lemon juice
- Salt and pepper
- Olive oil

Directions:
1. Heat your griddle to medium heat and cook the pancetta until crisp (about 5-7 minutes tossing often).
2. Remove the crisp pancetta from the heat and reserve for later. Add the mushrooms and butter to the pancetta fat with a bit of salt & pepper and toss to evenly coat. Cook for 3-4 minutes.
3. Add the garlic, cranberries and pancetta and toss to mix evenly. Cook for another 4-5 minutes.
4. Add a bit of water and the lemon juice. Cook for another 2 minutes to steam the beans.
5. Serve family style on a platter or in a large bowl.
6. Enjoy!

Bonzai Pipeline Tacos

Servings:1
Cooking Time:10 Min

Ingredients:
- 1 Lb. of Diced Boneless, Skinless, Chicken Breast
- 20 Oz. of Crushed Pineapple in Juice
- 1 Cup of Mr. Yoshida's Marinade & Cooking Sauce: Original Gourmet - Sweet & Savory
- Granulated Garlic to taste
- Salt & Pepper to Taste
- 2 Diced Jalapeños with Seeds Removed
- 1 Diced Red Onion
- 1 Green Pepper, Sliced
- 12 Flour Street Taco-Sized Tortillas (approximately 5" in diameter)
- 1 Bunch Fresh Chopped Cilantro

Directions:
1. Preheat the Blackstone griddle to high heat. When heated, coat the griddle top with light olive oil.
2. Drop diced chicken on one zone of the hot griddle top. Lightly season with granulated garlic, salt, and black pepper.
3. Drop jalapeño, onions, and green pepper onto another zone of the hot griddle top. Season with Salt.
4. Drop Crushed pineapple onto separate zone of the hot griddle top.
5. Mix and flip all ingredients on griddle top with spatula as they cook.
6. Cook Peppers until slightly blackened and onions until mostly translucent. Cook Pineapple until slightly blackened. Cook Chicken until done and outside is slightly blackened.
7. Turn griddle to low heat.
8. Add Mr. Yoshida's Marinade and mix all ingredients on griddle top together with spatulas.
9. Warm Tortillas on griddle top until brown. Do not let them burn.
10. Fill each Tortilla with an equal amount of hot mixed ingredients. Garnish with Fresh chopped cilantro to taste.
11. Enjoy the spicy sticky sweet taste of Bonzai Pipeline Tacos!

Mediterranean Pork Kabobs

Servings:8
Cooking Time:25 Min

Ingredients:
- 2 Lb. of Pork Tenderloin, Cubed
- 2 Red Bell Peppers, Cut into 1" Pieces
- 1 Large Red Onion, Cut into 1" Pieces
- 1/2 Cup of White Vinegar
- 1/2 Cup of Vegetable Oil
- 3 Tablespoons of Garlic Cloves, Finely Chopped
- 2 Tablespoons of Fresh Parsley, Finely Chopped
- 1 Teaspoon of Cumin
- 1/2 Teaspoon of Coriander

- 1/2 Teaspoon of Salt
- 1/4 Teaspoon of Pepper

Directions:
1. Mix all marinade ingredients in a gallon-sized resealable plastic bag.
2. Add cubed pork tenderloin and knead until evenly-coated in marinade.
3. Refrigerate 2-8 hours, turning occasionally.
4. Build your skewers by alternating threading pork, red pepper, and red onion pieces until the skewer is full (this recipe should make about 8 kabobs depending on the size of your skewer).
5. Heat your griddle to high heat and cover with a thin layer of olive oil.
6. Place skewers on your griddle and cook for 2 minutes.
7. Rotate 90 degrees and cook for 2 more minutes.
8. Continue cooking/rotating skewers until all sides have been cooked on your griddle and internal temperature of your pork is 145 degrees (8-10 minutes total).

Gochujang Sticky Steak Bites

Servings:4
Cooking Time:10 Min

Ingredients:
- 2, 1" thick NY strip steaks, cut into 1" cubes
- 3 tablespoons hoisin sauce
- 1/3 cup gochujang
- 2 tablespoon soy sauce
- The juice of 1 lime
- ¼ cup sliced green onion
- ¼ cup chopped cilantro
- 2 red chilis (or red jalapenos)
- ¼ cup beer (lager is best)
- 8 cloves fresh garlic, smashed
- 1 tablespoon sesame oil
- Salt and pepper
- Olive oil

Directions:
1. Preheat your griddle to high heat.
2. In a large mixing bowl, add the steak with a bit of olive oil and salt and pepper. Toss to evenly mix.
3. Heat your griddle to high heat and add the steaks pieces. Cook for 3-4 minutes tossing half way through.
4. In the same mixing bowl you used for the beef, add the gochujang, hoisin, soy sauce, sesame oil, lime juice and beer and whisk to evenly incorporate.
5. Once the steak as caramelized on all sides, add the some of the green onions, cilantro, red chilis and smashed garlic. Add ½ of the sauce over the top and toss. Cook for 2 minutes and then add the other half of the sauce and toss. Cook another 2 minutes and then add the steak to a platter.
6. Garnish with a bit more fresh cilantro and green onions and a sprinkle of sesame seeds.

S'mores Mini Pies

Servings:6
Cooking Time:15 Min

Ingredients:
- 6 mini Graham Cracker Pie Shells
- 1 cup Semi-Sweet Chocolate Chips
- 1 tbsp Butter
- 2 cups Mini Marshmallows

Directions:
1. In a microwave safe bowl, pour chocolate chips and butter. Melt at 30 second intervals until melted.
2. Spoon melted chocolate into pie shells, and top with a handful of marshmallows.
3. Set Air Fryer to high heat.
4. Put S'mores pies into air fryer tray and cook for 5-7 mins or until the tops are toasted.
5. Remove and serve immediately.

Fajitas

Servings:4
Cooking Time:25 Min

Ingredients:
- 16 Oz. of Flank Steak, Thinly Sliced
- 1 Red Pepper, Thinly Sliced
- 1 Green Pepper, Thinly Sliced
- 1 Onion, Thinly Sliced
- 4 Cups of Rice, Cooked
- 8 Oz. of Canned Green Chilles

- 8 Oz. of Canned Tomato Sauce
- Salt & Pepper to Taste
- 1/2 Teaspoon of Garlic Powder
- 1/3 Cup of Canola Oil
- 1/4 Cup of Lime Juice
- 1/2 Teaspoon of Cumin
- 1/2 Teaspoon of Garlic Powder
- Salt & Pepper to Taste
- 1/2 Cup of Sour Cream
- 2 Teaspoons of Chili Powder
- Juice from 1 Lime
- Salt & Pepper to Taste

Directions:
1. To make the sauce, combine sour cream, chili powder, juice from one lime, and salt & pepper in a bowl and thoroughly mix.
2. For the marinade, in a large re-sealable bag, mix the canola oil, lime juice, cumin, garlic powder, and salt & pepper.
3. Place the flank steak in the marinade and refrigerate for 1-2 hours.
4. Preheat Blackstone griddle to medium high. Apply a thin layer of oil to the griddle top.
5. Remove meat from marinade and place on the griddle, flipping occasionally until cooked.
6. Stir peppers and onion into the meat and sauté for 3-5 minutes until desired tenderness.
7. On a separate part of the griddle, add the rice ingredients and mix with a spatula. Cook until slightly reduced and well combined, about 4 minutes.
8. Serve immediately with warm flour tortillas, rice, and your favorite toppings.

Brussels Sprouts With Dried Cranberries

Servings:1
Cooking Time:10 Min

Ingredients:
- 2 bags Brussels Sprouts
- Olive Oil
- 2-3 Tablespoons of Butter
- 1 Onion, diced
- Salt & Pepper to Taste
- 1-2 Tablespoon of Sugar
- 1-2 Tablespoon of Balsamic Vinegar
- 1/3 Cup of Dried Cranberries
- 1/2 Cup of Chicken Stock

Directions:
1. Trim the stock and cut Brussels sprouts in half.
2. Put Brussels Sprouts and chicken stock in a microwave-safe bowl, cover, and microwave for 3-5 minutes.
3. Add olive oil and butter to the hot griddle with diced onions. Add Brussels sprouts and chicken stock to griddle.
4. Salt and pepper to taste. Continually stir the Brussels sprouts until they start to brown.
5. Add balsamic vinegar and sugar (adjust amounts to taste). Add dried cranberries at the end and cook for an additional minute or two.

Grilled Vegetable Italian Quinoa Bowl

Servings:x
Cooking Time:x

Ingredients:
- 1 Cup of Dry Quinoa
- 2 Cup of Vegetable or Chicken Broth
- Variety of Vegetables (you can use as much or as little as you want-all cut the same size)
- Red & Orange Bell Peppers
- Butternut Squash
- Zucchini
- Mushrooms
- Onion
- Garlic Salt & Pepper (or any Seasoning you prefer)
- Avocado Oil
- 1/2 - 1 Cup of Sun-dried Tomatoes in Oil (drain oil)
- Fresh Basil (cut into ribbons)
- Balsamic Glaze

Directions:
1. Cook quinoa according to package directions. Boil 2 c. chicken or vegetable broth and when boiling, add

quinoa. Reduce heat to low, and let cook for 15 minutes with the lid on, or until the liquid has absorbed. You can cook ahead of time and keep in fridge for several days.

2. Chop all vegetables a similar size so they cook evenly. Note: I use lots of onion because they give great flavor!

3. Heat Blackstone to a medium heat. Once hot, reduce to medium low and add avocado oil to coat the griddle.

4. Add cut vegetables and spread them evenly on the griddle.

5. Add garlic salt and pepper liberally to season all the vegetables.

6. Cook until soft, then remove from heat and enjoy!

Street Tacos With Pineapple Pickled Jalapeno Peppers

Servings:4
Cooking Time:10 Min

Ingredients:
- 1 Lb. of Thinly Sliced Steak (top round is a good cut for this)
- 2 Tablespoons of Blackstone Taco & Fajita Seasoning
- 2 Green Jalapeno Peppers, Sliced
- 2 Red Jalapeno Peppers, Sliced
- 1/4 Cup of Pineapple Juice
- 3 Tablespoons of Lime Juice
- 1 Teaspoon of Minced Garlic
- Fresh Cilantro
- Olive Oil
- 1/3 Cup of Sour Cream
- 3 Tablespoons of Lime Juice
- 1 Tablespoon of Blackstone Taco & Fajita Seasoning

Directions:

1. In a small bowl, add the sliced peppers, pineapple juice, lime juice, olive oil and minced garlic with a pinch of salt and pepper. Mix to evenly coat. Reserve on the side for later.

2. Using a large plate, add a drizzle of olive oil and season the steak with the Taco & Fajita Seasoning. Allow to sit for 10 minutes so the meat has a chance to marinate.

3. Heat your charcoal on your Blackstone Griddle Charcoal Grill Combo as hot as you can get it. Cook the thin steaks for 2 minutes per side and then dice.

4. Add a few corn tortillas to the griddle side of your Blackstone Griddle Charcoal Grill Combo and lightly toast.

5. To plate, add some of the steak to the bottom of each tortilla and then some of the sweet peppers, add a drizzle of the sauce and some fresh cilantro.

Sausage And Sage Thanksgiving Stuffing

Servings:8
Cooking Time:35 Min

Ingredients:
- About 2 loaves high quality sandwich bread or soft Italian or French bread, cut into 3/4-inch dice, about 5 quarts
- 4 TBLS butter
- 1 pound sage sausage
- 1 onion, finely chopped
- Celery, finely chopped
- 2 cloves garlic
- 2 teaspoons dried sage
- 2 cups chicken stock
- Finely chopped parsley leaves
- Salt and pepper to taste

Directions:

1. Brown the sausage ahead of time and set it aside.

2. Cut the bread into ¾" cubes. Add the butter, onions, garlic, and celery to the griddle.

3. Cook until they start to get soft. Add all of the bread and mix everything together.

4. Add the chicken stock about ½ cup at a time until it's all absorbed. Continue to cook until the bread starts to brown.

5. Add the sausage, sage, and salt and pepper to taste.

6. Finish by sprinkling with the fresh parsley.

7. Enjoy!

Fried Green Tomatoes

Servings:1
Cooking Time:10 Min

Ingredients:
- 3-4 Green Tomatoes
- 3 Cups of Italian Style Bread Crumbs
- 2 Cups of Flour
- 2 Teaspoons of Garlic Powder
- 3 Eggs
- 1/2 Cup of Milk
- Salt and Pepper to Taste
- Parsley Garnish, chopped
- Lemon Zest Garnish
- 3 Tablespoons of Butter
- 2 and 1/2 Tablespoons of Flour

Directions:
1. Set up your prep station with three separate deep containers. One with 3 eggs beaten with ½ cup of milk seasoned with salt and pepper. The second with 2 cups flour, 2 tsp garlic powder. The third with Italian seasoned bread crumbs.
2. Slice tomatoes ¼ to a ½ inch thick depending on how you like them. One at a time, coat the slices in the flour coating evenly and shaking off any excess flour, then dip and coat evenly in the egg wash, letting excess drip off, then into the breadcrumb, pressing slices into the crumbs to assure they coat completely.
3. Heat Blackstone Griddle to medium high heat and drizzle a generous layer of vegetable oil.
4. One at a time, place slices into the oil, pressing tomatoes gently into the oil. Add more oil underneath as needed.
5. Let the tomatoes cook 2-3 minutes until golden brown and crisp. Drizzle oil on the back side or lift the slices with your Blackstone spatula and add a drizzle of oil before flipping to cook the other side and let cook 2 more minutes.
6. Gently move slices to one side of the grill and turn heat to low and clean off the griddle top. Move slices back over and allow them to cook dry (no oil since you cleaned it) for a couple extra minutes on each side if needed.
7. Serve with White Pepper Gravy, garnished with chopped curly parsley and lemon zest (optional).
8. Now for the White Pepper Gravy, melt the butter in a small pot until bubbly. Then, whisk in the flour until completely mixed.

Bacon, Egg, And Cheese Pancake Sliders

Servings:6
Cooking Time:20 Min

Ingredients:
- Pancake mix (follow package directions)
- 6 strips of bacon
- 6 eggs
- 6 slices of cheddar cheese
- 2 TBS butter
- Syrup

Directions:
1. Follow pancake mix package directions to make 12 mini pancakes.
2. On one side of the griddle top, fry bacon. On the other side cook 12 mini pancakes.
3. Once the bacon is fried to desired crispness, remove and set aside on a paper towel. Remove pancakes and set to the side.
4. Scramble eggs 1 at a time and pour onto griddle.
5. Once egg is cooked top with cheese and cover with a pot lid or dome to help with the melting.
6. To assemble sliders, lay 6 pancakes on a platter. Top with egg, bacon, and then add another pancake to the top. Drizzle with syrup if desired.

Griddled Pineapple And Ice Cream

Servings:1
Cooking Time:10 Min

Ingredients:
- 1 Can Pineapple slices (or one fresh pineapple, sliced and cored)
- 1/2 Cup of Brown Sugar
- 1 Tablespoon of Lemon juice

- 2 Tablespoons of Honey
- 3 Tablespoons of Rum (or 1½ tsp Rum extract)
- 4 Tablespoons of Butter
- Vanilla Ice Cream

Directions:
1. Preheat Blackstone griddle to low heat.
2. In a large bowl combine brown sugar, lemon juice, rum, and honey in a bowl until smooth. Add pineapple rings to the bowl and spread mixture on both sides of each pineapple ring.
3. Melt the butter on the griddle.
4. Place pineapple rings on the griddle for 3-5 minutes, turning once until sugar mixture melts and pineapple is heated and tender.
5. Pour the remaining sugar mixture over pineapple rings and let it reduce. Keep the heat low and the sauce moving to avoiding burning the sugar.
6. Turn the griddle off and remove pineapple slices from the heat. Serve with scoop of ice cream and drizzle the sauce over the top.

Nate's Favorite Breakfast Sammich

Servings: 4
Cooking Time: 10 Min

Ingredients:
- 4 pieces of bacon
- 4 maple sausage patties
- 1/3 cup mayonnaise
- 1 tablespoon prepared horseradish
- 2 teaspoons Worcestershire sauce
- 4 eggs
- Blackstone Breakfast Blend Seasoning
- 4 slices American cheese
- 4 potato rolls, sliced

Directions:
1. Heat your Blackstone to medium-high heat and cook your bacon and sausage patties.
2. Move a bit of the bacon fat over and cook your eggs in the bacon fat sunny side up. Add a bit of Blackstone Breakfast Seasoning.
3. In a small mixing bowl, add the mayonnaise, horseradish and Worcestershire sauce. Using a whisk, mix evenly and reserve for later.
4. Once your sausage and bacon are fully cooked, stack the bacon on top of the sausage and add a piece of American cheese over the top to melt.
5. Toast your potato rolls and add some of the sauce to the bottom piece of bread then add the sausage, bacon and cheese.
6. Once your eggs are cooked the way you like, place them on the top of your sandwich and finish with the top bun.

Bacon Fried Corn 3.0

Servings: 3-4
Cooking Time: 20 Min

Ingredients:
- Diced Pancetta
- 2 bags of Frozen Corn
- 2 Tomatoes
- Red Onion
- Fresh Basil
- Fresh Parsley
- Parmesan Cheese
- Salt
- Pepper
- Garlic Powder
- Blackstone All Purpose Seasoning

Directions:
1. Preheat your griddle top on low. Start by adding diced pancetta and let it slowly cook so we can gently render the fat without cooking it too fast. Also, be sure to toss the pancetta occasionally to brown all sides.
2. While that is cooking dice up 2 tomatoes and mince half a red onion. By the time you finish that you should see that your pancetta is starting to brown. You can up your heat to medium if necessary.
3. While it finishes cooking chop up your fresh basil and parsley. The amount you chop is totally a preference. Your pancetta should be done cooking at this point.
4. Leaving all the fat on the griddle, add your frozen corn to the pancetta. Toss and coat the corn with the pancetta fat and season with salt, pepper, and garlic

powder. The last seasoning you'll need to add is the Blackstone All-Purpose Seasoning. Toss and incorporate all your seasonings.

5. The last step is to add your diced tomatoes, minced red onion, fresh basil, and parsley. Add this on the griddle top, toss with corn and pancetta.

6. Plate in a large dish garnish with grated parmesan and enjoy!

Shrimp Lejon With Thousand Island Dressing

Servings:8
Cooking Time:15 Min

Ingredients:
- 1 lb shrimp, peeled tails on
- ½ pack bacon, thin
- Prepared horseradish
- ¾ c Dukes mayo
- ¼ c ketchup
- 1 tbsp white vinegar
- ⅓ c sweet pickle relish
- 2 tsp sugar
- 2 tsp onion powder
- Pinch pink sea salt and pepper

Directions:
1. Run a knife along the top of the shrimp to butterfly, removing any veins.
2. Stuff each shrimp with horseradish.
3. Wrap each stuffed shrimp with half a piece of bacon in a single layer.
4. Place shrimp in the Blackstone Airfryer, preheated to medium to medium-high, checking after 3 minutes. Flip or move any around if needed and cook for another 3-5 minutes.
5. Serve with a thousand island dressing for dipping.

Frito Bandito

Servings:3
Cooking Time:15 Min

Ingredients:
- 1 pound 80/20 ground beef
- 1 cup diced sweet yellow onion
- Blackstone Steakhouse Seasoning
- 3 slices American Cheese
- 1 1/2 cup Chili Cheese Fritos
- 3 Wonder Bread Honey Bun burger buns
- BBQ Sauce
- Olive oil

Directions:
1. Pre-heat your griddle to medium-high heat. Add a tablespoon of olive oil to Blackstone. Add sliced sweet yellow onion to one heat zone on your Blackstone and toss in oil to caramelize for 4-5 mins.
2. Form the ground beef into 4 ounce meat balls. Place the meatballs on the griddle and smash thin. Add some Blackstone Steakhouse Seasoning over each patty and cook for 1-2 minutes each side.
3. Flip the burgers and add caramelized onions, Chili Cheese Fritos, BBQ Sauce and a slice of American Cheese.
4. Cover with a dome and melt the cheese. Once Cheese is melted add patty to a Wonder Bread Honey Hamburger bun and serve.

Bbq Chicken Bacon Pizza

Servings:1
Cooking Time:10 Min

Ingredients:
- 1 Crust of Pizza Dough
- 1/2 Cup of BBQ Sauce
- 1 Cup of Diced Chicken Breast (pre-cooked)
- 2 Tablespoons of Diced Red Onions
- 1/4 Cup of Chopped Bacon Pieces
- 1 1/2 Cups of Shredded Mozzarella Cheese

Directions:
1. Stretch out your pizza dough and spread BBQ sauce over it.
2. Add diced chicken, red onions, and bacon.
3. Add the mozzarella cheese.
4. Cook in the Blackstone Pizza Oven until done.

Korean Fire Chicken Lettuce Wraps

Servings: 4
Cooking Time: 30 Min

Ingredients:
- 2 LBS Chicken Thighs, boneless skinless
- 1 head Butter Lettuce
- 2 cups Mayonnaise
- 1 tbsp Rice Wine Vinegar
- 2 tbsp Sesame Oil
- 1/2+ c Blackstone Korean Fire Sear and Serve Sauce
- Green Onions, sliced and divided
- toasted Sesame Seeds
- 2 tbsp seasoned wok or stir-fry oil

Directions:
1. In a mixing bowl whisk to combine mayonnaise, rice wine vinegar, sesame oil, and Blackstone Korean Fire Sear and Serve Sauce. Depending on your heat level preference add more, or less, Korean Fire Sauce.
2. Slice green onions, separating the white ends and green ends.
3. Dice raw chicken breast into small bite sized pieces.
4. Toss chicken with 2 tbsp seasoned wok oil to coat evenly.
5. Preheat Blackstone to medium high heat and drop chicken down in a single layer to cook. Tossing every couple of minutes until chicken is golden brown.
6. Lower the heat to medium low and add about half of your sauce to coat chicken. Toss and allow to cook 2 minutes. Adding the white ends of the green onions to cook the last 1 minute.
7. Remove chicken and garnish with sesame seeds, the reserved green onions, and a drizzle of Korean Sweet Fire Sauce.
8. Serve separated lettuce leaves to fill with chicken, extra sauce, sesame seeds, and green onions.
9. Enjoy!

Octopus

Servings: 1
Cooking Time: 10 Min

Ingredients:
- 1 Package of Frozen Cleaned Octopus (17.6 oz-3 octopus)
- 2 Lemons
- 4 Tablespoons of Chopped Italian Parsley
- 2 Large Garlic Cloves
- 1 Bay Leaf
- 1/2 Cup of Dry White Wine or White Wine Vinegar
- 1 Tablespoon of Red Wine Vinegar
- 10 Whole Black Peppercorns
- Extra Virgin Olive Oil
- Sea Salt & Fresh Cracked Pepper to Taste

Directions:
1. Let octopus thaw overnight in fridge. Rinse and put in a stock pot, adding enough water to cover. Add the wine, 1 garlic clove (crushed), bay leaf, peppercorns and half a lemon. Boil for 45 minutes.
2. Remove octopus and rinse off. Slice off the head carefully, leaving the legs together. Place in a bowl to cool at room temp covered with plastic wrap for 30 min. Add a heavy drizzle of extra virgin olive oil to coat evenly, add 1 garlic clove chopped, and 2 ½ tbsp chopped parsley, squeeze of lemon, salt, and pepper. Let marinate on counter 30 minutes covered.
3. Heat your Blackstone to high heat and grill each side for 3-4 minutes. Remove and plate whole or cut portions (1 to 1-2 leg pieces) lightly drizzle extra virgin olive oil and season with sea salt, fresh cracked pepper, the rest of the chopped parsley and a squeeze of lemon. Serve with lemon wedges.

Caramelized Grilled Pineapple

Servings: 6
Cooking Time: 20 Min

Ingredients:
- 1 Fresh Pineapple cut into spears or cubes
- 3 Tablespoons of Cinnamon

Directions:
1. Heat your griddle to medium-high heat and coat evenly with a small amount of extra virgin olive oil.
2. Put pineapple spears (or cubes) into a large bowl and cover with cinnamon. Stir to coat evenly.

3. Place pineapple on griddle and rotate every 2 minutes until lightly browned and slightly caramelized on all sides.
4. Serve while still warm.

How To Make Crepes

Servings:5
Cooking Time:10 Min

Ingredients:
- 1 1/4 Cups of All Purpose Flour
- 3/4 Cup of Whole Milk
- 1/2 Cup of Water
- 2 Eggs
- 3 Tablespoons of Unsalted Butter, Melted
- 1 Teaspoon of Vanilla Extract
- 2 1/2 Tablespoons of Sugar

Directions:
1. In a large mixing bowl, add all the ingredients and mix evenly with a whisk. Be sure that the batter is smooth and blended. Cover and let rest for 1 hour (this allows the bubbles to subside and flour to fully hydrate.)
2. Heat your Blackstone Griddle to medium heat and add a thin layer of butter. Add about ¼ cup of the batter. Using your Crepe Spreading Tool, form your crepe and cook for 1-2 minutes. Use your Crepe Spatula and flip. Cook for another minute.
3. Repeat with remaining batter.

Maple Glazed Green Beans

Servings:x
Cooking Time:x

Ingredients:
- 2 12 Oz. of Bags of Frozen Green Beans
- 12 Oz. of Package of Bacon
- 1 Cup of Diced Onion
- Pure Maple Syrup
- Salt and Pepper to Taste

Directions:
1. Preheat griddle to medium heat.
2. Slice bacon into small strips. Cook on medium heat, mixing frequently. Adjust heat as necessary making sure not to burn the bacon. If the bacon appears to be cooking too quickly, turn a burner or two to low of off. Turn burner back up as necessary. The key is to make sure the bacon cooks but doesn't burn.
3. Add a small amount of cooking oil to an empty part of the griddle. Cook beans, adding salt and pepper to taste. Mix frequently.
4. At the same time, be sure to keep mixing and spreading bacon across the griddle top so it cooks quickly and evenly.
5. Once the bacon is nearly cooked, add onions, allowing them to cook in the bacon grease.
6. After 2 minutes, mix all ingredients together, allowing the bacon grease to flavor all ingredients.
7. Use a clean fork to test beans. As soon as the beans are completely hot, but still have somewhat of a snap to them, drizzle with maple syrup and mix for a few seconds.
8. Quickly remove from griddle and serve. Drizzle with additional maple syrup if desired.

Chicken Bruschetta

Servings:7
Cooking Time:10 Min

Ingredients:
- 4 Chicken Cutlets
- 3-4 Tablespoons of Blackstone Chicken and Herb Seasoning
- 4 Large Tomatoes, diced
- 3/4 Cup of Small Diced Red Onion
- 3 Tablespoons of Minced Garlic
- 6-8 Basil Leaves, chiffonade
- Sixteen 1" Thick Slices of French Bread
- Balsamic Glaze
- Olive Oil
- Salt & Pepper

Directions:
1. In a large bowl, add the tomatoes, red onion, garlic, basil with a drizzle of olive oil and some salt and pepper. Gently mix evenly.
2. Add a drizzle of olive oil and Blackstone Chicken and Herb Seasoning to the chicken cutlets and toss to evenly coat.

3. With your Blackstone set to medium-high heat, cook the chicken cutlets for 2-3 minutes per side or until fully cooked. Remove the chicken from the griddle and dice.
4. Add the chicken to the tomatoes and mix evenly.
5. Add a bit of olive oil to your Blackstone and lightly toast the slices of French bread.
6. To serve, add a few tablespoons of the chicken bruschetta over the toasted bread. Garnish with a drizzle of balsamic glaze and serve chilled.

Spicy Griddle Pineapple Margarita

Servings: 2
Cooking Time: x

Ingredients:
- Silver Tequila
- Triple Sec
- 1 Fresh Pineapple
- 3 Limes
- Sugar
- Water
- 3 Jalapeños
- Blackstone Tequila Lime Seasoning

Directions:
1. Cut off the top and bottom of the pineapple. Slice off one or two wheels for garnish.
2. Remove pineapple rind, core, and slice remains pieces into sections to place on the griddle
3. Before going on the griddle pat dry with paper towels to remove moisture, this helps the caramelization process.
4. Pre heat Blackstone to Medium High. Spray Blackstone non stick griddle spray on the flattop
5. Place pineapple on griddle and cook each side 3-4 minutes or till it's golden. Make sure to get every side
6. Slice Limes in half and pat dry of extra juices. Place on the griddle and cook until you see that it's toasted and golden.
7. In a jar or container add equal parts sugar and water. Then slice one fresh jalapeño and add to the water and sugar. Add lid and shake till sugar is dissolved.
8. In a blender add ice, half of your pineapple chunks, the lime juice from the griddle limes, 2-3 ounces of spicy simple syrup, 2-3 ounces of triple sec, 3-4 ounces of tequila and blend.
9. Rim glasses with pineapple juice and Tequila lime seasoning. Fill glass with contents from the blender and garnish with a piece of griddled pineapple and a fresh jalapeño.

Mango Tango Turkey Burger

Servings: 1
Cooking Time: 10 Min

Ingredients:
- 2 Lb. of Ground Turkey or Chicken
- 2 Tablespoons of Minced Garlic
- 1 1/2 Tablespoons of Organic Great Value Mango Habanero Seasoning (Walmart brand) or Jamaican Jerk Seasoning
- Fresh Mango Salsa (Available in Grocery Produce Coolers)
- 1 Cup of Mayonnaise
- 1 Tablespoon of Chili Garlic Sauce (Found Next to Sriracha Sauce)
- 1/2 Red Onion, Sliced
- 6 Fresh Jalapeño Peppers
- Monterrey Jack Cheese Slices
- 1 Bunch Fresh Cilantro
- 6-8 Torta Rolls

Directions:
1. Preheat the Blackstone griddle to high heat. When heated, coat the griddle top with light olive oil.
2. Mix ground turkey with Mango Habanero Seasoning and 2 Tbsp. Minced Garlic. Make medium sized patties.
3. Wash, remove seeds from, and slice Jalapeños.
4. Peel and slice red onion into large burger-sized slices.
5. Mix 1 Cup Mayo with 2 Tbsp Chili Garlic Sauce.
6. Wash and chop cilantro.
7. Drop the turkey patties on the hot griddle. Flip the patties when the bottom side is seared. Use your spatula to flatten your patties after they have been flipped.

8. Drop your Jalapeños onto the griddle. Drizzle oil and sprinkle salt on the peppers.
9. Add a slice of Monterrey Jack cheese to each burger patty as it nears completion. Top the cheese with the sautéed Jalapeños. Use Blackstone 12" Round Basting Cover to melt the cheese into the Jalapeños.
10. Meanwhile, placed sliced Torta roll inside down on oiled griddle top. Allow rolls to toast until golden brown.
11. Assemble the burger. Put the Chili Garlic Mayo inside the bottom roll. Place 2 onion slices on top of the mayo. Set your patty/cheese/Jalapeños on top of the onion. Cover in Mango Salsa and sprinkle with chopped cilantro. Add the top bun and serve.

Crab Cakes With Grapefruit Salad

Servings: 4
Cooking Time: 15 Min

Ingredients:
- ½ lb Jumbo Lump Crab Meat
- ½ lb Lump Crab Meat
- ½ cup Panko breadcrumbs
- 1/3 cup Mayonnaise
- 3 tablespoons Dijon Mustard
- 2 Eggs
- 1 tablespoon Worcestershire Sauce
- 1 tablespoon Hot Sauce
- 2 tablespoons Lemon Juice
- 4 cups Spring Greens
- The juice of half of a Grapefruit
- The juice of half of a Lemon
- 2-3 tablespoons finely chopped Flat Leaf Parsley
- Salt and Pepper
- Olive Oil

Directions:
1. In a large bowl, add the mayo, Dijon, eggs, Worcestershire sauce, hot sauce, panko, lemon juice and a pinch of salt and pepper. Whisk to evenly combine ingredients.
2. Add the crab meat and lightly mix to evenly incorporate.
3. Heat your griddle to medium heat and add a drizzle of olive oil.
4. Form the crab mix into cakes and cook in the oil for 2-3 minutes per side or until lightly golden and fully cooked.
5. In a large mixing bowl, add the spring greens, grapefruit juice, lemon juice, a drizzle of olive oil and a pinch of salt and pepper. Gently toss the salad to evenly coat.
6. To plate, add some of the salad to your plate and then the crab cakes over the top. Garnish with the parsley and a drizzle of hot sauce and serve hot.

Tumeric Cauliflower

Servings: 4
Cooking Time: x

Ingredients:
- 1 lb. fresh cauliflower or 1 12 oz. bag frozen cauliflower florets
- ¼ cup olive oil
- 1 tablespoon fresh minced garlic
- 1 tablespoon dried turmeric
- 1 tablespoon chicken soup base paste
- 1 tablespoon garlic salt
- 1 teaspoon black pepper

Directions:
1. Pre-heat the air fryer to medium high for 10 minutes.
2. If using fresh cauliflower, wash and pat dry. Using a paring knife, start at the stem and remove green leaf stalks, exposing the white stem. Cut the florets from the stem and remove them from the cauliflower head.
3. Chop cauliflower florets to about 1-inch pieces, making sure the thicker stem pieces are removed. Set aside.
4. Combine remaining ingredients in a large mixing bowl and whisk together, ensuring the entire soup base is incorporated with the oil and spices.
5. Add the cauliflower to the bowl and fold to coat with the olive oil and seasoning. Make sure the cauliflower is evenly coated.
6. Pour the cauliflower mixture into the air fryer basket and shake to achieve a single layer.

7. Cook for 10 minutes, then shake the air fryer basket well, moving the cauliflower florets around excessively.
8. Cook to finish an additional 3- 5 minutes or until the cauliflower has a crispy, browned exterior and is cooked through.

Spinach Omelette

Servings:1
Cooking Time:10 Min

Ingredients:
- 3/4 Cup of Whisked Eggs
- 1.5 Cup of Fresh Spinach
- 1 Tomato, Diced
- 1/2 Purple Onion, Diced
- 1/2 Avocado, Sliced
- Shredded Cheese
- Salt and Pepper
- Sour Cream (optional)
- Hot Sauce (optional)

Directions:
1. Turn griddle to medium heat, add a little oil or butter.
2. Add the onions, season with salt and pepper. Add the fresh spinach and cook until slightly wilted.
3. Set the spinach and onions aside. Spread a little more oil or butter on the griddle and slowly add the eggs.
4. Use a spatula to shape the eggs into a round omelette shape and season with salt and pepper.
5. Pour a little water around the omelette and cover with a basting dome to steam the top.
6. Add cooked spinach and onions. Then, add 1/2 of your diced tomatoes and all of your shredded cheese to the omelette.
7. Use the basting cover again to melt the cheese. Remove the cover, and fold the omelette in 1/2.
8. Plate the omelette. Top with sliced avocado, add more diced tomatoes, sour cream, and some hot sauce.

Grilled Shrimp & Arugula Salad

Servings:x
Cooking Time:x

Ingredients:
- 1-2 Lb. of Raw Shrimp, tail on (amounts will vary depending on how many shrimp per salad)
- 1 Lemon
- Salt and Pepper
- Garlic
- Arugula (can add romaine as well, if desired)
- Boiled Egg
- Grape Tomatoes
- Avocado (cut into chunks)
- White Sharp Cheese, any kind (I used Beehive Seahive cheese)
- Lemon White Balsamic Vinegar
- Extra Virgin Olive Oil

Directions:
1. Thaw shrimp in refrigerator overnight, or run under cold water in a colander until thawed.
2. Zest and juice lemon into a bowl large enough to marinate shrimp.
3. Mince garlic cloves (4-6) and add to the lemon juice.
4. Put thawed shrimp in with lemon juice and toss. Add salt and pepper to flavor shrimp. Drizzle with extra virgin olive oil. Toss again.
5. Heat Blackstone griddle to a medium heat and then turn to low.
6. Pour mixture onto Blackstone and spread shrimp evenly on the griddle. Add extra salt and pepper if desired. The shrimp cook quickly, so watch them. As they start to turn pink, turn them over. It might only take 1 minute or so on each side. After they are done cooking, remove and cover with a piece of aluminum foil to stay warm while you assemble the salads.
7. Assemble salads by layering with the Arugula on the bottom (add some Romaine lettuce or other lighter lettuce if straight Arugula is too peppery for you)
8. Add grape tomatoes, cut in half. Add boiled egg if desired and some ribbons of a white sharp cheddar cheese. I used Beehive Seahive cheese (local to Utah), but Parmesan would be good too! Add avocado chunks.
9. Top with cooked shrimp and drizzle with the lemon balsamic vinegar and some extra virgin olive oil. Enjoy!!

Amaretto Brioche French Toast With Chocolate Syrup

Servings: 4
Cooking Time: 15 Min

Ingredients:
- 4-6 Slices of Brioche French Bread
- 3 Eggs
- 1/2 Cup of Coffee Creamer (Amaretto Flavored)
- 2 Teaspoons of Sugar
- 3 Tablespoons of Salted Butter
- Chocolate Jimmies (sprinkles)
- Almonds, Slivered or Sliced
- 1/2 Cup of Sugar
- 1 Tablespoon of Special Dark Cocoa Powder
- Pinch of Sea Salt
- 3 Tablespoons of Water
- 1 Tablespoon of Salted Butter

Directions:
1. Start your chocolate syrup by whisking together the sugar, cocoa, and salt with the water until smooth in the Blackstone Sauce Pot or a small pot on the lowest heat setting on the Blackstone Griddle.
2. Add the butter and continue to whisk every few minutes until sauce comes together. Set aside while you make your french toast and the sauce will thicken some as it cools.
3. Beat eggs and sugar together, add the creamer and mix well. Spread around one tablespoon of butter to medium-low/low heated Blackstone.
4. Quickly dip one piece of bread into egg mixture, coating both sides of bread, and place in the butter. Let toast cook low and slow for about 4-5 minutes until golden brown and flip.
5. While the other side cooks for another 4-5 minutes, add a sprinkle of jimmies and almonds on each slice of bread.
6. Remove from griddle, plate, and garnish with a drizzle of warm chocolate syrup.

Cheese Chicken Sandwiches

Servings: 4
Cooking Time: 15 Min

Ingredients:
- 4 Chicken Cutlets
- 1 Sweet Yellow Onion, Julienne
- ½ Red Bell Pepper, Julienne
- ½ Green Bell Pepper, Julienne
- 1 cup Sliced Mushrooms
- 1/3 cup Ranch Dressing
- ¼ cup Buffalo Sauce
- 8 slices Pepper Jack Cheese
- Blackstone Cheesesteak Seasoning
- 4 Hoagie Rolls
- Salt and Pepper
- Olive Oil

Directions:
1. Pre-heat your griddle to medium-high heat.
2. Season the chicken cutlets with salt, pepper, and a good bit of Blackstone Cheesesteak Seasoning on both sides.
3. Add 2 tablespoons olive oil to the hot griddle and cook the chicken for 3 minutes per side.
4. Add a bit more olive oil next to the chicken and add the onions, bell peppers and mushrooms with a bit more Blackstone Cheesesteak Seasoning. Toss to evenly coat and cook for 3-5 minutes.
5. Once the chicken is nearly finished, using your spatulas or a knife and cut the chicken into bite sized pieces. Make 4 even piles of chicken and add some of the veggies over the tops of each. Add a couple pieces of pepper jack cheese over each stack and cover to melt.
6. In a small bowl, mix the ranch and buffalo sauce evenly and add to the bottom of each hoagie roll. Add the chicken stacks to the hoagie rolls, slice and serve hot.
7. Enjoy!

Chicken Parmesan Ranch Sandwich

Servings: 4
Cooking Time: 20 Min

Ingredients:
- 3 Chicken Cutlets
- Olive Oil
- Salt

- Pepper
- Blackstone Parmesan Ranch Seasoning
- Shredded Mozarella
- Pepperoni
- Martins Rolls Sandwich Buns
- Marinara
- Fresh Basil

Directions:
1. Pre heat Blackstone griddle to medium high.
2. On a plate add 3 chicken cutlets and lightly cover with olive oil, salt, pepper and Blackstone Parmesan Ranch Seasoning on each side.
3. On your griddle top add a light amount of olive oil and cook for 3-4 mins each side till cooked completely. Pull off the griddle and turn your heat to low.
4. Slice your chicken to fit into your egg rings.
5. Place Egg Rings on Griddle and add enough shredded mozzarella to inside of egg rings (not to much, just enough for a nice bed of cheese), chicken, pepperoni and top with mozzarella to liking.
6. Cover with a basting dome, spray water around egg rings before covering, and heat till cheese is melted.
7. While Cheese is melting place your Martins rolls on the griddle to lightly toast.
8. Remove dome when cheese is meted, place your rolls on a platter, slide a spatula under your egg rings and ingredients, and place on your toasted buns. Add a desired amount of marinara and freshly sliced basil.
9. Top with your bun crown and enjoy!

Buffalo Chicken Fritters

Servings:4
Cooking Time:20 Min

Ingredients:
- 1 Lb. of Boneless and skinless chicken breast, diced small
- 1/3 Cup of Shredded mozzarella cheese
- 1/4 Cup of Blue cheese crumbles
- 2 Tablespoons of Mayonnaise
- 3 Tablespoons of Buffalo Sauce (and extra to drizzle on top)
- 1/3 Cup of All-purpose flour
- 1 Egg
- Salt & Pepper to taste
- Olive Oil for Cooking
- Ranch for Dipping

Directions:
1. In a large mixing bowl, add all the ingredients except for the olive oil and ranch. Mix to evenly combine. Be sure there aren't any lumps of flour.
2. Heat your Blackstone Griddle to medium-low and add 2 tablespoons of the chicken mix. Press the chicken down so that it's a flat disc-like shape. Repeat with the remaining chicken mix.
3. Cook for 3-4 minutes per side or until the chicken is fully cooked. Serve with a bit more buffalo sauce and some ranch.

Salmon With Honey Soy Glaze

Servings:4
Cooking Time:13 Min

Ingredients:
- 4 Salmon Fillets (6 oz. each, skin on)
- 1/4 Cup of Honey
- 1/4 Cup of Soy Sauce
- 2 Limes
- 2 Tablespoons of Dijon Mustard
- 2 Tablespoons of Water
- Salt & Pepper to taste
- Olive Oil

Directions:
1. In a bowl, whisk together honey, soy sauce, juice from 2 limes, mustard, and water. Set aside.
2. Preheat the griddle to medium heat.
3. Check the salmon fillets for pin bones and remove any you find.
4. Coat the fillets with a little oil and season with salt and pepper.
5. Cook the salmon on each side for about 3 minutes (more or less depending on how thick your fillets are).
6. When the fillets are about 90% done, pour the honey soy glaze over them and let the sauce reduce for a minute. Move the sauce around with your spatula to evenly reduce it.
7. Remove the fillets and the sauce from the heat and serve with steamed asparagus.

Cranberry Jalapeño Sausage Stuffing

Servings: 11
Cooking Time: x

Ingredients:
- 16 Oz. of Breakfast Sausage
- 1 Cup of Diced Red Onion
- 1/2 Cup of Diced Jalapeño
- 1 Cup of Dried Cranberries
- 1 Large Loaf Bakery Fresh French Bread, Cubed int 1/2" Squares
- 1 Cup of Chicken Stock
- Salt and Pepper to Taste

Directions:
1. Preheat griddle to medium heat.
2. Cook sausage, breaking it apart with spatulas as it cooks. Adjust heat as necessary, making sure sausage cooks evenly, but does not burn. Mix frequently.
3. Add onion and Jalapeño when sausage is getting close to done. Allow the onion and Jalapeño to cook in the sausage grease, mixing frequently. Cook for a few minutes, until soft.
4. Add cranberries and mix, allowing to cook in sausage grease. The cranberries should remain chewy. Allow the cranberry's sugar to release and sauté with the recipe, but don't let the cranberries lose their moisture and turn hard.
5. Add bread and mix together with other ingredients.
6. Add chicken stock and quickly mix ingredients allow stock to soak into all the bread. You can add an addition ½ cup of chicken stock if needed, so long as bread does not get soggy.
7. Allow bread to slightly toast on some edges while mixing, adding salt & pepper to taste.
8. Remove from griddle and serve.

Beer Battered Fish & Chips

Servings: 2
Cooking Time: x

Ingredients:
- 4-5 Large Idaho Russet Potatoes, Peeled and Cut into Strips
- 3-5 Pieces of Meaty White Fish like Grouper, Cod, or Haddock
- 1 Cup of Flour
- 1 Beer (Heineken is used in this Recipe)
- 1 Tablespoon of Baking Powder
- 1/2 Tablespoon of Old Bay Seasoning
- 1 Tablespoon of Corn Starch
- Vegetable Oil in a Squirt Bottle

Directions:
1. Soak cut fries in cold salted water for 15 minutes, then dry well using a clean dish towel.
2. Prep your fish, cutting if needed; you don't want too thick of a piece because we are trying to deep fry on a griddle. Pat each fish fillet well with a paper towel to dry.
3. Whisk flour, baking powder, cornstarch, and old bay together, then whisk in beer. If the batter is too thin, add more flour.
4. Heat griddle to medium heat and drizzle vegetable oil and add fries. Cook until crispy, adding more oil with your Blackstone squirt bottle as needed throughout turning to cook all sides.
5. You want lower heat the first half of cooking. Turn heat to medium-high / high heat and continue cooking, turning and adding oil as needed. Don't rush them! When they are close to done move them to one side of your Blackstone.
6. On the opposite side using medium-high to high heat add vegetable oil, dipping your fish in the batter than adding to the hot oil.
7. Using your squirt bottle add more oil to the front of each piece of fish, closest to you, so the oil slides back and under the fish. Cook 3-4 minutes on each side adding oil before flipping.
8. Season fish and chips with sea salt. Serve with tartar sauce and malt vinegar!

Ricotta Lemon Griddle Cakes

Servings: 4
Cooking Time: 20 Min

Ingredients:
- 1 cup all purpose flour
- 1 tbsp baking powder
- 1 tbsp baking soda

- 2 tbsp sugar
- ¼ tsp salt
- 1 ¼ cup whole milk ricotta
- 2 eggs
- ⅔ cup milk
- Juice from one large lemon
- 1 ½ tsp pure vanilla extract
- Butter for cooking
- Zest from one large lemon

Directions:
1. In two separate mixing bowls combine the wet ingredients in one and the wet in the other. Whisk the wet ingredients together.
2. Slowly add the dry ingredients to the wet mixing to combine. Let sit 10 minutes or while the Blackstone heats up to medium heat.
3. Swirl butter to melt where you will cook the pancakes, using a ¼ cup measuring cup per pancake.
4. Cook about 2 minutes per side, or until bubbles appear, flipping once.
5. Enjoy!

Portobello Mushrooms

Servings:1
Cooking Time:10 Min

Ingredients:
- 4-5 Portobello Caps, sliced
- 3 Garlic Cloves
- 3 Tablespoons of Curly Parsley, chopped
- 1/4 Cup of Extra Virgin Olive Oil
- Sea Salt & Fresh Cracked Pepper to Taste
- Pinch Red Pepper Flake (optional)
- 1 Tablespoon of Butter

Directions:
1. Wash and dry mushrooms. Slice Â½ inch slices. Add the chopped garlic, chopped parsley, Salt, Pepper, Red Pepper Flakes and olive oil. Toss to coat. Cover and let sit 20 minutes.
2. Drizzle Blackstone with a little oil and add 1 tbsp butter, spreading around, on medium high heat. Add the mushrooms in single layer and let cook 3 minutes. Flip and cook additional 2 minutes. Plate and garnish with reserved parsley.

Ultimate Breakfast Platter

Servings:6
Cooking Time:20 Min

Ingredients:
- Bacon
- Sausage Links
- Pancakes
- Eggs
- Strawberries
- Raspberries
- Blackberries
- Oranges
- Juice
- Mini Bagels (toast on griddle top for a couple minutes)
- Salmon
- Cream Cheese
- Cucumbers
- Red Onions
- Sesame Seeds
- Strawberry Yogurt
- Granola
- Fresh Raspberries

Directions:
1. Begin by sautéing your bacon and sausage. Then use your favorite pancake mix to make your pancakes.
2. Set your Air Fryer to low, and place eggs on the tray. Set a timer for 15 minutes and have a large bowl of ice water ready and waiting.
3. Once your timer goes off, remove the eggs, and let them set in the ice bath until cooled.
4. On a large platter, start to arrange all of your ingredients in a presentable manner. Your guests will be wowed by its beauty and will want to dig right in!

Ramen Burger

Servings:1
Cooking Time:10 Min

Ingredients:
- 6 Ramekins
- 5 Packages of Ramen
- 5 Hamburger Patties

- 5 Eggs
- 2 Pinches Sea Salt
- 2 Pinches - Black Pepper
- 2 Pinches Granulated Garlic
- 1 Cup of KC Masterpiece BBQ Sauce
- 1-2 Tablespoons of Mr. Yoshida's Teriyaki Sauce
- 1/4 Cup of Chopped Green Onion

Directions:
1. Boil and strain packages of Ramen noodles
2. Crack eggs into a bowl, add a few pinches of Sea Salt, Black Pepper, and Granulated Garlic. Mix everything together in bowl.
3. Pour egg mixture into a bowl of boiled Ramen noodles. Mix everything thoroughly.
4. Fill 6 ramekins with Ramen noodles and cover the top with plastic wrap. Place ramekins in the fridge for 15 minutes.
5. Add KC Masterpiece BBQ Sauce into a bowl. Add Mr. Yoshida's Teriyaki Sauce and chopped green onion. Mix everything thoroughly and set aside.
6. Preheat griddle on high, add olive oil. Place Ramen patties and hamburger patties on the griddle. Season burger patties with granulated garlic. Place strips of turkey bacon on griddle. Flip Ramen patties when golden brown. When the hamburger patties are almost done glaze each one with the sauce. Once everything is cooked, place a hamburger patty, some turkey bacon, and shredded lettuce in between the two Ramen buns. Enjoy!

Philly Cheesesteak

Servings:1
Cooking Time:10 Min

Ingredients:
- 2 Lb. of Thinly Sliced Beef (Rib-Eye Roast, Sirloin, Tri-Tip Roast, Rump Roast, or Flank Steak)
- 1 Onion, Sliced
- 1 Green Pepper, Sliced
- 1 Red Pepper, Sliced
- 1 Teaspoon of Garlic Powder
- 2 Tablespoons of Butter
- Salt & Fresh Ground Black Pepper to Taste
- 3 Tablespoons of Red Wine Vinegar (or apple cider vinegar)
- 12-18 Slices of Provolone Cheese
- 1 Jar of Cheese Whiz
- 6 Hoagie Rolls

Directions:
1. Preheat the griddle to medium high heat.
2. Add 1 tablespoon of butter and some oil to the griddle.
3. Add the onions, green peppers, and red peppers to the hot griddle.
4. Season with salt, pepper, vinegar, and ½ tsp of garlic powder. Toss to combine and coat evenly.
5. Add another tablespoon of butter and some oil to the other side of the griddle.
6. Add the thinly sliced beef to the griddle. Chop it up with your metal spatulas to help it all cook evenly. Season the meat with salt, pepper, and another ½ tsp of garlic powder.
7. When the meat is cooked, divide it evenly on the griddle into 6 piles.
8. Turn the heat down to medium.
9. Add a few tablespoons of Cheese Whiz to each pile of meat, then add the veggies to each pile.
10. Add 2-3 slices of provolone cheese to each pile of meat and veggies.
11. Split your hoagie rolls and toast them on the griddle.
12. When the provolone cheese is melted, place each pile of meat into a toasted hoagie roll and serve hot.

Bbq Reuben Pork Sandwich

Servings:2
Cooking Time:60 Min

Ingredients:
- 8-10 Oz. of Pork Loin Chops
- Kosher Salt to Taste
- Pepper to Taste (Freshly Ground)
- BBQ Pork Seasoning to Taste
- Swiss Cheese
- 1 Garlic Clove
- 1 Cup of Mayonnaise
- 3 Tablespoons of Sriracha
- 4 Tablespoons of Lemon Juice (Freshly Squeezed)

- 4 Rosemary Olive Loaf Bread Slices
- 3 Tart Apples
- 2 Fennel Heads (Small)
- 1 Red Onion (Small, Thinly Sliced)
- 1/4 Cup of Olive Oil
- Salt, Pepper, and Parsley (To Taste)
- 2 Tablespoons of Lemon Juice

Directions:

1. To make the sriracha mayonnaise, mix garlic, mayonnaise, sriracha, and lemon juice in a small bowl. Season with salt, then cover the bowl and chill it in the fridge.
2. To make the apple and fennel slaw, pour the lemon juice in a large bowl. Cut an apple in half, core, and julienne, then toss it in the lemon juice. Add the other ingredients in the bowl and let the mix marinate for 20 minutes.
3. Turn on the Blackstone Griddle. Set half to high heat and the other to low. You'll use the high heat zone for the chops and the low heat for other ingredients.
4. Lightly coat chops with olive oil and season evenly.
5. Cook each side of your pork chops for 4 minutes. Use a thermometer - they should have an internal temperature of 145 degrees.
6. Take the pork chops off the griddle and let rest for 15 minutes. Then, slice.
7. Place sliced Pork from 1 Loin in a pile on the low side of the griddle. Chop up and cook âcheesesteakâ style for 1 minute.
8. Place 2 slices of Swiss Cheese on top of the pork and cover with basting cover to melt.
9. Coat slices of rosemary olive loaf with sriracha mayonnaise. Place on low-heat zone of the griddle.
10. Put the pork loin chop with melted cheese on top of 2 bread slices.
11. Place apple and fennel slaw on top of the pork loin and cheese.
12. Add more sriracha mayonnaise to taste and then top off with remaining slices of bread for each sandwich.

Bacon Blue Cherry Brussels

Servings:6-8
Cooking Time:20 Min

Ingredients:

- 2 lb bag of brussel sprouts, shredded
- 8 slices bacon, thick cut
- 3-4 garlic cloves, grated
- 1 tbsp duck fat (sub olive oil)
- 5 oz bag dried cherry and walnuts (salad toppers)
- 4 oz blue cheese wedge
- black pepper

Directions:

1. If the brussel sprouts are not pre shredded, use a mandolin or sharp knife to shred the brussel sprouts. Slice sprouts in half, then slice into ribbons to shred and set aside.
2. Turn Blackstone on low heat, while that is preheating, cut bacon into bite sized pieces. Add bacon to the Blackstone and cook for 3-4 minutes.
3. Add the shredded brussel sprouts to the bacon and bacon fat. Toss to coat adding a tablespoon of duck fat or olive oil. Continue to toss every couple of minutes allowing bacon to finish cooking and sprouts to get tender and slightly char. Season with black pepper.
4. Mix in dried cherries and walnuts, these are found in the produce department with salad toppers or you can but dried cherries and walnuts separately. Let cook one minute.
5. Plate and top with crumbled blue cheese.

Strawberries And Cream Pancakes

Servings:6
Cooking Time:45 Min

Ingredients:

- 2/3 cup all purpose flour
- 2 tsp baking powder
- 1 tbsp sugar
- a pinch of salt
- 2 tsp lemon zest
- 5 strawberries chopped into bits
- 1 egg, separated
- 1/2 cup milk
- 1/3 cup ricotta cheese
- 2 tbsp melted butter

- 1tsp pure vanilla extract
- Whipped cream (for finishing)
- 12 oz cream cheese, room temperature
- 1/4 cup sugar
- 1 cup whipping cream
- 2 tbs lemon juice
- 1 pint of Strawberries cut into to chunks
- 1/4 cup sugar
- 2 tbs lemon Juice

Directions:
1. In a mixing bowl, combine all dry ingredients.
2. In a separate bowl, mix egg yolk, milk, ricotta, butter, vanilla. Slowly, add dry ingredients and mix on low until combined.
3. Whisk egg white until stiff peaks form, and gently fold into pancake mix. Then gently fold in strawberry bits.
4. Set to the side while you prepare your filling and syrup.
5. In a stand up mixer, whisk together cream cheese, sugar, and lemon juice. Turn to low speed and add in whipped cream. Place in refrigerator until your syrup is done.
6. In a sauce pan add chopped strawberries, sugar, lemon juice and simmer until juices have slightly thickened. About 20-25 mins.
7. Preheat Griddle to medium. Melt a tablespoon of butter on griddle. Pour 1/4 cup of pancake mix onto griddle and let cook until bubbles start to form and edges are slightly browned. About 3-4 minutes. Flip and cook another 3 minutes.
8. Once all of your pancakes are cooked, grab a plate and start layering your pancakes. Begin with a pancake, then spread some of the cream cheese filling, and top with some of the strawberry chunks. Repeat steps until you have a nice stack. Top with remaining strawberry syrup and a dollop of whipped cream.

Crispy Steak Bites

Servings:4
Cooking Time:x

Ingredients:
- 16 oz New York Strip Steak
- 1 egg
- 2 tablespoons oil
- 2 cups panko breadcrumbs
- 1 tablespoon garlic salt
- 1 tablespoon smoked paprika
- 1 tablespoon cracked black pepper

Directions:
1. Trim any fat or silver skin from the exterior of the steak.
2. Slice the steak into about 12 one-inch cubes. Cut across the grain of the meat.
3. Whisk together the egg, oil, garlic salt, paprika, and black pepper until oil is well combined with the egg and spices.
4. Dredge steak pieces into the egg mixture, then the panko breadcrumbs one at a time.
5. Preheat air fryer to maximum heat for 10 minutes.
6. Air fry for about six minutes or until panko is browned and steak is cooked to your desired doneness.
7. Serve with barbecue sauce, steak sauce, or ranch dressing for dipping.

Crunchy Crab Melts

Servings:8
Cooking Time:20 Min

Ingredients:
- 2 artisan loaves, sliced roasted garlic bread
- 1 lb lump crab meat
- 1 - 8 oz block muenster cheese, shredded
- 1 - 8 oz block cheddar cheese, shredded
- Old Bay seasoning
- Dukes mayo
- parsley

Directions:
1. Shred both blocks of cheese and mix together, set aside.
2. Spread mayonnaise on each outer side of each slice of bread.
3. Place bread mayo side down on low to medium-low preheated Blackstone.
4. Add cheeses to both slices. Add crabmeat to one side. Season with old bay and parsley.

5. When cheese is melted and outside of bread is toasted to perfection, sandwich the two slices together.
6. Serve as whole sandwiches or slice into halves or quarters for bit sized appetizers!

Marinated Flat Iron Steak

Servings:6
Cooking Time:140 Min

Ingredients:
- 1 1/2 Lb. of Flat Iron Steak
- 2 Tablespoons of Olive Oil
- 1/2 Cup of Soy Sauce
- 1/2 Cup of Brown Sugar
- 1/2 Teaspoon of Seasoned Salt
- 1/4 Teaspoon of Ground Ginger
- 1/4 Teaspoon of Black Pepper
- 1/4 Teaspoon of Garlic Powder

Directions:
1. Add all marinade ingredients to a gallon-sized resealable bag. Seal the bag and mix well.
2. Add steak to the bag, seal the bag closed, and knead until steak is completely coated.
3. Place bag in the fridge and allow steak to marinade for at least 2 hours (or up to 8 hours).
4. Heat your griddle to high heat and coat with a thin layer of olive oil or butter.
5. Remove steak from marinade, shake off excess, and discard marinade.
6. Cook steaks on hot grill to desired doneness (internal temperature of 130-135 degrees for medium-rare).

Airfryer Mini Spinach And Cheese Quiche

Servings:4
Cooking Time:20 Min

Ingredients:
- 1 Package Pie Crust Dough
- 3 Eggs
- 1 Cup Milk
- 1/2 Cup Shredded Cheese
- 2 Pieces Crumbled Bacon
- 2 Cups Spinach
- 1/2 Yellow Onion Diced
- 1 tsp Minced Garlic
- 1/8 tsp of nutmeg
- Cooking Spray
- Salt/Pepper

Directions:
1. Heat griddle top to medium/high. Sauté bacon and onions. Remove bacon and place on a paper towel. Toss the onions in some of the bacon grease.
2. Add minced garlic and spinach to onions. Sauté until spinach is wilted. Remove and set to the side.
3. Roll out the pie crust, and cut circles with a cookie cutter. Ball up the excess dough, roll out, and cut again until you have 12 circles.
4. Preheat air fryer to medium, and spray silicone muffin cups with cooking spray.
5. Press 1 pie crust in each cup. Put a spoonful of spinach, onions, and bacon in the bottom of each cup.
6. In a pyrex cup, whisk together eggs, milk, cheese, nutmeg, salt/pepper.
7. Pour the egg mixture into each cup until it reaches the top of the pie crust.
8. Cook in the air fryer about 10 mins, or until the tops are golden brown.
9. Enjoy!

Buttermilk Syrup

Servings:1
Cooking Time:10 Min

Ingredients:
- 3 Cups of White Sugar
- 1 Cup of Buttermilk
- 1 Cup of Butter
- 1/4 Cup of Corn Syrup
- 2 Teaspoons of Baking Soda
- 4 Teaspoons of Vanilla Extract

Directions:
1. In a large pot, stir together all ingredients.
2. Bring to a boil, and cook for 3 minutes stirring continually.
3. Remove from the heat. Serve warm with Buttermilk Pancakes, French Toast, or Waffles.

Classic Margherita Pizza

Servings:1
Cooking Time:10 Min

Ingredients:
- 1 Crust of Pizza Dough
- 8 Oz. of Fresh Mozzarella
- 8 Fresh Basil Leaves
- 1/2 Cup of Vine Ripened Crushed Tomatoes or San Marzano Tomatoes
- 1 Tablespoon of Extra Virgin Olive Oil
- 1 Pinch of Sea Salt

Directions:
1. Turn your Pizza Oven on to medium high heat.
2. Stretch your pizza dough and add the crushed tomatoes.
3. Add the fresh mozzarella torn into chunks.
4. Put fresh basil on top and drizzle with a little olive oil. Sprinkle the top with a little pinch of sea salt if you'd like.

Mini Chicken Pot Pies

Servings:4
Cooking Time:30 Min

Ingredients:
- 1 package of Pillsbury refrigerated pie crust
- 2 chicken breasts
- 1 tbsp olive oil
- 1 egg white
- 2 carrots chopped
- ½ yellow onion chopped
- 1 cup peas
- 1 cup chopped green beans
- 1 cup corn
- 1 can cream of chicken soup
- ½ cup whole milk
- 1 tsp Blackstone Chicken and Herb Seasoning
- salt and pepper
- cooking spray

Directions:
1. Chop carrots and parboil for 5 minutes.
2. Chop all other vegetables and set to the side.
3. Pour cream of chicken soup and milk in a bowl and stir. Pour over all vegetables and mix together. Set aside.
4. Chop chicken into small bite size pieces.
5. Set Griddle to high and coat with 1 tbsp olive oil. Cook chicken until no longer pink. Add salt and pepper and Blackstone seasoning. Remove from griddle and add to the veggie mixture.
6. Roll out pie crust and cut 8 – 5" circles.
7. Spray 4" silicone pie liners with cooking spray, and push 1 pie crust into the liner.
8. Scoop vegetable mixture into pie crust and pre-cook in the air fryer on high for 5 mins.
9. Remove and press the other 5" pie crust on top of the veggie mixture. Brush with egg white.
10. Place back into the air fryer on low heat for 10 minutes.
11. Remove from the air fryer, let cool for a few minutes before removing the liner, so the crust has time to firm up.

Air Fryer Spinach, Feta, And Sun-dried Tomato Stuffed Chicken

Servings:x
Cooking Time:x

Ingredients:
- 4 Chicken breasts
- 4oz of Feta Cheese
- 4oz shredded Mozzarella
- 1 Beefsteak Tomato, Sliced
- 1 Small Jar of Sun-Dried Tomatoes, cut into little bits
- 1 Small Bundle of Spinach
- 3 Tablespoons of Olive oil
- 1 Tablespoon Herbs de Provence
- 1 Tablespoon Garlic Powder
- 1 Teaspoon Salt/pepper
- Cooking spray

Directions:
1. Butterfly all 4 pieces of chicken by slicing in half, but not all the way through the other side. Drizzle olive oil over the chicken and gently rub.

2. Layer the inside with spinach, sliced tomatoes, sun-dried tomatoes, feta, and mozzarella cheese.
3. Fold chicken over and seal with a toothpick if necessary. Sprinkle the tops of the chicken with all of the spices.
4. Preheat Air-Fryer to medium.
5. Spray Air-Fryer trays with cooking spray, and place the chicken breasts on the tray. Be careful not to allow the goodies inside to fall out.
6. Cook the chicken breasts for 10 minutes, or until the top of the chicken is golden brown. Carefully, flip the chicken and cook another 4-5 minutes.
7. Remove from tray, serve with green beans or your favorite vegetable.

Steamed Ranch Carrots

Servings:5
Cooking Time:17 Min

Ingredients:
- 12 Petite Carrots
- 1 Packet Dry Ranch Dressing/Seasoning Mix
- 2 Extra Virgin Olive Oil
- Water

Directions:
1. In a large bowl, combine carrots, ranch seasoning mix, and olive oil. Stir until well-combined and all the carrots are coated evenly with oil and seasoning.
2. Heat griddle to medium-high heat and cover evenly with a small amount of olive oil.
3. Add carrots to the griddle and let cook for 2-3 minutes, turning occasionally.
4. Add 2-3 Tbsp water to the pile of carrots to generate steam. Cover carrot pile with basting cover or similar metal dish.
5. Every 2-3 minutes remove basting cover, toss carrots, add 2-3 Tbsp water, and re-cover with basting cover to continue steaming.
6. Cook carrots for approximately 12 minutes or to desired tenderness.

Sweet Dessert Sandwich

Servings:1
Cooking Time:10 Min

Ingredients:
- 1 Cup of Nutella Spread
- 8 White Bread Slices
- 2 Banana, Sliced
- 16 Marshmallows, Halved
- Butter
- Powdered Sugar

Directions:
1. Preheat Blackstone griddle to medium low.
2. Pair up slices of bread and spread Nutella on half of each.
3. Apply banana slices to 4 pieces of bread and marshmallows to other 4 pieces. Match up each banana side with a marshmallow side and sandwich together.
4. Spread a light layer of unsalted butter to the outside of sandwich.
5. Cook on griddle until each side is golden brown.
6. Remove from heat and dust with powdered sugar.

Rosemary Garlic Potatoes

Servings:4
Cooking Time:15 Min

Ingredients:
- 1 pound red potatoes, quartered
- 8 large garlic cloves, smashed
- 3 large sprigs rosemary
- 2 tablespoons unsalted butter
- Salt & pepper
- Olive oil

Directions:
1. Heat your griddle to medium heat.
2. In a large mixing bowl, add the potatoes, a pinch of salt and pepper and 1-2 tablespoons of olive oil. Toss to evenly incorporate ingredients.
3. Add the potatoes to the griddle and cook for 4-5 minutes, tossing often.
4. Reduce the heat of your griddle to low and add the garlic and rosemary and toss to incorporate. Cover with a dome and cook for another 4-5 minutes.
5. Add the butter and toss all ingredients together. Cover with a dome and cook another 4-5 minutes. When the potatoes are fully cooked, remove and serve hot.

Slammin' Cajun Salmon

Servings:4
Cooking Time:x

Ingredients:
- 12-16 oz. salmon fillets
- Olive oil, to taste
- Blackstone Crazy Cajun Seasoning, to taste
- 1 lb linguine or fettuccine
- 1/2 c unsalted butter
- 4-6 garlic cloves
- 1 Jalapeno pepper, cored and diced
- 1 pint heavy whipping cream
- 2 cups fresh tomatoes, diced
- Fresh basil leaves, to taste
- 1-3 tbsp flour (enough to thicken)
- Louisiana (cayenne-based) hot sauce, to taste
- Fresh lemon juice, to taste
- Green onion, sprinkled for garnish

Directions:
1. Preheat griddle top on medium to high heat. Exact setting will depend on your griddle size & number of burners. Make sure griddle top is hot enough to sear.
2. Cut salmon fillets into 4 serving-sized portions.
3. Rub salmon fillets with olive oil.
4. Rub flesh sides of salmon fillets (the pink meat side) with Blackstone's Crazy Cajun Seasoning. The seasoning will stick to the olive oil.
5. Meanwhile, fill Deep Fryer Attachment with water, set burner to high, and allow water to boil. Add salt and olive oil to water for flavor.
6. Place a cast iron or seasoned steel skillet on the hot griddle top
7. Add butter to skillet. Allow butter to melt. Stir butter to ensure butter doesn't burn.
8. Add minced garlic to butter. Stir garlic and butter to keep garlic from burning.
9. Add diced jalapeño to butter & garlic.
10. Add heavy whipping cream to skillet, stirring as you go. You might need to adjust the burner below your skillet to keep sauce simmering but to avoid boiling and burning. Continue stirring as necessary.
11. Add pasta to deep fryer basket, submerge in boiling water, pressing pasta down as necessary.
12. Lay salmon fillets flesh/seasoning side down on the hot griddle top.
13. Flip salmon fillets over once first side is seared.
14. Check pasta and stir as necessary to make sure pasta is not sticking. Pasta cooking times will vary but you'll want to cook your pasta until it's al dente.
15. Lift fryer basket and allow pasta to drain over steaming water while you finish the rest of the steps in the recipe.
16. Add diced tomatoes and basil leaves to the sauce as desired. Continue to stir.
17. Thicken sauce with flour. It should only take a few tablespoons of flour to thicken a skillet full of sauce. Slowly add flour and stir sauce until it reaches desired thickness.
18. Add Louisiana hot sauce to pasta sauce. Add enough sauce to change color of pasta sauce from white to a pinkish or peach color. Sprinkle a few drops at a time until desired amount of hot sauce is dispensed. Continue stirring.
19. Add fresh squeezed lemon juice to sauce.
20. Remove salmon fillets when salmon is flaky and pulls apart easily with a fork. Set aside.
21. Using tongs, place pasta in creamy Cajun sauce skillet. Gently turn pasta until it is completely covered in sauce.
22. Plate portions as needed. Start with a bed of pasta with sauce, sprinkle with chopped green onion, Blackstone Crazy Cajun Seasoning, and a salmon fillet. Sprinkle salmon fillet with fresh squeezed lemon juice.

Airy Fryer Breakfast Biscuit Bombs

Servings:x
Cooking Time:x

Ingredients:
- 6 slices thick bacon
- 1 tablespoon unsalted butter
- 4 large eggs, beaten
- 1/2 green bell pepper diced
- 1/2 yellow onion diced
- 1/4 teaspoon cracked black pepper
- 1 can refrigerator biscuits

- 2 oz sharp cheddar cheese, cut into 3/4-inch cubes
- 1 egg
- 1 tablespoon whole milk

Directions:

1. On your griddle top cook bacon over medium-high heat until crisp. Add peppers and onions to griddle top and sauté for 3-4 minutes. Remove and place on paper towel. Add butter to griddle and melt over medium heat. Add 2 beaten eggs and pepper. Cook until eggs are thickened, but still moist, stirring frequently. Remove from heat; stir in bacon, onions, peppers. Set aside.
2. Separate dough into 5 biscuits. Press each into 4-inch rounds. Spoon 2 heaping tablespoonful egg mixture onto center of each round. Top with one piece of the cheese. Gently fold edges up and over filling; pinch to seal.
3. In small bowl, beat remaining egg and milk. Brush biscuits on all sides with egg wash.
4. Preheat Air Fryer to 325°F; spray cooking spray on the tray. Place 5 of the biscuit bombs, seam sides down, in air fryer basket. Place the remaining biscuit bombs in the 2nd air fryer drawer.
5. Cook 8 minutes. Using tongs, carefully flip biscuits. Cook 4 to 6 minutes longer or until cooked through and golden brown.

Thanksgiving Turkey Breast

Servings:1
Cooking Time:10 Min

Ingredients:

- Turkey Breast (Skin On)
- Parsley (About a Handful, Finely Chopped)
- 1 Tablespoon of Dried Sage
- 2-3 Tablespoons of Butter
- 1 Lemon
- Olive Oil
- 1/2 Cup of Chicken Stock
- Salt and Pepper

Directions:

1. Drizzle olive oil in a tin tray pan.
2. Slice lemon and lay in pan.
3. Put turkey breast on top of lemon slices.
4. In a separate bowl, mix butter, sage, and chopped parsley together.
5. Pull the skin of the turkey back and spread ¾ of the butter mixture under the skin.
6. Lay the turkey skin back down and spread the rest of the butter mix all over the turkey breast.
7. Drizzle top with more olive oil and salt and pepper to taste.
8. Pour chicken broth in the bottom of the pan.
9. Cover with aluminum foil.
10. Bake in the Blackstone Patio Oven at about 350-400°F for about 20-25 minutes.
11. Remove the foil to brown and crisp the turkey skin for an additional 5 minutes.
12. Let the turkey rest for 5-10 minutes before slicing it.

Bbq Chicken Stir-fry

Servings:4
Cooking Time:35 Min

Ingredients:

- 4 Chicken Breasts (Deboned and Skinless)
- 1/2 Cup of BBQ Sauce
- Salt and Pepper or BBQ Rub
- 4 Eggs
- 3 Tablespoons of Soy Sauce (Chef Recommends Maggi Sauce)
- 3 Tablespoons of Ponzu Sauce
- 1 Garlic Clove (Minced)
- 1/4 Teaspoon of Ginger (Minced)
- 1/4 Teaspoon of Black Pepper
- 1 Large Sweet Onion (Sliced)
- 1 Medium Green Pepper (Medium, Cut into Strips)
- 1 Sweet Red Pepper (Medium, Cut into Strips)
- 12 Oz. of Peas and Carrots (Frozen)
- 1 Cup of Corn (Frozen)
- 4 Cups of Jasmine Rice (Pre-Cooked)

Directions:

1. Preheat your griddle to medium-high heat and oil the surface.
2. Coat the chicken with salt and pepper or BBQ rub to taste. Cook a few minutes on each side. Dice the

chicken into small pieces and continue cooking. Add BBQ sauce and cook to desired doneness.

3. Start sautéing the peppers and onions and cook until they start to get soft. Add garlic, ginger, and black pepper. Cook until fragrant.

4. Add more oil beside the onions on the griddle. Then, place the frozen peas, carrots, and corn on the griddle separate from the garlic and ginger mix. Incorporate the cooked diced chicken as well.

5. Add the cooked rice on top of the onion, garlic, and ginger mix. Toss to combine.

6. When the peas, carrots, corn, and chicken are finished, combine with the rice and mix.

7. Melt the butter on the griddle and add the eggs. Scramble until fully cooked then incorporate into the rice.

8. Add shoyu sauce and ponzu sauce to the rice. Toss to combine.

9. Remove from griddle and serve warm.

Quick Collards

Servings:4
Cooking Time:20 Min

Ingredients:
- 1 pound shredded collard greens
- 8 strips thick cut bacon
- 1/3 cup chopped yellow onion
- ½ cup chicken stock
- 2 tablespoons red wine vinegar
- 2 teaspoons red pepper flake
- Salt & pepper
- Olive oil

Directions:

1. Heat your griddle to medium heat and add the bacon. Cook for 5-6 minutes or until crisp and fully cooked. Remove from the griddle and drain on a few pieces of paper towel.

2. Add the onion to the griddle and cook for 4-5 minutes, tossing often.

3. Add the collard greens with a pinch of salt, a large pinch of pepper and toss to incorporate. Cook for 4-5 minutes, tossing often.

4. Add ½ of the chicken stock and cover with a dome. Cook for 3-4 minutes.

5. Add the remaining chicken stock, red wine vinegar and red pepper flake. Toss to evenly combine ingredients. Cover and cook for another 4-5 minutes then serve hot.

Betty's Italian Cutlets

Servings:5
Cooking Time:30 Min

Ingredients:
- 2-3 large boneless skinless Chicken Breast
- 4 Eggs
- 1 ½ cup Parmesan Cheese
- 2 c plain Bread crumbs
- 1 bunch flat leaf Parsley, chopped
- 1 tsp Paprika
- 1 tsp Garlic Powder
- ½ tsp Onion Powder
- Salt & Pepper
- Oil for frying, extra light tasting Olive Oil preferred
- Coarse Sea Salt, optional

Directions:

1. Slice each chicken breast into 4-6 pieces then using the flat side of a meat mallet flatten out each chunk of chicken pulling the mallet towards the outside. Repeat for each chicken breast. You should get 4-6 cutlets per chicken breast. Set them aside and set up your dredging station.

2. Line up two shallow dishes or containers. In one add the eggs, a big handful of Parmesan cheese (about ½ - ¾ cup) and a handful of chopped parsley (about ¼ cup). Whisk together to combine, then and add the cutlets to the cheesy eggs. Note this step can be done ahead of time and cutlets in egg mixture can sit in the refrigerator until ready to use up to overnight or use immediately.

3. In the second shallow bowl add bread crumbs, paprika, garlic and onion powder. Season with salt and pepper. Mix in a handful of cheese and chopped parsley.

4. Remove one cutlet from the egg mixture and place in the bread crumb mixture flipping and patting bread

crumbs onto the chicken until completely coated. Repeat with each cutlet.

5. Allow the BLACKSTONE to heat to medium to medium low heat. Place a cooling rack on one side of the griddle or nearby.

6. Using a BLACKSTONE squirt bottle filled with oil lightly squirt cooking area with a little oil and place cutlets into oil a few at a time, adding a small amount of more oil before each set of cutlets. Allow to cook 3-4 minutes or until golden brown. Flip cutlets adding a light squirt of oil to allow cutlets to shallow fry evenly for another 3-4 minutes. Low and slow frying without rushing or burning breadcrumbs.

7. Remove cutlets to rest as each one cooks onto a cooling rack immediately sprinkle cutlets with cheese and or coarse sea salt. Once all cutlets are fried, plate and enjoy!

Griddled Chicken Street Tacos

Servings:8
Cooking Time:25 Min

Ingredients:
- 3 Chicken Breasts (cut into strips)
- 1 Teaspoon of Cumin
- 1 1/2 Teaspoons of Chili Powder
- 1 Teaspoon of Garlic Powder
- 1/2 Teaspoon of Salt
- 1/2 Teaspoon of Pepper
- 8 Small Corn Tortillas (4.5" "street taco" size)
- 1/4 Cup of Ctoija Cheese
- 1/2 Yellow Onion, Diced
- 2 Roma Tomatoes, Diced
- 2 Limes, Divided
- 1/2 Cup of Cilantro, Chopped
- 1/2 Jalapeno Pepper

Directions:

1. Heat your griddle to medium-high heat and cover with a thin layer of olive oil.

2. In a small bowl, combine seasonings including cumin, chili powder, garlic powder, salt, and pepper.

3. Add chicken to your hot griddle and coat evenly with seasoning mix. Turn a few times to combine.

4. Cook 8-10 minutes, turning occasionally, until chicken's internal temperature reaches 165 degrees.

5. Remove from griddle.

6. To make the pico topping: In another bowl, combine onion, tomatoes, juice from 2 limes, cilantro, and jalapeño. Stir until well-mixed.

7. On a small corn tortilla, place a few strips of your grilled chicken. Top with pico and a teaspoon of cotija cheese.

Jamaican Jerk Seasoning

Servings:1
Cooking Time:10 Min

Ingredients:
- 1 Tablespoon of Allspice
- 1/4 Teaspoon of Ground Cinnamon
- 1/4 Cup of Brown Sugar
- 1/2 Teaspoon of Red Pepper Flakes
- 1/4 Teaspoon of Ground Cloves
- 1/2 Teaspoon of Ground Cumin
- 2 Teaspoons of Salt
- 1 Teaspoon of Black pepper
- 2 Tablespoons of Canola or Vegetable Oil
- 1 Freshly Squeezed Lime
- 3-4 Tablespoons of Coconut Milk

Directions:

1. Combine all dry ingredients and store in an airtight container.

2. To use the spice mixture for Kabobs, put about 2 pounds of your choice of meat pieces in a zip-top bag. Boneless skinless chicken thighs work well for this but you can use chicken breast, beef, vegetables, or pineapple.

3. In a bowl, mix canola oil, lime juice, and coconut milk, and pour into the bag with the meat.

4. Add 2-4 tablespoons of the dry Jerk Seasoning to the bag (more or less to taste). Seal the bag and mix all the contents together until well coated. Let meat marinade for at least 10 minutes.

Betty's Bite Sized Chinese Meatballs

Servings: 6
Cooking Time: 30 Min

Ingredients:
- 1 lb Ground Pork
- 1.5 tbsp Cornstarch
- 1 tsp fresh Ginger, grated
- 3-4 Garlic Cloves, grated
- 3 tsp Brown Sugar
- 3 tsp Soy Sauce
- 1 tsp Five Spice
- 5 Green Onions, sliced (3 for the mixture and 2 for a garnish)
- Stir Fry Oil or Olive oil for cooking
- Sesame Seeds for garnish
- 1/4 c Honey
- 1/2 c low sodium Soy Sauce

Directions:
1. With a spoon mix together first 8 ingredients. (Make sure to leave roughly 2 stems of green onion on the side for a garnish) Roll in small bite size meatballs. Recipe about makes 24.
2. On medium heat spread olive oil onto the Blackstone Griddle and cook meatballs on each side until browned. About 5 minutes per side, adding a little more oil if needed when rolling onto each side to cook.
3. Use the Blackstone dome towards the end to help meatballs cook through.
4. Garnish with sliced green onions & sesame seeds, serve with dipping sauce!
5. Enjoy!

Pulled Pork Breakfast Tacos

Servings: 1
Cooking Time: 10 Min

Ingredients:
- 1 Lb. of Wood Smoked Pulled Pork (without seasoning)
- 12 Large Eggs
- 1 Lb. of Hash Brown Potatoes
- 1 Lb. of Shredded Cheddar Cheese
- Salt to Taste
- Pork Rub or Rib Seasoning of Your Choice
- Hickory Barbecue Sauce of Your Choice
- 12 Small Taco-Sized Flour Tortillas (Approximately 5" in Diameter)

Directions:
1. Preheat the Blackstone griddle to medium heat. When heated, coat the griddle top with light Olive oil.
2. Steps 3-5 are to be cooked at the same time.
3. Heat 1 lb. already smoked (cooked) pulled pork on griddle top. Season to taste with Pork rub or Rib seasoning. Use spatula to turn meat as it browns.
4. Crack and cook 12 large Eggs sunny side up. Season to taste with salt. Remove from griddle top when yolk is still runny.
5. Cook 1 lb. shredded Hash browns on griddle top, flipping when bottom sides are browned.
6. Add shredded Cheddar cheese to taste on top of Hash browns when they are almost finished cooking.
7. Warm 12 small Taco-sized flour tortillas on griddle until slightly browned.
8. Plate it up: Put equal amounts of Hash browns/Cheese, Eggs, and Pulled pork on each Tortilla. Top with Hickory flavored barbecue sauce.

Cj's Rooty Tooty Fresh And Fruity Breakfast

Servings: 2
Cooking Time: 20 Min

Ingredients:
- Milk
- Bacon
- Breakfast Sausage links
- Eggs
- Fresh Fruit 1/2 cup Strawberries 1/2 cup Raspberries 1/2 cup Blackberries
- Whiskey
- Brown sugar
- Honey
- 1/2 cup Strawberries
- 1/2 cup Raspberries
- 1/2 cup Blackberries

Directions:
1. Preheat one zone of your Blackstone on high and one zone on medium or low. Place a skillet on your hot zone to the side/corner with the handle away from the griddle top (it'll get hot if it's directly over the griddle top)
2. While the Blackstone is preheating you can cut and prepare your fruit. Cut the stem off and remove the top of your 1/2 cup of strawberries, and slice the strawberries into quarters. You don't have to but this helps them cook a little quicker when they're cut.
3. Once your strawberries are prepped you can add the strawberries, raspberries and blackberries to your skillet on the Blackstone. Also in your skillet you will now add 1-1 1/2 cups of a whiskey. 1/4 cup of brown sugar and 3-4 tablespoons of honey. Stir occasionally to incorporate the ingredients. You'll quickly notice little bubbles that pop quickly. We're looking to have large bubbles that pop slowly. This is when you know you've reached the optimal reduction of the syrup. And don't worry, the alcohol in your whiskey will burn off leaving that beautiful flavor in your syrup.
4. While your syrup reduces let's place down 4 strips of thick cut bacon on the other zone pre heating on medium. You can also add your sausage links at this point. Both the bacon and sausage won't take much time to cook.
5. While your bacon and sausage are cooking you can prep your pancake batter. Simply follow the directions on the back of the box. Usually this consists of milk, eggs and mixing in a large bowl. This doesn't take long at all so be sure to check in on your syrup string occasionally and flipping your bacon and sausage.
6. Your syrup is probably done reducing now, so pull that off and let it cool. You should see that your fruit has softened up, changed color a bit and your whiskey reduced down to a thicker consistency. Once it's cooled down a bit you can place that in a small bowl or jar. Or you can serve it straight from the skillet.
7. By this time your bacon should be done so remove that and drain on paper towels. Sometimes I like to cook the sausage a little longer than bacon. But that's up to you. BUT DO NOT GET RID. OF ALL THE BACON FAT. We want to cook our pancakes in that bacon fat.
8. Let's make the pancakes. Keeping your heat on medium ladle out your pancake batter on to the Blackstone to your preferred size. You'll know it's time to flip, usually about 2 minutes per side, when you see little bubbles starting to pop in the batter. This won't take long so you can start on your eggs. But be sure to flip once you see those little bubbles and remove when done.
9. Crack 4 eggs onto your Blackstone, still using the bacon fat from before and cook eggs to your liking. Be sure to add salt and pepper to taste. The classic Rooty Rooty breakfast always shows eggs sunny side up, but I'm not a sunny side up kinda guy.
10. Now your plate should be ready to serve with two pancakes, two pieces of bacon, two pieces of sausage, and two eggs. Spoon as much of that fresh fruit bourbon syrup one your pancakes and enjoy!

Thanksgiving Leftovers Grilled Cheese Sandwich

Servings:1
Cooking Time:10 Min

Ingredients:
- 8 Slices French Bread (Sourdough or Other Artisan Bread)
- 4 Slices Provolone Cheese
- 4 (Heaping) Cranberry Sauce
- Leftover Stuffing
- Leftover Turkey
- 4 Butter (Room Temperature)
- 1 Dried Sage

Directions:
1. Turn your griddle on to Medium Low heat (This is a thick sandwich so you want the ingredients in it to heat up before the outside burns).
2. In a small bowl, mix the butter and sage together.
3. Lay out the slices of bread.
4. Top one side of the bread with a slice of provolone cheese, a layer of stuffing, turkey, and finally top with cranberry sauce.

5. Put the other piece of bread on top and butter the outside of the bread with the sage butter.
6. Grill both sides of the sandwich until golden brown and heated through.

Onchos

Servings: 2
Cooking Time: 20 Min

Ingredients:
- 2 Servings of Frozen Onion Rings
- 1 lb Ground Beef
- Blackstone Taco Fajita Seasoning
- 1/2 Cup Black Beans
- 1 Cup Cheddar Jack Cheese
- Romaine Lettuce
- Tomato
- Salsa Verde
- Jalapeños

Directions:
1. Set Air-fryer to Medium Low. Add 2 servings of Onion Rings to Airfryer.
2. Pre Heat Griddle to Medium High and cook 1lb of 80/20 ground beef. When Beef is almost done add Blackstone Fajita Taco Seasoning.
3. Chop and dice Lettuce and Tomato for toppings.
4. When onion rings are crispy and done place in Blackstone cast iron serving platter. Add cooked beef, Black beans and Shredded cheese.
5. Place back on griddle top, spray some water on griddle top to create steam and cover till cheese is melted. When cheese is melted pull off and add lettuce, tomato, jalapeños and salsa verde.

Apple Stuffed French Toast With Bourbon Caramel Sauce

Servings: 4
Cooking Time: 25 Min

Ingredients:
- 8 thick slices of French Bread
- 3 cups Bourbon
- 2/3 cup White Sugar
- 2 large Green Apples, small dice
- ½ Green Apple Brunoise (finely diced)
- 8 oz. softened Cream Cheese
- 2 tablespoon Cinnamon Sugar
- ¼ cup Whole Milk
- 4 Eggs
- 1 tablespoon Cinnamon Sugar
- ¼ cup Milk

Directions:
1. Using a large sauté pan over medium-high heat, add the apples, bourbon and sugar. Bring to a boil and reduce until it has the consistency of maple syrup then remove from the heat.
2. In a large mixing bowl, add the cream cheese, cinnamon sugar finely diced apples and milk. Mix to evenly incorporate.
3. In a casserole dish, add the egg mix ingredients and whisk to mix evenly.
4. Add the some of the cream cheese mix to one side of the read and make a sandwich with a second piece of bread. Repeat with remaining bread.
5. Place the sandwiches into the egg mix and coat on both sides. Add a bit of oil or non-stick spray to you griddle over medium heat and add the French toast sandwiches. Cook for 3-4 minutes per side.
6. Once the french toast is fully cooked, slice in half and add it to your serving plate. Drizzle the caramel sauce over the top with some of the cooked apples. Garnish with fresh mint or powdered sugar and serve.

Huckleberry Pancakes

Servings: x
Cooking Time: x

Ingredients:
- 1 1/4 Cups of All-Purpose Flour
- 1/2 Teaspoon of Salt
- 1 Tablespoon of Baking Powder
- 1 1/4 Teaspoons of Sugar
- 1 Egg
- 1 Cup of Milk
- 1 Tablespoon of Butter (melted)
- 1/2 Teaspoon of Vanilla Extract
- 1/2 Cup of Huckleberries

Directions:

1. In a bowl, mix together flour, salt, baking powder, and sugar with a whisk or fork.
2. In a separate bowl, beat egg, milk, melted butter, and vanilla. Gently add huckleberries to the mixture and lightly whisk to incorporate the huckleberries.
3. Combine both bowls, using a whisk to mix dry and wet ingredients together.
4. Set your griddle between medium and low heat. Spray griddle top with nonstick cooking spray once griddle top has reached the desired heat.
5. Pour approximately 1/4 cup of batter on the griddle top. Repeat and evenly space your pancakes until the batter has been used.
6. Carefully fip pancakes when the edges have bubbled and the bottom is golden brown.
7. Allow second side of pancake to cook until golden brown.
8. Remove pancakes, top with butter, fresh huckleberries, huckleberry syrup, or other topping of your choice.
9. Enjoy!

Marinated Balsamic Pork Chops

Servings:4
Cooking Time:25 Min

Ingredients:
- 1/3 Cup of Balsamic Vinegar
- 1/3 Cup of Worcestershire Sauce
- 1/4 Cup of Reduced-Sodium Soy Sauce
- 2 Tablespoons of Olive Oil
- 2 Garlic Cloves, minced
- 1/2 Teaspoon of Black Pepper
- 1/4 Teaspoon of Cayenne Pepper
- 4 Bone-In Pork Chops (3/4-in thick)

Directions:
1. Whisk together balsamic vinegar, Worcestershire sauce, soy sauce, oil, garlic, black pepper, and cayenne pepper.
2. Place pork chops in a gallon-sized resealable bag and pour marinade over pork chops.
3. Refrigerate 3-4 hours (or up to overnight).
4. Remove pork chops from fridge 15 minutes before grilling.
5. Heat griddle to high heat and cover with a thin coat of olive oil.
6. Place pork chops on griddle and cook approximately 2-3 minutes per side, or until internal temperature reaches 145 (medium rare) to 155 (medium) degrees.

California-style Salmon Tacos

Servings:4
Cooking Time:25 Min

Ingredients:
- 1 1/2 - 2 Lb. of Salmon Fillet
- 5 Bacon Slices
- 1 Green, Red, or Yellow Peppers (Finely Chopped)
- 1/2 White Onion (Finely Chopped)
- 2 Pineapple Slices (Fresh, Finely Chopped)
- 2 Garlic Cloves (Finely Chopped)
- 2 Limes
- 1/4 Tablespoon of Celery Salt
- 1/4 Tablespoon of Paprika
- Cilantro (Bunch, Finely Chopped)
- 4 Corn Tortillas

Directions:
1. Preheat the griddle with all burners set on medium temperature
2. Place the strips of bacon on the griddle and cook them thoroughly. Take out the bacon strips and make sure the grease remains on the griddle.
3. Spread the grease from the bacon thoroughly on the surface of the griddle and then place the salmon with the skin facing down on it. Add paprika and celery salt and let it cook from five to seven minutes.
4. While the salmon is cooking, take advantage of the bacon fat, and start cooking on one side of the griddle the green peppers, pineapple, onions, and garlic. Use the spatulas to spread the vegetables and cook them evenly. To season the vegetable mix, sprinkle a little bit of celery salt (be careful; celery salt is strong and can overpower the flavors of the vegetable mix).
5. Once the skin side of the salmon is cooked, flip the salmon and let it cook between four and seven minutes.
6. Once the vegetable mix is cooked, remove from the griddle.

7. Once the salmon is cooked, place the fillet on a large cutting board, break the bacon into small crumbs, and mix them thoroughly with the vegetable mix. Place the mix on top of the salmon and sprinkle fresh cilantro.

8. Heat tortillas, assemble the tacos and squeeze lime drops on top of the salmon.

Griddled Grapefruit Shandy

Servings:4
Cooking Time:15 Min

Ingredients:
- 2 Grapefruits, Cut in Half
- 4 Oz. of Simple Syrup
- 4 Oz. of Grapefruit-flavored Vodka
- Corona Beer

Directions:
1. Set griddle to high heat. Slice both grapefruits in half and dry off with a paper towel. Using a paper towel, spread a very thin layer of vegetable oil on the griddle top to assist with the caramelization. Place grapefruit halves on griddle top and cook until caramelized.
2. For our Simple syrup add equal parts sugar and water to a plastic container with a lid and shake for about 20-30 seconds or until you see the sugar has completely dissolved.
3. On a plate add 1 TBSP of sugar, 1 Tsp of salt and a dash of cayenne pepper. Coat the glass rim with grapefruit juice and season the glass rim.
4. In your glass strain and squeeze one half of the grapefruit 1 ounce of simple syrup, 1 ounce of grapefruit flavored vodka, give that a stir and pour in your ice cold Corona, and garnish with a grapefruit wedge.

Salmon Street Taco

Servings:4
Cooking Time:25 Min

Ingredients:
- 4-6 oz Salmon filets, diced large cubes
- 1 tbsp Wok oil
- 1 tbsp Sesame oil
- 1 tbsp Sesame seeds
- 12 Flour Tortillas, street taco size
- 2 Avocados
- 2 c Green Cabbage, sliced thin
- ½ cup Green Onions, sliced
- 1-2 c Cilantro, rough chopped
- 1 juice of Lime plus Zest
- 2 tsp Wok oil
- 2 tsp Sesame oil
- BLACKSTONE Tequila Lime seasoning to taste
- 1 c Mayo, Dukes or Kewpie preferred
- ½- ¾ c Sriracha
- 2 tbsp Sesame Oil
- 1.5 tbsp Ponzu sauce
- 2 Garlic cloves, grated

Directions:
1. Cube salmon and toss in sesame oil, wok oil and sesame seeds. Let marinate while you make the slaw and sauce.
2. Mix cabbage, cilantro and green onions in a large bowl. Toss with wok oil, sesame oil, lime juice and zest of the lime. Season with BLACKSTONE tequila lime seasoning to taste. Set aside.
3. Mix all ingredients for spicy Mayo adding more or less sriracha depending on spice level. Set aside.
4. Preheat BLACKSTONE griddle to medium high heat, add salmon to sear 1 minute per side.
5. While salmon cooks, warm the tortillas for 1-2 minutes per side on medium heat. Place heated tortillas in the BLACKSTONE taco rack, add slaw then salmon, a slice of avocado and drizzle with spicy mayo.

Loaded Italian Pork Sandwiches

Servings:4
Cooking Time:15 Min

Ingredients:
- 4-8 Pork Cutlets
- ¾ cup Blackstone Loaded Italian Sear and Serve
- ½ cup Mayonnaise
- 3 tablespoons Lemon Juice
- 8 slices Salami
- 4 slices Coppa
- 8 slices Provolone
- ½ a large Red Onion, thinly sliced
- 2 cups shredded Romaine Lettuce

- 4 Potato Rolls
- Salt & Pepper
- Olive Oil

Directions:
1. Pre-heat your griddle to medium-high heat.
2. Season one side of the pork cutlets with a bit of salt and pepper. Add a few tablespoons of olive oil to the griddle and cook the pork for 3-4 minutes.
3. In a small mixing bowl, add the mayo, lemon juice, a pinch of salt and pepper, and 2 tablespoons of the Loaded Italian Sear and Serve. Mix to evenly combine.
4. Flip the pork cutlets and add the remaining Loaded Italian Sear and Serve over the top.
5. Add 2 slices of salami and 1 slice of coppa over the cutlets and then top with 1 or 2 pieces of provolone. Cover with a basting dome to melt.
6. Lightly toast the buns.
7. To build, add some of the sauce to the toasted bottom bun then some lettuce and red onion. Add 1 or 2 of the pork cutlets over the top. If desired, add more sauce to the top bun and serve hot.
8. Enjoy!

Tequila Party Cake

Servings:4
Cooking Time:x

Ingredients:
- 8 slices pound cake
- 4 tbsp butter, unsalted
- 1 8oz can pineapple, crushed or chunks
- 1.5 tbsp dark brown sugar
- 2 tbsp cilantro, plus some for garnish
- Pink sea salt
- Zest of one lime
- ¼ cup tequila
- 1 c heavy whipping cream
- ½ c powdered sugar
- Splash tequila
- 1 tsp fresh lime juice

Directions:
1. Beat together the ingredients for the cream with electric beaters until thickened. About 5 minutes. Set in the refrigerator.
2. On medium heat cook the pineapple and brown sugar mixing together to coat pineapple evenly for 3 minutes, adding half of the cilantro during the last minute. Remove and set aside.
3. Melt half the butter on medium to medium low preheated Blackstone.
4. Working quickly, dip the bottom end of each piece of pound cake, about ¼ inch, quickly into tequila and lay them in the melted butter.
5. Fry for about 2 minutes or until golden brown.
6. Add remaining butter and carefully flip the cake onto the other side to fry until golden brown.
7. Plate fried cake slices, top with a sprinkle of pink sea salt, pineapple, drizzle with cream and garnish with cilantro and lime zest.

Blackstone Betty's Blackstone Airfryer Cannolis

Servings:x
Cooking Time:x

Ingredients:
- 15 oz whole milk ricotta cheese
- 8 oz mascarpone cheese
- 1⁄2 c powdered sugar
- 1.5 tsp vanilla
- 3⁄4 tsp cinnamon
- 1 cup mini chocolate chips, divided in half
- 1 package wonton wrappers
- 1⁄4 c vegetable oil
- tin foil
- powdered sugar, for dusting

Directions:
1. Mix the first five ingredients plus 1⁄2 cup of mini chocolate chips. Place mixture in a storage bag and place in the refrigerator.
2. Cut strips of tin foil about 2 inches wide and roll into tubes. Use the handle of a rounded wooden spoon to help roll tubes.
3. Using fingers or a rubber brush, coat wontons one at a time with a thin layer of oil and wrap around a tube of foil. Place finger inside tube to help press the wonton to seal at the corners.

4. Place wontons seam side down into air fryer, preheated to high. Wontons will cook quickly in just 3-6 minutes, so check every two minutes and turn halfway through. Wontons are ready when they reach a golden brown color.

5. Remove and let cook a few minutes. Carefully pull tin foil out.

6. Cut the corner of the storage bag with the cannoli filling and fill each cannoli, squeezing filling into each side of the cannoli shells.

7. Dip each filled end into the remaining 1/2 cup of chocolate chips (optional), dust with powdered sugar and enjoy!

Buttermilk Pancakes

Servings:1
Cooking Time:10 Min

Ingredients:
- 3 Cups of All-Purpose Flour
- 3 Tablespoons of Sugar
- 3 Teaspoons of Baking Powder
- 1 1/2 Teaspoons of Baking Soda
- 3/4 Teaspoon of Salt
- 3 Eggs
- 1/3 Cup of Melted Butter
- 3 Cups of Buttermilk
- 1/2 Cup of Milk

Directions:
1. In a large bowl, combine dry ingredients.
2. In a separate bowl, whisk the eggs and melted butter together. Add the buttermilk and milk. Keep the two mixtures separate until you are ready to cook.
3. Pour the wet mixture into the dry mixture, using a wooden spoon or rubber spatula to blend. Stir until itâs just blended together. Do not over mix.
4. Let the batter rest for 5 minutes. This will give the batter time to activate and create the bubbles necessary for fluffier pancakes.
5. While the batter is resting, turn on the griddle to medium-high heat. When you flick water on the griddle it should sizzle and dance across it.
6. Spray the griddle with cooking spray (or use butter). Pour about 1/2 Cup of batter onto the griddle per pancake. Periodically check the bottom of the pancakes and adjust the heat as needed.

Sweet & Spicy Parmesan Pickle Chips

Servings:4
Cooking Time:x

Ingredients:
- 16 oz jar sweet pickle chips
- 1 cup flour
- 2 eggs
- 1 tablespoon Sriracha
- 2/3 cup panko breadcrumbs
- 1/3 cup grated Parmesan cheese

Directions:
1. Drain pickle chips from pickling liquids and arrange them in a single layer on a few sheets of paper towel. Cover with additional paper towel sheets and allow them to dry enough to remove any standing liquid.
2. Create a dredge station by mixing the eggs with Sriracha sauce.
3. Mix the panko breadcrumbs with Parmesan cheese.
4. Dredge the pickle chips first into the flour to lightly coat then into the egg wash, and on to the Parmesan and breadcrumb mixture.
5. Preheat your air fryer to 400F.
6. Cook the Parmesan pickle chips for 8-10 minutes in batches turning once until the pickle chips become golden brown and are crispy.
7. Serve immediately with ranch dressing for dipping.

Chili Lime Chicken Fajitas

Servings:6
Cooking Time:25 Min

Ingredients:
- 1/4 Cup of Lime Juice
- 1 Clove Garlic (minced)
- 1 Teaspoon of Chili Powder
- 1/2 Teaspoon of Salt
- 1/2 Teaspoon of Cumin
- 1/4 Cup of Olive Oil
- 1 1/2 Lb. of Chicken Breast (sliced into fajita strips)

- 1 Yellow Bell Pepper (sliced)
- 1 Green Bell Pepper (sliced)
- 1 Red Bell Pepper (sliced)
- 1 Medium Onion (sliced)
- 12 Fajita Tortillas (6-8 inches)
- Shredded cheese
- Sour Cream
- Salsa
- Tomatoes
- Guacamole

Directions:
1. In a resealable, gallon-sized plastic bag, mix lime juice, garlic, chili powder, salt, cumin, and oil until well-combined.
2. Add chicken, seal bag, and knead to coat evenly.
3. Let marinade 30 minutes - 6 hours (I don't recommend more than 6 hours as the acid from the lime juice can break down the chicken, affecting its texture).
4. Heat your griddle to medium-high heat and cover the surface with olive oil.
5. Add the peppers and onions to half your griddle and cook for 2-3 minutes, turning occasionally.
6. Add the chicken and marinade mixture to the other half of your griddle and cook for 8-10 minutes, turning occasionally. Chicken's internal temperature should be 165 degrees.
7. Serve on tortillas, top with cheese, sour cream, guacamole, and tomatoes.

Flank Steak With Chimichurri Sauce

Servings:1
Cooking Time:10 Min

Ingredients:
- 1 Lb. of Flank Steak
- Kosher Salt
- Freshly Ground Pepper
- Canola Oil
- 2 Cups of Packed Fresh Italian Flat Leaf Parsley
- 4 Medium Garlic Cloves
- 1/4 Cup of Packed Fresh Oregano Leaves (or 4 tsp dried Oregano)
- 1/4 Cup of Red Wine Vinegar
- 1/2 Teaspoon of Red Pepper Flakes
- 1/2 Teaspoon of Kosher Salt
- Freshly Ground Black Pepper
- 1 Cup of Extra Virgin Olive Oil

Directions:
1. CHIMICHURRI SAUCE: Combine parsley, garlic, oregano, vinegar, red pepper flakes, salt, and pepper in a food processor. Pulse a few times until everything is roughly chopped. Then turn the food processor on and slowly add the olive oil. Put it in an air tight container and put it in the fridge for at least 2 hours to let the flavors combine.
2. If you don't have a food processor just finely chop the parsley, oregano, and garlic and combine with all the other ingredients.
3. FLANK STEAK: Season steak generously with Kosher salt and freshly ground black pepper. Coat with a little canola oil on each side (we're using canola oil here instead of olive oil because it can handle the high heat of the griddle better).
4. Turn your griddle to high heat. This would also work well to cook the steak on the Grill+Kabob with the included grill grates.
5. Cook the steak on each side for about 4-5 minutes. Take the steak off the griddle when you've reached the desired doneness and let it rest for 5 minutes. Slice it against the grain and top it with the Chimichurri sauce.

Twice Cooked Griddle Baked Potatoes

Servings:6
Cooking Time:35 Min

Ingredients:
- 6 Russet Potatoes (cut into 1/2" slices)
- 2 Tablespoons of Olive Oil
- 2 Teaspoons of Fresh Ground Black Pepper
- 2 1/2 Teaspoons of Garlic Powder
- 2 Teaspoons of Dried Rosemary
- Salt to Taste

Directions:

1. In a large pot, boil sliced potatoes until fork tender (about 10 minutes). This can be done on a range top or Blackstone griddle.
2. Transfer potatoes from water into a large bowl. Add olive oil, black pepper, garlic powder, rosemary, and salt. Toss until potatoes are evenly coated.
3. Heat your griddle to high heat and coat with a very thin layer of olive oil or butter.
4. Add potatoes to griddle and cook approximately 5-6 minutes each side or until crispy, light brown crust coats the outside of the potato slices.
5. Remove from heat and serve.

Bacon Wrapped Beer Battered Deep Fried Pickles

Servings:4
Cooking Time:20 Min

Ingredients:
- 4 Slices thick Cut Bacon
- 4 Large Dill Pickles
- 1 Cup of All Purpose Flour
- 1 Teaspoon of Salt
- 2 Teaspoons of Black Pepper
- 1 Teaspoon of Garlic Salt
- 1 Teaspoon of Smoked Paprika
- 3/4 Cups of Beer (Lager is best)
- 2 Quarts Vegetable Oil
- Ranch Dressing for Dipping
- Tooth Picks

Directions:
1. Using the Blackstone Griddle Range Top Fryer accessory, heat the vegetable oil to 365 degrees.
2. Wrap the bacon evenly around the pickles from top to bottom and secure both ends with a toothpick.
3. Fry the pickles in the vegetable oil for 3-4 minutes, or until the bacon is crisp. Remove the pickles from the oil and drain on a bit of paper towel.
4. In a large bowl, add the flour, salt, pepper, garlic salt, and smoked paprika and mix evenly with a whisk. Add the beer and whisk to fully incorporate.
5. Remove the toothpicks from the pickles and place them into the batter. Turn the pickles in the batter to evenly coat on all sides. (Be sure to lift the pickles out of the batter with tongs and let the excess batter drip off before adding them back to the fryer.)
6. Add the battered pickles to the vegetable oil and fry for 3-4 minutes or until they are golden and crispy.
7. Slice and serve with ranch dressing.

Amish Onion Patties

Servings:1
Cooking Time:10 Min

Ingredients:
- 1 Cup of All Purpose Flour
- 2 Teaspoons of Sugar
- 2 Teaspoons of Baking powder
- 1/2 Teaspoon of Salt
- 1/2 Teaspoon of Black Pepper
- 1/2 Teaspoon of Garlic Powder
- 2 Tablespoons of Cornmeal
- 2 1/2 Cups of Chopped Onion
- 1 Cup of Milk
- Vegetable Oil
- Hot Sauce

Directions:
1. Mix dry ingredients together, add the onions and mix so the onions get coated well.
2. Mix in milk and hot sauce (about 10-15 dashes is good).
3. Add extra flour and cornmeal if you want a thicker patty.
4. Turn the Blackstone griddle on medium to medium-low heat.
5. Drizzle a heavy coating of vegetable oil where you will be cooking and begin dropping spoonfuls, about ¼ cup, of onion batter in the oil.
6. Cook until golden brown, and flip. Adjust heat if needed.
7. Serve with ketchup, spicy ketchup, buttermilk ranch dressing or your favorite dipping sauce!

Corn Fritters

Servings:1
Cooking Time:10 Min

Ingredients:
- 1/2 Cup of All-Purpose Flour
- 1/2 Cup of Corn Meal
- 1 Teaspoon of Baking Powder
- Salt & Pepper to taste
- 1/2 Cup of Milk
- 1 Fresh Corn Ear
- 1/4 Cup of Cilantro, chopped
- 1/4 Cup of Mayonnaise
- 1/4 Cup of Sour Cream
- 2 Tablespoons of Honey
- 1/2 Teaspoon of Chipotle Chili Powder
- 1/2 Teaspoon of Smoked Paprika
- 1 Lemon

Directions:
1. In a large bowl mix flour, corn meal, baking powder, and milk. Season with a pinch of salt and pepper.
2. Cut the kernels off of a fresh ear of corn and mix it in the batter.
3. Add chopped cilantro.
4. Heat the griddle to medium-high heat.
5. Lightly oil the griddle and add spoonfuls of the batter to griddle and spread them out slightly.
6. Cook each side until they're golden brown.
7. Serve warm with the dipping sauce and sprinkle with more chopped cilantro.
8. To make the sauce: In a bowl mix the mayo, sour cream, honey, chipotle powder, smoked paprika, salt and pepper, and juice from half a lemon.

Tamari Ponzu Salmon With Sweet Chili Broccoli And Potato Crisps

Servings:4
Cooking Time:25 Min

Ingredients:
- 4, 6-8 oz skinless Salmon Filets
- 2 Large Russet Potatoes, cut into ¼ inch chips
- 12 oz Broccoli florets
- ½ tablespoon Ground Ginger
- ½ tablespoon Garlic Powder
- ¼ cup Tamari
- 3 tablespoons Ponzu
- 3 tablespoons Honey
- 1 tablespoon Sesame Oil
- ¼ cup sweet Thai Chili Sauce
- ¼ cup thinly sliced Green Onion
- 1 tablespoon toasted Sesame Seeds
- Salt and pepper
- Olive oil

Directions:
1. Pre-heat your griddle to medium-high heat.
2. Season the sliced potatoes with salt and pepper and a touch of garlic powder.
3. Add a drizzle of olive oil to the griddle and then the sliced potatoes. Cook for 2-3 minutes then flip.
4. Season the salmon on both sides with a light drizzle of olive oil, ground ginger, garlic powder and a bit of salt and pepper. Then add the hot griddle. Cook for 3-4 minutes per side or to desired doneness.
5. Add a bit of oil and the broccoli with a pinch of salt and pepper. If desired, add a splash of water and a dome to steam the broccoli for 4-5 minutes.
6. In a small mixing bowl, add the tamari, ponzu, honey and sesame oil. Mix evenly and pour ½ of the liquid over the fish for the last minute of cooking. Repeat if more glaze is desired.
7. Add the sweet Thai chili sauce to the broccoli and toss to incorporate.
8. To serve, lay out the potatoes in a fan pattern then add the broccoli. Place the salmon over the top and garnish with the sliced green onion and sesame seeds.
9. For an additional sauce, mix a bit of the sweet Thai chili sauce into the remaining tamari mix and drizzle over the top of the fish.

New York Style Pizza Dough (cold Rise)

Servings:1
Cooking Time:10 Min

Ingredients:
- 4 Cups of Bread Flour
- 1 and 1/2 Cups of Warm Water
- 1/2 Teaspoon of Instant Dry Yeast
- 2 Teaspoons of Salt
- 4 Teaspoons of Olive Oil

Directions:
1. Add water, flour, yeast, and salt together in a large bowl. Don't add the oil yet. You want the flour to hydrate first before adding oil.
2. Mix the dough until most of the flour is incorporated.
3. Add the oil and knead your dough for 10 minutes.
4. Cover dough and let it rise for 45 minutes to an hour.
5. Divide the dough into 3 pieces and round into balls. Wipe the dough balls with oil or cooking spray.
6. Place the dough balls in airtight containers and place in fridge for 12-24 hours (up to 4 or 5 days).
7. Remove from fridge and let come to room temperature before using (about an hour or two).

Airfryer Biscuits And Maple Sausage Gravy

Servings:4
Cooking Time:20 Min

Ingredients:
- 4 Pillsbury Homestyle Biscuits
- 1 pound maple sausage
- 2 ½ cups whole milk
- ¼ cup all purpose flour
- Blackstone Breakfast Blend Seasoning

Directions:
1. Pre-heat you Airfryer to medium-low heat. Spray a bit of canola oil to the bottom of the Airfryer basket and add your biscuits. Cook for 9-11 minutes or until lightly browned and fully cooked.
2. Heat your griddle to high heat and place an oven-safe pan on top. Add the maple sausage and cook until slightly crisp and fully cooked (about 6 minutes). Chop the sausage up to the desired size.
3. Once the sausage is fully cooked add 1 ½ cups of the milk, 1 tablespoons of Blackstone Breakfast Blend Seasoning and stir to combine. Heat the milk until its simmering, about 4 minutes.
4. In a small mixing bowl, add the flour and remaining milk. Whisk to evenly incorporate. Be sure to whisk out any lumps.
5. Once the milk and sausage is simmering, add the milk and flour combination slowly. Be sure to whisk constantly to evenly incorporate the milk and flour into the sausage. As the milk heats back up the gravy will begin to thicken. Cook for 4-5 minutes or until the flour has fully cooked and the gravy has thickened up to your liking.
6. If you gravy is too thick, add a splash of milk and whisk.
7. To plate, add the cooked biscuits to a plate and pour some of the sausage gravy over the top. Enjoy!

Greek Tzatziki Sauce

Servings:x
Cooking Time:x

Ingredients:
- 2 Cups of Greek Yogurt
- 2 Cucumbers, peeled and seeded
- 1 Garlic Clove, finely minced
- 2 Tablespoons of White Wine Vinegar
- 1 Bunch Fresh Dill, finely chopped (or 3 tsp dry dill)
- 3 Tablespoons of Olive Oil
- Salt & Pepper to taste

Directions:
1. Peel the cucumbers, cut them in half, and spoon out the seeds from the middle. Grate with a cheese grater.
2. Combine the cucumber, yogurt, garlic (minced), 2 tablespoons white wine vinegar, and 3 tablespoons of olive oil.
3. Mix until well combined.
4. Add pepper and salt to taste.
5. Add the finely chopped fresh dill.
6. Refrigerate for at least an hour to let the flavors combine.

Crispy Smashed Potatoes With Bacon And Cilantro

Servings:4
Cooking Time:15 Min

Ingredients:
- 1 pound yellow potatoes
- 4-6 strips thick cut bacon
- 1/3 cup sour cream
- 1 tablespoon Blackstone Tequila Lime Seasoning
- 1 tablespoon lime juice
- 1-2 tablespoons beer (lager is best)
- 2-3 tablespoons chopped cilantro
- 2 teaspoons garlic powder
- Salt and pepper
- Olive oil

Directions:
1. Pre-heat your Blackstone griddle to medium-low heat. Add 1-2 tablespoons of olive and oil and then the potatoes. Cook for 2-3 minutes covered. Lift the dome and add ¼ cup of water. Cover with a dome and steam for 3-4 minutes. Add another ¼ cup of water and steam another 3-4 minutes or until soft.
2. Cook your bacon crisp and well done then drain on a bit of paper towel.
3. Move your potatoes into the bacon fat and cook for 2-3 minutes, tossing often.
4. In a mixing bowl, add the sour cream, Tequila Lime Seasoning, Lime juice and beer. Mix evenly.
5. Using a heavy spatula or burger press, smash the potatoes into the bacon fat. Add some salt & pepper and garlic powder. Cook for 2 minutes and then flip to cook the other side.
6. Chop the bacon as small as you like.
7. To plate, add the crispy potatoes to a serving platter, garnish with chopped cilantro and chopped bacon. Finish with a drizzle of the sauce and serve hot.

Pepperoni Pizza

Servings:1
Cooking Time:10 Min

Ingredients:
- 1 Crust of Pizza Dough
- 1/2 Cup of Pizza sauce (or vine ripened crushed tomatoes)
- 8 Oz. of Shredded Mozzarella Cheese
- 16-20 Slices Pepperoni
- 1/8 Cup of Shredded Parmesan Cheese

Directions:
1. Turn your Pizza Oven to medium high heat.
2. Stretch out your pizza dough.
3. Add your sauce. You can use pizza sauce or a can of vine ripened crushed tomatoes. Cento brand crushed tomatoes are available in most big box grocery stores. San Marzano tomatoes work great for pizza sauce as well.
4. Add your mozzarella cheese and pepperoni slices.
5. Top with freshly grated parmesan cheese.
6. Cook until the crust is golden brown.

Olive Oil Flatbread

Servings:4
Cooking Time:120 Min

Ingredients:
- 2 Cups of Water (Warm, 105Â° Farenheit)
- 2 1/4 Teaspoons of Dry Yeast
- 1/2 Tablespoon of Kosher Salt
- 4 1/2 Cups of All-Purpose Flour
- 8 Tablespoons of Olive Oil
- Salt to Taste
- Pepper to Taste

Directions:
1. In a large mixing bowl, combine flour and yeast and mix well. Add warm water and 4 tbsp. olive oil - stir until dough comes together
2. Let it rest for 5 minutes.
3. Sprinkle kosher salt over the dough and mix well until salt is combined
4. Cover with plastic wrap and set in a warm spot to rise for 1 hour
5. In a baking pan, add 4 tablespoons of olive oil and spread evenly with your fingers
6. Now, with your olive oil-covered fingers, remove the plastic wrap - gently punch dough down and knead a few times in the bowl. Transfer dough to the baking pan and shape it into a flat rectangle. Sprinkle salt and

pepper over dough and let it sit for 30 minutes - you don't need to cover it again with the plastic wrap

7. Preheat your Blackstone griddle on high, then turn it down to medium-low heat

8. Add 2 tbsps. of oil to the hot griddle and spread it with your spatula. Carefully place bread dough onto the griddle. Quickly dimple the top of the bread with your fingers, and then pour any remaining olive oil over the top of the bread

9. Cook for 6-8 minutes. Then, flip over and cook the other side for the same time

10. Remove from the griddle. Now, simply cut it up to enjoy!

Thai Sweet Chili Chicken Pizza

Servings:1
Cooking Time:10 Min

Ingredients:
- 1 Crust of Pizza Dough
- 1/2 Cup of Sweet Chili Sauce (we used Mae Ploy Brand)
- 1 Cup of Diced Chicken Breast (pre-cooked)
- 1 - 1 1/2 Cup of Shredded Mozzarella Cheese
- 1 Tablespoon of Chopped Cilantro
- Olive Oil (To Drizzle)
- 1 Cup of Veggie Slaw (recipe below)
- 1 Cup of Chopped carrots, broccoli, and cabbage (typically can be bought in a bag pre-chopped)
- 2 Teaspoons of Apple Cider Vinegar
- 1 Teaspoon of Sugar
- 1 Teaspoon of Oil
- Pinch of Salt

Directions:
1. Stretch out your pizza dough and spread Sweet Chili sauce over it.
2. Add diced chicken and sprinkle with a pinch of chopped cilantro.
3. Add mozzarella cheese and drizzle with a little olive oil.
4. Cook in the Blackstone Pizza Oven until done.
5. Slice pizza and top with Veggie Slaw and more fresh chopped cilantro.

6. Veggie Slaw Recipe: Mix all ingredients together and toss to combine. Let sit for 5-10 minutes for flavors to combine.

Griddle Girl Air Fryer Apple Fries

Servings:x
Cooking Time:x

Ingredients:
- 2 large green apples
- 1 cup graham cracker crumbs
- ¼ cup sugar
- 2 eggs
- 1 cup flour
- cooking spray
- caramel dip

Directions:
1. Peel apples and cut into thin slices.
2. In a bowl, mix graham cracker crumbs and sugar. In a separate bowl, scramble two eggs. In the third bowl, pour flour.
3. Working in batches, coat apple slice with flour, then egg mixture, then graham crumbs.
4. Spray Air fryer tray with cooking spray. Heat to medium.
5. Add apple slices to tray and cook 5 minutes.
6. Flip and cook for 3 more minutes.
7. Remove and serve with caramel apple dip.
8. Enjoy!

Chicken Piccata Pasta

Servings:1
Cooking Time:10 Min

Ingredients:
- 2 Large Boneless Skinless Chicken Breasts (or 1 lb. of Chicken Tenderloins)
- 1/2 Cup of Flour
- 2 Tablespoons of Extra Virgin Olive Oil
- 2 Tablespoons of Butter
- 2 Garlic Cloves, Minced
- 1/2 Cup of White Wine
- 1/2 Cup of Chicken Broth

- 1 or 2 Lemons (Juiced and Zested)
- 1/4 Cup of Capers (drained and rinsed)
- 1 Lb. of Cooked Spaghetti (Al Dente)
- 2 Tablespoons of Chopped Flat-Leaf Parsley
- Salt & Pepper to Taste

Directions:
1. Butterfly each chicken breast all the way so you have 4 equal pieces.
2. Season chicken with salt and pepper, then dredge each piece in flour. Shake off excess flour.
3. Turn griddle to medium heat. Add 2 tablespoons of butter and 2 tablespoons of olive oil to griddle.
4. In a bowl mix the wine, chicken stock, lemon juice, lemon zest, and capers together.
5. Add chicken to the butter and olive oil. Cook chicken until browned on both sides.
6. While the chicken is still cooking, add 2 tablespoons of butter next to it on the griddle. Add the minced garlic and cook 30 seconds. Add the cooked pasta to the butter and garlic. Toss to coat.
7. Start adding the lemon wine sauce to the pasta and toss to coat and reduce the sauce. Add about ¼ Cup of the sauce to the chicken to deglaze the griddle and coat the chicken.
8. Add any remaining sauce to the pasta and continue to toss and reduce the sauce. Take it off the griddle when all the pasta is coated with sauce and thickened enough. Garnish with chopped parsley.

Chorizo Breakfast Hash

Servings:4
Cooking Time:25 Min

Ingredients:
- 8 strips thick cut Bacon
- 8 Eggs
- 1 lb Red Bliss Potatoes, quartered or diced
- ½ cup diced Chorizo
- 1 large Sweet Onion, large dice
- 1 Red Bell Pepper, small dice
- 1 Green Bell Pepper, small dice
- 1 tablespoon minced Garlic
- ¾ cup shredded Asiago Cheese
- Hot Sauce
- Chopped Chives
- Salt and Pepper

Directions:
1. Set your griddle to medium heat and cook the bacon until desired doneness then remove from the heat.
2. Add the potatoes to the bacon fat with a pinch of salt and pepper and cook for 5-6 minutes tossing often.
3. Add the chorizo and cook for an additional 2-3 minutes tossing often.
4. Add the onions and peppers and toss to incorporate. Cook for an additional 4 minutes.
5. Using either 4 small cast iron skillets or 1 large family style skillet, add all the vegetables. Using tongs, make small wells for the eggs.
6. Break up the bacon and add over the top and then add the shredded cheese. Crack the eggs into each of the wells with a pinch of salt and pepper and cover with a dome for 4-5 minutes to cook the eggs.
7. Once the eggs are cooked garnish with the chives and hot sauce then serve immediately.

Griddle Chili Dogs

Servings:8
Cooking Time:20 Min

Ingredients:
- 8 All Beef Hotdogs
- 8 Hotdog Buns
- 1 Cup of Grated Cheddar Cheese (for topping)
- 1 Tablespoon of Olive Oil
- 1 Large Yellow Onion, Diced (for topping)
- 1 1/2 Lb. of Ground Beef
- 2 Teaspoons of Ground Cumin
- 1 Tablespoon of Chili Powder
- 1 Cup of Ketchup (or substitute with one 14.5 oz. can of diced tomatoes)
- 2 Tablespoons of Mustard
- 1/4 Cup of Water
- 1 Jalapeño (Diced)
- Salt and Pepper to Taste

Directions:
1. Add oil to griddle on medium heat. Add the onion, jalapeño, garlic powder, and cumin. Cook until it is soft and translucent.

2. Add the ground beef, breaking it up with the metal spatula.
3. Add salt, pepper, and the chili powder and cook until browned.
4. Stir in the ketchup (or diced tomatoes) and mustard.
5. Let the chili reduce on the griddle top until thickened. If the chili gets too thick just add a couple tablespoons of water to thin it out (if using diced tomatoes you probably won't need the extra water since it has more liquid already). When the chili is done, put it in a metal bowl and leave on the griddle top to keep warm.
6. Crisscross slice the hotdogs on two sides. Add some olive oil to the griddle and roll the hotdogs around in it to coat them. Cook until crispy on the outside.
7. Spread butter on the hotdog buns and toast on the griddle until golden brown.
8. Put the hotdog in the bun and top with hotdog chili, shredded cheddar cheese, and diced onions.

Mexican Breakfast Molletes

Servings:8
Cooking Time:35 Min

Ingredients:
- 4 Bolillos (Mexican Bread)
- 16 Oz. of Refried Beans
- 12 Oz. of Chorizo (Mexican Sausage)
- 2 Tomatoes (Medium-Sized, Finely Chopped)
- 1/2 White Onion (Finely Chopped)
- Cilantro (Bunch, Finely Chopped)
- 1 Lime
- 1 Avocado (Finely Chopped)
- 1 Serrano Pepper (Deveined and Finely Chopped)
- 4 Eggs
- 2 Teaspoons of Vegetable Oil
- Salt (to Taste)

Directions:
1. In a big bowl place the tomatoes, onion, serrano peppers, avocado and cilantro. Add lime juice, salt to taste, and mix well.
2. Slide the bolillos in half lengthwise.
3. Preheat the griddle. Set the center burners at medium, and the side burners at low.
4. Spread two teaspoons of vegetable on the center of the griddle. Place the chorizo. As it cooks, break it into small pieces - make sure not to let any grease leak out.
5. Once the chorizo is half cooked, smear some grease on all bolillo halves. Place them on the griddle face down for toasting. Make sure you flip the bolillos from time to time.
6. Use the chorizo grease on the griddle again to heat the refried beans. As soon as the bolillos are toasted and the beans hot, take the ingredients off the flat top. Place beans, chorizo, and pico de gallo on top of the bread and set them aside.
7. Use the remaining chorizo grease to cook the four eggs. Cook sunny-side up, and place on top of mollets. In the end, you'll have four mollets with eggs and four without.

Pork Cutlets

Servings:x
Cooking Time:x

Ingredients:
- 1 Lb. of Prime Pork Cutlets, sliced thin (about 6-7)
- 1 Cup of Italian Seasoned Bread Crumbs
- 1/2 Cup of Pecorino Romano Cheese
- 1 Teaspoon of Thyme
- 2 Eggs
- 1/4 Cup of Milk
- 1 Teaspoon of Garlic Powder
- Salt and Pepper to taste
- Oil for Shallow Frying (Extra Virgin, Safflower, or Vegetable work great)

Directions:
1. Using two separate containers or shallow dishes, mix bread crumbs, cheese, and thyme in one. In the other beat eggs with milk, garlic powder, and salt and pepper.
2. Coat one cutlet at a time into egg wash and then the breadcrumbs and lay on a tray until all cutlets are coated evenly.
3. Set Blackstone Griddle to medium low heat or about 350 degrees.
4. Using a squirt bottle, drizzle oil into a spot the size of your cutlet and place cutlet into oil. Repeat for each

cutlet. Cook about 2-3 minutes or until golden brown (cooking time depends on thickness of pork, if thicker start with lower heat and cook longer).

5. Drizzle oil over cutlet before flipping to cook the other side, another 2-3 minutes until golden brown. You may need to lift cutlet using tongs or spatula and squirt a little extra oil under.

6. Place on cooling rack and sprinkle a little coarse sea salt and pecorino cheese.

Gouda Ale Sliders

Servings:4
Cooking Time:15 Min

Ingredients:
- 1 Lb. of Smoked Gouda (shredded)
- 1 Cup of Parmesan Cheese (shredded)
- 1.5 Lb. of Roast Beef (sliced)
- 12 Oz. of Ale
- Salt & Pepper to Taste
- Granulated Garlic to Taste
- Hoagie Slider Rolls
- Potato Sticks

Directions:
1. Place a cast iron skillet or sauce pan on griddle or side burner. If using a side burner, set your heat to low. If placing directly on the griddle top, you can adjust the heat accordingly. Combine shredded gouda, parmesan, and ale in skillet. Stir frequently. Keep at a simmer.
2. Meanwhile, set your griddle, or griddle zone, to high. Lightly coat with olive oil. Place 1.5 lbs. sliced roast beef on hot griddle top. Use griddle scraper or spatula to chop beef into smaller pieces.
3. Season roast beef to taste with black pepper, granulated garlic, and salt.
4. The roast beef is already cooked and safe to eat. Mix beef until the outside is caramelized and the meat is steaming hot.
5. Once the beef is caramelized, remove it from the griddle top and combine it with the gouda ale mixture.
6. Stir and allow mixture to simmer for a few minutes.
7. Place hoagie slider rolls on griddle top and turn until they are warm to the touch.
8. Slice hoagie rolls, place roast beef and cheese in rolls.

Pancake Kabobs

Servings:4
Cooking Time:20 Min

Ingredients:
- 1 Cup Pancake Mix
- 3/4 Cup Water
- 1 tsp Vanilla
- 5 Large Strawberries cut in 1/2' slices
- 3 tbsp Nutella
- 1 Medium Banana
- 3 tbsp Peanut Butter
- Syrup
- Butter
- Kabob Sticks cut into 4" pieces

Directions:
1. In a mixing bowl, combine pancake mix, water, and vanilla to make the pancake batter. Set to the side.
2. Heat griddle top to medium. Melt a couple of teaspoons of butter.
3. Drop 1 teaspoon of pancake batter onto the griddle. Continue until you have about 20 mini pancakes. Once they begin to bubble, flip them, and cook another minute or two.
4. Remove the pancakes from the griddle, and let them cool on a plate for a few minutes while you cut your fruit.
5. Begin with the strawberry and Nutella kabobs. Spread a little Nutella on a pancake, top with a strawberry slice, and another pancake. Continue until you have 4 layers.
6. Then, spread a little peanut butter, top with banana, and add another pancake and continue until you have 4 layers.
7. Poke a kabob stick in the middle of your stack, place on a plate, and drizzle with syrup.
8. Enjoy!

Buffalo Blue Cheese Chicken Balls

Servings: 1
Cooking Time: 10 Min

Ingredients:
- 3 Lb. of Ground Chicken
- 3 Eggs
- 2 Cups of Plain Panko Bread Crumb
- 1/3 Cup of Sliced Green Onions
- 1/3 Cup of Carrots, Sliced & Diced Small
- 1 Celery Stalk (the Center leafy stalks are best, use the leaves too!)
- 3 Oz. of Blue Cheese (crumble bigger pieces)
- 1/4 Cup of Sweet Baby Rays Buffalo Sauce
- 1 Teaspoon of Garlic powder
- Sea Salt & Fresh Cracked Pepper to Taste

Directions:
1. Slice green onions, slice and dice carrots and celery into small pieces, crumble blue cheese into small pieces.
2. In a large mixing bowl combine all ingredients with a spoon. Roll out 30 meatballs (10 meatballs per 1 pound of chicken).
3. Drizzle Blackstone with vegetable oil and cook meatballs on medium heat, turning every so often to cook each side. Use a dome and steam halfway through. Continue to drizzle vegetable oil as needed throughout. Cook time may vary depending on size of meatballs and temp but for 30 took 15 minutes total.

Crispy Cod

Servings: 2
Cooking Time: 23 Min

Ingredients:
- 2 Fresh Cod Loin pieces
- 3 Tablespoons of Mayonnaise
- Lemon Juice (1 lemon is enough)
- 1 1/2 Teaspoon of Old Bay Seasoning
- 1 Garlic Clove, minced
- 1 heaping Curly Parsley, chopped
- 1 1/2 Cup of Panko Breadcrumbs
- Salted Butter
- Vegetable Oil

Directions:
1. Rinse cod and pat dry with paper towels. Set aside on paper towels to absorb any extra liquid while preparing your sauce.
2. Put panko breadcrumbs onto a plate and set aside.
3. For the sauce, whisk together the mayo, lemon, garlic, parsley, and old bay rub. (Note: if using regular old bay start with 1 tsp and check flavors, the rub is less salty and has a touch of brown sugar.)
4. Take half of your sauce and brush a thick layer all over the cod. Place cod into the panko and with your hands gently press the bread crumbs to evenly coat all sides.
5. Heat the Blackstone Griddle to medium to medium/low heat and place 1 tbsp each oil and butter to melt together.
6. Gently place your cod for about 4-5 minutes per side, depending on thickness, turning once. Add more butter and oil to cook the other side.
7. Your Blackstone basting dome can be used after the first flip for 3 minutes, letting the fish finish cooking uncovered.
8. Serve fish with the reserved sauce, lemon wedge and garnish with parsley. Serve as is, over a salad, tacos or as a sandwich in your favorite bread.

Ground Turkey Taco Stir Fry

Servings: 5
Cooking Time: 25 Min

Ingredients:
- 2 Tablespoons of Extra Virgin Olive Oil
- 1 Lb. of Ground Turkey
- 1 Onion (diced)
- 2 Cups of Cooked Brown Rice
- 1/4 Cup of Water
- 1 Packet Taco Seasoning Mix
- 1 Jar of Salsa (16 oz.)
- 1 Can of Corn (15 oz.) (drained)
- 1 Cup of Shredded Mexican or Taco Cheese Blend
- 1 Large Tomato (chopped)
- 1/2 Cup of Reduced-Fat Sour Cream

Directions:

1. Heat your griddle to high heat and cover the surface evenly with olive oil.
2. Cook ground turkey and onion together for 5-7 minutes, turning regularly. When you start cooking your turkey, add your cooked rice to a separate part of your griddle, turn occasionally to make a "fried rice".
3. Add the seasoning mix and water to the turkey. Mix thoroughly.
4. Add salsa, corn and green chilies to the turkey and stir to combine.
5. Combine fried rice with ground turkey mixture until thoroughly mixed.
6. Sprinkle with cheese and let melt.
7. Once served on plates, top mixture with lettuce, tomato and sour cream.

Blt Hot Dogs With The Blackstone Air Fryer Combo

Servings:8
Cooking Time:15 Min

Ingredients:
- 100% beef hot dogs(beef franks)
- Bacon, thin slices
- Tomatoes, diced
- Lettuce, shredded
- Blackstone Steakhouse Seasoning
- Mayonnaise
- Hot dog buns

Directions:
1. Preheat Blackstone Air Fryer Combo fryer baskets on medium heat.
2. I recommend using very thin bacon. Thick-cut bacon will take longer to cook and won't adhere to the hot dogs as well. Wrap bacon around each hot dog(frank) in a spiral motion.
3. Place hot dogs in fryer basket and season the tops with Blackstone's Steakhouse Seasoning or seasoning of your choice.
4. Allow hot dogs to cook.
5. Meanwhile, dice the desired amount of fresh tomatoes for topping.
6. Use pre-shredded lettuce, available in most grocery stores. Otherwise, shred desired amount of your favorite lettuce
7. It's not necessary to toast your hot dog buns. If you prefer a toasted hot dog bun, toast buns on griddle top using a low heat setting for a minute or two.
8. Bacon-wrapped hot dogs are done when both the hot dog and the bacon are cooked to your liking.
9. Garnish buns with mayonnaise, lettuce, and tomato.
10. Enjoy your BLT hot dog!

Garlic Soy Pork Chops

Servings:1
Cooking Time:10 Min

Ingredients:
- 5-7 Thick Cut Pork Chops
- 3-4 Garlic Cloves
- 1/2 Cup of Extra Virgin Olive Oil
- 1/2 Cup of Low Sodium Soy Sauce
- 1/2 Teaspoon of Garlic Powder
- 1/2 Teaspoon of Sea Salt
- 1 Teaspoon of Fresh Cracked Black Pepper
- 1/2 Cup of Curly Parsley
- 1/2 Stick Real Butter
- Extra Virgin Olive Oil for griddle top

Directions:
1. I buy a huge pork loin from Sam's Club or BJ's and slice the chops myself. I usually get 4 freezer bags with five to seven 1-¼ inch thick chops per bag. Freezing the extra 3 bags of chop's airtight! Or buy a pack of thick cut chops ready to go or ask your butcher to cut them thick for you!
2. In a small mixing bowl mix fresh chopped garlic, olive oil, soy sauce, salt and pepper, parsley (reserving some for garnishing), garlic powder. Add the mixture and chops into a freezer bag and close tight, massaging everything to combine. Marinate in fridge 30 min - 6 hours.
3. Take out pork chops and set on counter for 20-25 minutes, still in freezer bag, to reach room temp.
4. Turn Blackstone Griddle on medium to medium-high heat. Add a drizzle (about 1-½ tbsp) of olive oil and spread 1-½ tbsp butter around, mixing with the

oil. One at a time, place your chops on the grill (NOT dumping the entire bag of marinade onto the griddle, but making sure the chops have garlic and parsley on them. I like to spoon on extra marinade to spread on top of each chop too). Let cook 4-5 minutes, adding a little cracked black pepper before flipping. Flip and add 1.5 tbsp butter and spread around underneath the chops, let cook 3-4 minutes.

5. Add a splash (about 2 tbsp) of low sodium soy sauce over and around the chops. Cook 2-4 more minutes, then turn griddle to medium or medium low and flip 1-2 more times until chops are cooked through.

6. Spread 1 tbsp softened butter (a little more doesn't hurt) across a serving dish (one that can hold some liquid) and place chops on top of butter. Let REST without cutting into them for 10 minutes. Top with chopped parsley. After 10 minutes your dish will be full of dipping juices! Slice chops thin and dip.

Cherries Jubilee

Servings:4
Cooking Time:10 Min

Ingredients:
- 2 Tablespoons of Butter
- 2 Tablespoons of Sugar
- 2 Teaspoons of Cinnamon
- 1 Teaspoon of Vanilla Extract
- 1/3 Cup of Orange Juice (low or no pulp preferred)
- 2 Cups of Fresh Cherries (pitted)
- 2/3 Cup of White Rum
- Vanilla Ice Cream

Directions:
1. Place a skillet on the Blackstone Tailgater burner or Range Top Combo side burner. Turn the burner to low. Add butter, sugar, cinnamon, vanilla extract, orange juice, and cherries.
2. Mix ingredients and bring to a simmer and cook for 4-5 minutes or until the mixture has reduced by half.
3. Add 1/4 cup rum.
4. Tilt skillet, allowing burner flame to ignite rum in skillet or simply use a lighter to ignite (flambe) the rum.
5. Allow the flambe to continue for 5-10 seconds before giving the ingredients a few final stirs and cook for another 3-4 minutes or until the sauce has reduced by half.
6. Pour the cherries and sauce over scoops of vanilla ice cream.
7. Top with a light dusting of cinnamon, if desired. Enjoy!

Shrimp Scampi

Servings:4
Cooking Time:20 Min

Ingredients:
- 1 pound peeled and deveined Shrimp
- 4 Shallots, thin julienne
- 4-6 Garlic Cloves, thinly sliced
- 3 sprigs fresh Oregano
- 2 cups Pinot Grigio
- ½ cup Chicken Stock
- ½ bunch fresh flatleaf Parsley
- 2 cups grape Tomatoes, sliced in half
- 2 teaspoons Red Pepper Flakes
- 3 tablespoons Unsalted Butter
- 2 tablespoons Lemon Juice
- 1 tablespoon Chili Powder
- 1 teaspoon Garlic Powder
- 4 1 inch sliced of Baguette or French Bread
- ½ cup finely shredded Parmesan Cheese
- Salt & Pepper
- Olive Oil

Directions:
1. Using a large sauté pan over a burner on medium-high heat. Add a drizzle of olive oil and the shallots. Cook for 3-4 minutes then add the garlic and oregano. Cook an additional 2-3 minutes.
2. Add the wine, chicken stock, and half of the parsley (stems and all). Add a pinch of salt and pepper and turn the heat to high. Cook for 7-8 minutes or until the liquid reduces by about 60% and begins to thicken up.
3. Add the tomatoes, red pepper flakes, and butter. Stir consistently until the butter fully melts and emulsifies.
4. Preheat your griddle to medium-high heat.

5. In a medium sized mixing bowl, add the shrimp, a bit of olive oil, a pinch of salt and pepper, chili powder, and garlic powder. Toss to evenly coat the shrimp.
6. Add the shrimp to the griddle and cook for 3-5 minutes or until lightly caramelized then add them to the sauté pan with the sauce. Chop the remaining half of the parsley and add to the pan with the lemon juice. Stir to incorporate.
7. Add a bit of olive and salt and pepper to one side of the sliced bread and toast on the griddle top.
8. To plate, add 1 piece of toasted bread to each plat and then top with some of the shrimp. Pour some of the sauce over the tops of each and garnish with a bit of lemon and shredded parmesan.
9. Enjoy!

Breakfast Sausage & Egg Baskets

Servings:15
Cooking Time:4 Min

Ingredients:
- 6 Eggs
- 1 ½ cups All-Purpose Flour
- 2 tablespoons White Sugar
- 1 teaspoon Ground Cinnamon
- 1 teaspoon Ground Chipotle
- 1/3 cup Whole Milk
- 4 Breakfast Sausage Patties
- ½ cup shredded Cheddar Cheese
- Maple Syrup
- Powdered Sugar

Directions:
1. Cook the sausage patties over medium heat until fully cooked. Remove and reserve for later.
2. In a large mixing bowl, add the flour, sugar, 1 egg, cinnamon, chipotle, and milk. Whisk to evenly incorporate all ingredients. Add a bit more milk if your batter is too thick.
3. Add the mix to a narrow nozzle squeeze bottle. Squeeze the batter onto the griddle making a criss-crossed pattern. Cook for 2-3 minutes and gently flip. Repeat.
4. Crack 1 egg into the center of the pancake basket, break the yolk, and spread the egg out to the edges. Add a pinch of salt and pepper, 1 sausage patty and a bit of cheese. Using 2 spatulas, fold the side of the basket over into the center creating a square. Cook for 1 more minute and flip.
5. For presentation, cut away any over-hanging pancake batter from the sides to even out the shape. Serve hot with a bit of maple syrup and powdered sugar.
6. Enjoy!

Savory Candied Sweet Potatoes

Servings:4-6
Cooking Time:10 Min

Ingredients:
- 3-4 large sweet potatoes, diced small
- 1 lb savory sage ground sausage, bob evans
- 2 tbsp oil
- 4-5 tbsp butter, unsalted
- 1-1.5 c brown sugar
- Salt & pepper
- Dried parsley

Directions:
1. Dice sweet potatoes into small pieces and place in large mixing bowl. Toss to lightly coat with oil and season with salt and pepper.
2. Preheat Blackstone to medium or medium low heat. Add sausage and crumble to cook on one side and potatoes to cook on the other side. The smaller the dice the quicker they cook. When tender to your liking mix the cooked sausage with the potatoes.
3. Turn Blackstone to the lowest heat setting. Create a well in the center of your sausage and potato mixture. Add butter to the center to melt then add brown sugar and mix with the butter slightly then toss everything together to coat evenly. Cook 1-2 minutes adding a light sprinkle of parsley.
4. Plate and garnish with more parsley if desired.

Wild Caught Jumbo Scallops With Shredded Sprouts & Prosciutto

Servings:1
Cooking Time:10 Min

Ingredients:
- 1-1 1/2 Lb. of Brussels Sprouts
- 4 Oz. of Diced Prosciutto
- 3 Garlic Cloves
- 1 1/2 Tablespoons of Extra Virgin Olive Oil
- Sea Salt & Fresh Cracked Pepper to Taste
- Juice of Half Lemon
- Zest of Half a Lemon
- 1/4 Cup of Fresh Grated Locatelli Pecorino Romano Cheese

Directions:
1. Wash/Rinse the Brussels Sprouts (don't worry about draining too well, the little bit of extra water helps steam on the grill). Cut in half and slice thin, season with sea salt, fresh cracked pepper, and garlic powder. Toss with 5 tbsp extra virgin olive oil. Cover and let sit while you prep everything else.
2. Dice your Prosciutto. Crush 3 garlic cloves and dice. Rinse and pat dry scallops. Season with Sea Salt and Cracked Black Pepper.
3. Using ½ tbsp butter, saute garlic and prosciutto for about one minute. Add sprouts on medium heat about 5 minutes total, moving everything around throughout cook time. (I like to pre-season with oils and spices, especially with veggies, so that no extra oil is needed usually while cooking)
4. At the same time on the other side of the griddle, melt 2 tbsp butter on med-med/high heat. Cook the scallops in the butter for 3-4 min, flip over and add the juice of half a lemon and 1 tbsp butter, let cook 3-4 min.
5. Garnish with Lemon Zest and freshly grated Locatelli Pecorino Romano Cheese (or whatever cheese you like).

Croque Madame

Servings:6
Cooking Time:25 Min

Ingredients:
- 1 loaf crusty sour dough bread
- 1 wedge gruyere cheese, grated
- 1 lb ham, tavern, black forest, or your favorite
- 1/4 lb baby swiss cheese
- 1/4 lb muenster cheese
- Dijon mustard
- butter
- 6 eggs
- 2 tbsp butter
- 2 tbsp flour
- 1 cup milk
- 1 tsp nutmeg
- black pepper

Directions:
1. Slice loaf of bread into 1/2-1 inch thick slices and begin assembling sandwiches by spreading Dijon mustard on the inside of each slice of bread and layer muenster cheese, ham, gruyere cheese, ham, baby swiss cheese. You want your cheese against the bread as well as in the center, the cheese is the glue to holding our sandwich together. Set aside.
2. Heat a small pot directly on the Blackstone surface or on the Blackstone side burner using low heat. Add the butter to slowly melt then whisk in the flour. Continue whisking until golden brown and fragrant and then slowly whisk in the milk a 1/4 cup at a time. Sauce will thicken as it cooks. Season with nutmeg and black pepper.
3. On low to medium low heat spread butter over Blackstone surface and add sandwiches to toast up until golden brown on both sides. Low and slow is key so that the cheeses inside heat and melt through.
4. Cook sunny side up eggs just before the sandwiches are done.
5. Assemble sandwiches by plating. Top each sandwich with béchamel sauce, grated gruyere cheese, and a sunny side up egg.
6. Enjoy with a fork and knife!

Greek Turkey Burger

Servings: 8
Cooking Time: 21 Min

Ingredients:
- 2 Lb. of Ground Turkey Breast
- 1 Egg
- 1 (6 oz) Package Crumbled Feta Cheese
- 1/3 Cup of Finely Chopped Red Onion
- 1 Teaspoon of Dried Oregano
- 1 Teaspoon of Lemon Zest
- 1/2 Teaspoon of Salt
- 6 Whole Wheat Hamburger Buns
- Lettuce Leaves
- Tomato Slices
- Thinly Sliced Cucumber
- 1 Cucumber (peeled and seeded)
- 16 Oz. of Plain Greek Yogurt
- 2 Cloves Garlic (crushed)
- 1 Teaspoon of Red Wine Vinegar
- 1/2 Teaspoon of Lemon Juice
- 1/4 Teaspoon of Dried Dill Weed

Directions:
1. One hour before serving, make tzatziki sauce.
2. Shred or grate the cucumbers and blot them with a paper towel or clean kitchen towel to get rid of as much moisture as possible.
3. Mix together the shredded cucumbers, strained yogurt, garlic, vinegar, and lemon juice.
4. Add dill and salt and pepper to taste. Cover and keep in the fridge until serving.
5. In a large bowl, stir together ground turkey, egg, feta cheese, red onion, oregano, lemon zest, and salt. Shape mixture into 8 (1/2-inch-thick) patties.
6. Heat griddle to medium-high heat and cover with a thin layer of olive oil.
7. Add patties to hot griddle; cook approximately 5 minutes on each side or until done.
8. Serve each patty on a hamburger bun with homemade tzatziki sauce and desired burger toppings.

Fall Harvest French Toast

Servings: 1
Cooking Time: 10 Min

Ingredients:
- 6 Eggs
- 1/4 Teaspoons of Salt
- 1 Tablespoon of Brown Sugar
- 2-3 Teaspoons of Ground Cinnamon
- 1/2-1 Teaspoon of Ground Nutmeg
- 1/4 Cup of Pecans
- 1 Can Pumpkin (15oz.)
- 1 1/4 Cup of Heavy Whipping Cream
- Additional Toppings of your Choice

Directions:
1. Slice bread into desired thickness
2. Crack your 6 eggs into a large mixing bowl, and beat them
3. Add salt, brown sugar, ground cinnamon, ground nutmeg, pecans, can of pumpkin, and heavy whipping cream.
4. Mix all ingredients together in the mixing bowl.
5. Heat your Blackstone griddle to low temp and apply a light coat of cooking oil.
6. Submerge bread slices in the mixing bowl batter to coat, then gently place on the griddle.
7. Wait til one side is cooked and flip, being careful not to burn.
8. Plate and garnish with desired toppings.

Tomato Salad

Servings: x
Cooking Time: x

Ingredients:
- 6 Large Tomatoes (slicing tomatoes like Big Beef, Early Girl or Beefsteak are perfect)
- 1 Long Hot Pepper
- 6 Fresh Cloves of Garlic
- 1 Handful of Basil
- 1 Handful Flat Leaf Italian Parsley
- Extra Virgin Olive Oil
- Salt and Pepper
- Ice Cubes
- Loaf Crusty Italian Bread

Directions:

1. Slice tomatoes in half, slice each half into quarters and place in a glass bowl. Season tomatoes with salt and pepper.
2. Peel, smash, and chop garlic cloves, the more the better! Add garlic to glass bowl.Â
3. Remove stem from long hot pepper and slice into bite sized strips. Remove or keep any seeds depending on how hot you like your salad. Adjust pepper amount to your heat level preference.Â
4. Wash fresh basil and parsley well, cut the bottom stems off (about 1 inch) and discard. Chop parsley and basil (I prefer to tear apart by hand). Add to the glass bowl.
5. Drizzle extra virgin olive oil around everything, about 1/3-1/2 cup. Mix everything together.
6. Place about 8-10 ice cubes all around the salad on top, pushing some in between and down into the tomatoes. Cover tightly with plastic wrap and allow to sit out on the counter for 20-30 minutes. Ice cubes will melt and mix in with the oil. Mix well before serving, adding more salt or oil if needed. Serve with a crusty loaf of Italian bread, torn apart into pieces for dipping!

S'mores Pancakes

Servings:6
Cooking Time:20 Min

Ingredients:
- Your favorite Pancake mix. (My favorite is Member's Mark Buttermilk Pancake Mix available at Sam's Club)
- Graham crackers
- Brown Sugar
- Cinnamon
- Mini or small marshmallows
- Semi-sweet or dark chocolate chips
- Chocolate Syrup
- Caramel Syrup

Directions:
1. Preheat griddle to medium or medium-low heat. Heat settings will vary depending on the size of your griddle and the number of burners on your griddle. TIP: A general rule of thumb is that pancakes cook best with a griddle surface that is over 375 ° Fahrenheit.
2. Mix desired amount of pancake batter per manufacturers instructions. Add marshmallows, chocolate chips, cinnamon, brown sugar, and crumbled graham crackers to taste. Add enough ingredients to assure a s'mores surprise in each bite, but make sure batter maintains its somewhat runny consistency.
3. Spray griddle top with your favorite nonstick cooking spray.
4. Use ladle to drop batter on to hot griddle top.
5. Use thin spatula to check bottom side of pancake. Flip pancake when bottom side is golden brown.
6. Allow second side of pancake to cook until golden brown.
7. Place cooking/cookie sheet on empty side of griddle.
8. Remove pancakes from griddle top and place on the elevated cooking/cookie sheet while you are making more pancakes.
9. If pancakes are thick, I suggest allowing them to sit on the cooking/cookie sheet for a few minutes until the insides of the pancakes are completely cooked and not runny.
10. Remove cooked pancakes
11. Garnish with marshmallows, chocolate chips, chocolate syrup, caramel syrup, graham crackers, and a dusting of cinnamon.
12. Enjoy your fabulous S'mores Pancakes!

Pickle Chic Sandwiches

Servings:8
Cooking Time:x

Ingredients:
- 4 boneless skinless chicken breast
- 1 cup pickle juice
- 1 tbsp All Purpose Blackstone Products Seasoning
- ¼ cup mayonnaise, Dukes preferred
- 1 8-pack brioche buns
- 8 slices muenster cheese
- 8 slices sharp cheddar cheese
- 1 box FarmRich crispy dill pickles
- Horsey Sauce
- ½ c mayonnaise
- ¼ c prepared horseradish
- Dash each salt pepper and paprika

- Red Cabbage Slaw
- 2 cups red cabbage, shredded
- ¼ cup green onions, chopped
- 2 tbsp extra virgin olive oil
- 2 tbsp red wine vinegar
- Salt and pepper to taste

Directions:
1. Using a meat tenderizer, pound out the chicken breast until ½ inch thick and even all around. One breast should make for two sandwiches, so cut each breast into two portions. Add chicken to a storage bag with pickle juice, remove air, seal, and marinate overnight.
2. Prepare slaw by shredding or thinly slicing the cabbage. Add green onion, oil, vinegar, salt and pepper to the cabbage and toss to coat evenly in a mixing bowl. Set aside.
3. Combine ingredients for the horsey sauce and set aside.
4. Drain chicken and pat dry, toss chicken with mayonnaise and Blackstone All Purpose Seasoning to coat evenly.
5. Turn Blackstone Griddle to medium heat and Blackstone Airfryer to high heat.
6. Place chicken on on the Blackstone. Cooking for 3-4 minutes per side.
7. Place Farmrich pickles into preheated airfryer and cook for 4-5 minutes or until crispy and heated through.
8. Add one slice of each cheese to chicken the last minute of cooking before removing chicken. Allow chicken to rest while you toast the buns in the grease left behind from the chicken.
9. Assemble sandwiches by layering chicken, cheese, slaw, pickles and horsey sauce. Enjoy!

Caribbean Jerk Vegetables

Servings:6
Cooking Time:45 Min

Ingredients:
- 1 Tablespoon of Onion Powder
- 1 Tablespoon of Ground Allspice
- 1 Teaspoon of Five-Spice Powder
- 1 Teaspoon of Ground Ginger
- 1 Teaspoon of Ground Nutmeg
- 1/2 Teaspoon of Garlic Powder
- 1/2 Teaspoon of Cayenne Pepper
- 1 Tablespoon of Dried Thyme
- Salt and Pepper, to taste
- 1 Zucchini, thickly sliced
- 1 Yellow Zucchini Squash, thickly sliced
- 1 Bunch of Asparagus, tough ends removed
- 1 Cup of Sliced Mushrooms
- 1 Red Bell Pepper, sliced
- 1 Orange Bell Pepper, sliced
- 2 Tablespoons of Olive Oil

Directions:
1. In a small bowl, mix together all spices for jerk seasoning.
2. Wash, cut, and prepare vegetables as directed.
3. Place vegetables in a single layer on a large cookie sheet. Drizzle with olive oil and sprinkle jerk seasoning over the vegetables, then gently toss so that the vegetables are equally coated.
4. Let vegetables sit for 10 minutes.
5. Heat your griddle to medium-high heat and coat with a thin layer of olive oil.
6. Add vegetables to griddle and cook for 10-15 minutes or until desired doneness, turning occasionally.

Bacon Pancakes With Strawberry Whiskey Syrup And Whipped Cream

Servings:2
Cooking Time:20 Min

Ingredients:
- Pancake Mix
- 1 lb Bacon
- 1 Cup Milk
- 2 Eggs
- Fresh Strawberries
- Honey
- Whiskey
- Heavy Whipping Cream
- Powdered Sugar

Directions:

1. Pre Heat 17" Blackstone range top combo griddle to Medium High. Add 4 strips of bacon and cook. Once done remove bacon and drain on paper towels. Remove most, but not all, bacon fat from griddle. (You'll need this to cook your pancakes in)

2. In a medium sized skillet add 2 cups of whiskey, 2-3 table spoons of honey stir and reduce. When bubbles are large in skillet add fresh cut strawberries and reduce heat. Stir occasionally. Add more whiskey if syrup is too thick.

3. In a mixing bowl add 2 cups of pancake mix, 2 eggs, and 1 cup of milk. Stir till incorporated and add to Blackstone pancake batter dispenser.

4. Cut bacon in half and back4 pieces to griddle at medium High. Cover bacon with pancake batter and flip when golden brown. Remove pancakes from griddle when both sides are cooked.

5. In a bowl add 1 cup of heavy Whipping cream. Add a teaspoon of powdered sugar and beat. Incorporate more powdered sugar as needed when whipping cream begins to thicken. You'll know it's done when there are large peaks on the tip of your whisk.

6. Plate your bacon pancakes, add strawberry whiskey syrup and fresh whipped cream on top and enjoy.

Green Chile Chicken Quesadilla

Servings:8
Cooking Time:25 Min

Ingredients:
- 1 Burrito-Sized Tortilla 8-10 count Package
- 2 Cups of Shredded Pepper Jack Cheese (Monterey Jack also works well)
- 2 Cups of Cooked, Shredded Chicken (Cook on griddle before hand or pre-cooked works)
- 1/4 Cup of Green Onions Diced
- 1 Red Bell Pepper Diced
- 1 Green Bell Pepper
- 2 Tablespoons of Butter Melted

Directions:
1. Heat your griddle to medium heat and cover with a thin coat of olive oil.
2. Cook peppers, onions, and chiles until tender (approximately 5-10 minutes) and set aside.
3. Top half of a tortilla with shredded cheese, chicken, onions, chiles, and peppers. Fold tortilla in half and press down.
4. Put a small amount of melted butter on your griddle. Place the folded quesadilla on the griddle and cook for 1-2 minutes or until desired doneness.
5. Flip to other side and cook an additional 1-2 minutes.
6. Repeat with all remaining ingredients.
7. Serve with salsa, guacamole, and/or sour cream.

Bacon Chicken Party Dip

Servings:x
Cooking Time:x

Ingredients:
- 3 chicken breast, diced small
- 1 package bacon, diced small
- 1 heaping cup of mayo, Dukes preferred
- 2 blocks cream cheese, softened
- 1 bunch green onions, chopped
- 1 8 oz block cheddar cheese, grated
- 3 garlic cloves, grated
- 1-4 oz jar pimentos, drained
- Blackstone Parmesan Ranch Seasoning

Directions:
1. Dice chicken and bacon into small bite sized pieces. Cook chicken and bacon on medium low heat separately on the Blackstone. Season chicken with Blackstone Parmesan Ranch seasoning. Set aside when done.
2. In a large mixing bowl mix cream cheese, mayonnaise, garlic, pimentos, half of the green onions, and about one tablespoon of the Parmesan Ranch seasoning.
3. Mix in the chicken and half of the bacon.
4. Put mixture into a casserole or baking dish. Top with cheddar cheese and remaining bacon. Dip can be reheated in oven before serving or served hot off the Blackstone. Add remaining green onions when ready to serve!

Hawaiian Meat Marinade And Sauce For Chicken Or Pork

Servings:x
Cooking Time:x

Ingredients:
- 1-1.5 Lb. of Boneless Skinless Chicken Breast or Pork Shoulder Butt
- 1.5 Cup of Soy Sauce
- 1.5 Cup of Pineapple Juice
- 1 Cup of Brown Sugar, packed
- 1 Tablespoon of Brown Sugar, packed
- 8 Garlic Cloves, chopped
- 2 Tablespoons of Fresh Ginger, chopped

Directions:
1. In a large mixing bowl combine soy sauce, pineapple juice, garlic, and ginger.
2. Before adding the brown sugar, take one cup of the sauce mixture and place into a separate bowl and add 1 TBSP brown sugar, this will be to marinate your meat. Add 3/4 cup brown sugar to the original marinade bowl and mix both bowls until sugar dissolves.
3. Place meat in freezer bag and add your meat marinade. If using pork shoulder butt, slice meat into bite sized chunks suitable for skewers, adding meat to skewers after the meat marinates overnight in the freezer bag.
4. Refrigerate sauce overnight.
5. Place sauce in a small sauce pan to gently boil on low heat, stirring every few minutes. Sauce will thicken slightly. This can be done directly on your Blackstone Griddle in a sauce pan!
6. With Blackstone set to medium high heat, drizzle a light coating of vegetable oil and add chicken thighs or pork skewers. Cook time will vary on thickness of meat.

Cinnamon Apple

Servings:6
Cooking Time:12 Min

Ingredients:
- 4 Apples (your preferred variety)
- 1 Tablespoon of Butter
- Cinnamon to Taste (approximately 1 tsp; more or less depending on taste)
- 2 Cups of Water

Directions:
1. Heat your griddle to medium heat and cover with butter.
2. Peel your apples and slice into wedges.
3. Place apples on hot griddle and add cinnamon.
4. Slowly add 1/2 cup water and mix thoroughly.
5. Continue to add 1/2 cup water every 2-3 minutes as it evaporates off the griddle. You want to keep them moist.
6. Add water and stir apples every 2-3 minutes until the desired doneness is achieved (approximately 10 minutes).
7. Optional - serve with whipped cream, vanilla ice cream, or granola.

Fluffy Protein Pancakes

Servings:6
Cooking Time:10 Min

Ingredients:
- 1 Cup of Rolled Oats
- 1 Ripe Banana
- 2 Eggs
- 1/2 Cup of Egg Whites
- 4 Teaspoons of Baking Powder
- Pinch of Salt
- Pinch of Cinnamon
- 1-2 Scoops Protein Powder (Vanilla tastes best with this recipe)

Directions:
1. Place all ingredients in the blender and blend until smooth.
2. Heat griddle to medium high heat and coat with a thin coat of cooking oil or butter.
3. Pour about 1/4 cup of batter onto a hot griddle.
4. Cook 1-2 minutes (until bubble start to form) and then flip pancake.
5. Cook 1-2 minutes on the other side, plate, and serve.
6. Serve with your favorite fruit, nut butter, or syrup on top (alters nutrition content below). Nutrition facts will vary slightly depending on which protein powder you use.

Peanut Butter & Banana Crepes

Servings:1
Cooking Time:10 Min

Ingredients:
- 1 Cup of Yogurt
- 1/2 Cup of Peanut butter
- 1/2 Teaspoon of Cinnamon
- 2 Bananas
- 1 Cup of Flour
- 1 1/4 Cup of Milk
- 2 Teaspoons of Water
- 1 Teaspoon of Butter (per Crepe Cooked)
- Chocolate for Drizzle

Directions:
1. In a medium bowl, put in your peanut butter, yogurt and cinnamon and mix until smooth and consistent, then set aside.
2. In a separate bowl, add in your milk and sift in your flour. Whisk until there are no clumps.
3. Add water to your flour and milk mixture and stir until consistent.
4. Put your Blackstone Griddle on high.
5. Add one teaspoon of butter, don't be scared if it scorches, it should do that. Make sure it covers the size of crepe you want.
6. Add ⅓ cup of the mixture to the pan and using a batter spreader (found in the Blackstone crepe kit), or a large metal spatula, spread the batter wide enough for a nice thin layer.
7. Cook for about 25 seconds, flip and cook for an additional 25 seconds.
8. Remove from griddle and lather one side with your peanut butter mixture.
9. Add as many banana slices as you want. I like mine loaded so I put about 12 slices.
10. Roll the crepe and enjoy!

The Lippy Spritz Cocktail

Servings:x
Cooking Time:x

Ingredients:
- Bud Light Seltzer
- Malibu Rum 1.5 oz
- Pineapple Juice 1 oz
- Lime

Directions:
1. Add ice to a rocks glass. Start with 5 oz of Malibu Coconut Rum. 1 oz of pineapple juice, more if you would like it sweeter. Top off with Bud Light Seltzer and a squeeze of lime juice.

Buttermilk Bathed Rosemary Chicken Thighs

Servings:4
Cooking Time:x

Ingredients:
- 8 chicken thighs with bone and skin
- 2 tablespoons kosher salt
- 1 pint buttermilk
- 1 oz fresh rosemary or about 8 sprigs

Directions:
1. Pat the chicken thighs dry with paper towels. Season both sides of the thigh with kosher salt and place in a zipper top bag.
2. Strip the rosemary from the stalks and add it to the chicken.
3. Allow the chicken to sit in the refrigerator for 2 hours.
4. Add the buttermilk to the chicken and allow the chicken to soak overnight in the brine.
5. Drain the chicken in a colander and allow as much of the buttermilk mixture to drip away as possible.
6. Preheat the air fryer to 375F.
7. In batches, cook the chicken thighs, 4 in each fry basket. Cook for 35 minutes, flipping every 10 minutes until the chicken skin is crispy and the meat safely reaches a minimum temperature of 165F internal.

Betty's Ricotta Doughnuts

Servings:4
Cooking Time:20 Min

Ingredients:
- 1 C whole milk ricotta cheese
- 1 large egg

- 1 tbsp white rum
- Zest of ½ - 1 whole lemon
- 1 C all purpose flour
- 2 tbsp white sugar
- 2 tsp baking powder
- Canola or Vegetable oil for frying
- Sturdy pan for deep frying
- Powdered Sugar

Directions:
1. Turn Blackstone onto high heat and place a small sturdy pan with oil of choice to heat.
2. In a large bowl mix together ricotta, egg, rum and lemon zest.
3. In a separate bowl mix together flour, sugar and baking powder.
4. Slowly add the dry ingredients, ¼ cup at a time, into the wet ingredients and mix to combine. Dough should be thick and sticky.
5. Using a wooden chopstick or toothpick carefully dip it into the oil, if bubbles appear around the wooden stick oil should be ready for frying (or use a thermometer oil should be perfect between 350-375 degrees)
6. Using two spoons, slowly drop a ball of dough into the oil. Allow to fry until deep golden brown in color, about 3-5 minutes. If donuts do not flip on their own gently flip donuts for even cooking.
7. Remove from oil and let drain on paper towels.
8. Serve with a dusting of powdered sugar.

Sweet Potato Pizza

Servings:1
Cooking Time:10 Min

Ingredients:
- 1 Sweet Potato
- 1/4 Cup of Chopped Pecans
- 6 Tablespoons of Butter, Room Temperature
- 4 Tablespoons of Brown Sugar
- 3 Tablespoons of Flour
- 1/2 Teaspoon of Cinnamon
- 1 Cup of Mini Marshmallows

Directions:
1. Preheat Pizza Oven to 325 degrees. NOTE: You want the Pizza Oven at a fairly low temperature because the sugar in the marshmallows and crumble mix will burn if it's too hot.
2. Prep Sweet Potato: Wash and skin potato. Pat dry and slice to be roughly 1/8 of an inch. Place them in a pot of water and boil till soft. Once done, drain and let cool.
3. Prep Pizza Dough: Roll out dough and spread 1 TBSP of butter around on the dough.
4. Roll out dough and spread 1 TBSP of butter around on the dough.
5. Prep Crumble: Combine remaining butter, sugar, flour, and cinnamon in bowl and set aside. NOTE: Don't put this on the pizza yet. The sugar will burn too quickly in the Pizza Oven.
6. Cook Pizza the pizza for about 2 and a half minutes or until crust starts to brown. Remove pizza and spread crumble and marshmallows over the top and return to the oven for another minute until the marshmallows are slightly toasted.

Reversed Sear Ribeye With Smoked Garlic, Zucchini, And Squash

Servings:2
Cooking Time:45 Min

Ingredients:
- 1, 1 ½ pound boneless ribeye steak
- 6-10 large garlic cloves
- Blackstone Steakhouse Seasoning
- 2 tablespoon unsalted butter
- 2 zucchini, quartered lengthwise
- 2 squash, quartered lengthwise
- 1 cup applewood chips
- 2 sprigs rosemary
- Olive oil
- Small Aluminum Tray
- Torch
- Blackstone Resting Rack
- Blackstone XL Dome

Directions:
1. Place the steak, garlic and aluminum tray on the resting rack. Add the wood chips to the aluminum tray

and light with the torch. Once the wood chips are burning, blow out the fire to create smoke. Cover the entire resting rack with an XL Dome or close the hood. Allow the meat and garlic to smoke for 20-30 minutes.

2. Heat your griddle to medium-high heat and add a bit of olive oil. Wait for the oil to start smoking before adding the steak.

3. Season the steak generously with Blackstone Steakhouse Seasoning and place into the smoking oil. Cook for 2-3 minutes and flip. Flip as often as you like and don't forget to turn the steak on its side to sear all surface areas.

4. For the last few minutes of cooking, add the garlic to the oil and lightly caramelize.

5. Move the garlic to the cooler side of the griddle, add the rosemary and a bit of water over the top and cover with a dome to finish cooking.

6. Once the steak is cooked to the desired doneness, remove it from the griddle and let rest for 5 minutes.

7. Add the butter to the beef fat on the hot side of the griddle and then the zucchini and squash. Add a bit of Blackstone Steakhouse seasoning if desired. Cook for 2-minutes per side.

8. To plate, slice the steak and serve over the sliced veggies family style. Garnish with the garlic and rosemary over the top.

Garlic Parmesan Zucchini

Servings:4
Cooking Time:15 Min

Ingredients:
- 3 Medium Zucchinis, sliced (try to get the width as consistent as possible)
- 1 Tablespoon of Olive Oil
- 1 Tablespoon of Grated Parmesan Cheese (more or less to taste)
- 1/2 Teaspoon of Garlic Powder (more or less to taste)
- 1/4 Teaspoon of Fresh Cracked Black Pepper

Directions:
1. Heat your griddle to med-high heat and cover the cooking surface evenly with olive oil.

2. Once oil is heated, add sliced zucchini and sautÃ© for about 3 minutes, turning occasionally.

3. Add parmesan cheese, garlic powder, and pepper and continue sautÃ©ing until zucchini is tender (an additional 4-6 minutes).

4. Serve immediately.

Betty's Burrata Sandwiches

Servings:x
Cooking Time:x

Ingredients:
- 4 slices Panini bread, Sourdough or Italian
- 1 container Burrata, BelGioioso 4-2 oz "minis"
- 4 slices Provolone Cheese
- 4 slices Prosciutto
- 4 slices Soppressata or Genoa Salami
- 4 slices Capicola
- roasted Red Peppers, Cento
- Arugula
- 2 tbsp Mayonnaise, Dukes preferred
- Blackstone Parmesan Ranch seasoning

Directions:
1. Remove burrata from the container and pat dry between paper towels, set aside.

2. Turn Blackstone griddle on low to preheat.

3. In a small bowl mix mayonnaise and 1 tbsp of the Blackstone Parmesan Ranch seasoning. Spread mayo mixture on one side of each slice of bread and place mayo side down on the Blackstone.

4. Place provolone cheese on top of each slice of bread. Layer Italian meats evenly between sandwiches. Adding a handful of arugula and desired amount of roasted peppers.

5. Place two burrata minis on each sandwich and lightly dust with Blackstone Parmesan Ranch seasoning.

6. When the crust is golden brown, sandwich the two pieces of bread together, and place on a cutting board. Cut the sandwich in half.

7. Enjoy!

Corn Bread Thanksgiving Stuffing

Servings: 8
Cooking Time: 30 Min

Ingredients:
- 16 Oz. of Dry Corn Bread Mix
- 2 Tablespoons of Butter
- 3 Stocks of Celery, Chopped
- 1 Onion, Diced
- 2 Cups of Chicken Stock
- 2 Tablespoons of Dried Sage
- Salt & Pepper to taste

Directions:
1. Make the cornbread according to the instructions on the box.
2. When the cornbread is done, let it cool.
3. Put the butter on the griddle.
4. Add the onions and celery and cook until they start to get soft.
5. Add all the cornbread and use a metal spatula to roughly chop it up.
6. Add the chicken stock about ½ cup at a time to let the corn bread absorb it.
7. Add the sage and salt and pepper to taste. Continue to cook the stuffing until it starts to brown.

Mongolian Chicken Lettuce Wraps

Servings: 1
Cooking Time: 10 Min

Ingredients:
- 2 1/2 Lb. of Boneless Skinless Chicken Thighs
- 1/2 Cup of Corn Starch (more if needed to coat all of the chicken)
- 1/4 Cup of Vegetable Oil
- 3/4 Cup of Soy Sauce
- 1/2 Cup of Brown Sugar
- 1 Tablespoon of Minced Fresh Ginger
- 2-4 Cloves Minced Garlic
- 1/2 Cup of Water
- 4 Green Onions, Sliced
- 2 Heads of Butter Lettuce

Directions:
1. Trim the chicken and cut into 2" pieces. In a large bowl, combine the chicken and corn starch. Toss until all the chicken is coated. Add extra corn starch if need to make sure all chicken is coated.
2. In a saucepan or microwave safe bowl combine the soy sauce, water, brown sugar, garlic, and ginger. Heat until all the sugar is dissolved.
3. Preheat griddle to medium high heat.
4. Add the oil to the griddle.
5. Add the chicken to the griddle and cook until it's crispy on the outside.
6. Add the sauce and half the sliced green onions to the chicken and let the sauce thicken for about 1 minute.
7. Remove the chicken from the heat. Serve in individual lettuce leaves and garnish with sliced green onions.

Air Fryer Stuffed French Toast

Servings: 4
Cooking Time: 15 Min

Ingredients:
- 8 Slices Soft Bread
- 8 Tablespoon Raspberry Jam
- 8 Tablespoons Cream Cheese, Softened
- 1/4 cup powdered sugar
- 2 Large Eggs
- 2 Tablespoon Milk
- 1/4 Cup Powdered Sugar (for sprinkling)
- Maple Syrup (optional)

Directions:
1. In a small bowl, mix softened cream cheese and powdered sugar.
2. On a clean surface, lay out bread.
3. Place a tablespoon of the raspberry jam in the center of a piece of bread and a tablespoon of cream cheese in the center of another piece. Smooth out the cream cheese and jam leaving space on the edges.
4. Place the jam and cream cheese slices together. Cut off the crusts. Using a fork press the edges pinching them together to make a seal.
5. Repeat steps to complete all 8 pieces of bread.

6. In a shallow dish, whisk together the eggs and milk.
7. Preheat air fryer to 380°F for 2 minutes.
8. Spray air fryer basket with cooking spray. Dip sealed sandwich into egg mixture, place in air fryer and cook 5 minutes, flip sandwich over and cook for an additional 2 minutes.
9. Sprinkle with powdered sugar or dip in maple syrup.

Johnny Cakes With Bourbon Salted Caramel Sauce

Servings:4
Cooking Time:25 Min

Ingredients:
- 1 cup All-purpose Glour
- 1 cup coarse Cornmeal
- 1 tablespoon Baking Powder
- 2 tablespoons Sugar
- 3 large Eggs
- ¼ cup liquid Bacon fat
- 1 cup Buttermilk
- ½ cup Bourbon
- ¼ cup Water
- 1 cup granulated Sugar
- 3 tablespoon Unsalted Butter
- 1 cup Heavy Cream
- 1 teaspoon Vanilla Extract
- 2 teaspoons kosher Salt

Directions:
1. In a large sauté pan, add the bourbon, water and sugar. Bring to a simmer over medium-high heat until the bubbles get large and the color changes to a slight amber color. Add the butter and stir consistently until it is all melted and fully incorporated. Add the heavy cream, vanilla extract and salt. Stir to incorporate and remove from the heat to cool.
2. In a large mixing bowl, add the flour, cornmeal and baking powder.
3. To a separate mixing bowl, add the eggs and bacon fat and whip evenly.
4. Add the eggs and bacon fat to the flour and cornmeal bowl. Add ½ of the buttermilk and mix evenly with a spatula. Add more buttermilk to get to the consistency you prefer.
5. Heat you griddle to medium-low heat and add a bit of butter or oil. Using a ladle, add your batter onto the griddle and cook for 3 minutes per side or until fluffy, golden and fully cooked.
6. To plate, add a few johnny cakes to the plate and drizzle the bourbon salted caramel sauce over the top.

Whiskey-honey Salmon With Cajun Stir Fried Rice

Servings:4
Cooking Time:10 Min

Ingredients:
- 4, 6 ounce fillets of skinless salmon
- 3 cups cooked white rice
- ¼ cup diced yellow onion
- ¼ cup sliced okra
- ¼ cup diced bell pepper
- Blackstone Crazy Cajun Seasoning
- ¼ cup whiskey
- 3 tablespoons honey
- Olive oil

Directions:
1. Heat one side of your griddle to medium-high heat and the other to low heat. Add a drizzle of olive oil to the hot side. Add the onion, okra, and bell pepper. Add a few shakes of Blackstone Crazy Cajun Seasoning and toss to incorporate. Cook for 3-4 minutes.
2. Season each salmon fillet with Blackstone Crazy Cajun Seasoning on all sides.
3. Slide the veggies over to the cooler side of the griddle. Add a bit more olive oil to the hot side and then the salmon fillets. Cook for 3 minutes per side or cooked to the desired doneness.
4. In a small mixing bowl, add the whiskey and honey and mix evenly.
5. Add the rice over the veggies and toss to evenly mix.
6. Once the salmon is 90% finished, add 75% of the whiskey honey mix over the tops of each fillet. Flip them over as the liquid begins to reduce. The sweet syrup

should coat the fish on all sides. Add the remaining whiskey over the rice and toss to incorporate.

7. To plate, add the rice to a plate and then the salmon over the top. Serve hot.

Crispy Salmon Belly Salad With Honey Soy Glazed Shiitakes And Arugula

Servings:4
Cooking Time:10 Min

Ingredients:
- 1 pound salmon belly
- 2 teaspoons sesame oil
- 3 cups sliced shiitake mushrooms
- 1 teaspoon garlic powder
- 1 tablespoon honey
- 2 tablespoons soy sauce
- The juice of 1 lemon
- 2 cups baby arugula
- Salt and pepper
- Olive oil

Directions:
1. Heat one side of your griddle to medium-high heat and leave the other side off. Add a bit of olive oil and the mushrooms to the hot side of the griddle. Toss and cook for 3-4 minutes then move the mushrooms to the cool side of the griddle.
2. Increase the hot side of your griddle to High heat.
3. Season the salmon belly with a bit of salt & pepper and garlic powder. Sear for 2 minutes per side or until the fish is crisp and golden.
4. In a small bowl, mix the honey, soy sauce and sesame oil. Pour over the mushrooms and toss to evenly incorporate.
5. In a mixing bowl, add the arugula, lemon juice, a pinch of pepper and a drizzle of olive oil. Toss gently to evenly coat the arugula.
6. Once the fish is 90% finished, slide the mushrooms back over to the high heat side of your griddle and toss to caramelize the honey and soy sauce (about 1 minute).
7. To plate, add some of the mushrooms to the center of your plate and then a loosely packed handful of the arugula. Slice the fish into strips and add few over the top of the arugula. Garnish with cracked black pepper or sesame seeds.

Pasta Primavera

Servings:x
Cooking Time:x

Ingredients:
- 1 Lb. of Campanelle Pasta
- 1 Red Onion sliced
- 1 Cup of Shredded Carrot Matchsticks
- 1 Cup of Broccoli, chopped
- 1 Zucchini, sliced into 1 inch pieces
- 1 Yellow Squash, sliced into 1 inch pieces
- 1 Red Bell Pepper, sliced
- 4 Fresh Garlic Cloves, chopped
- 8 Oz. of Cherry Tomatoes, sliced in half
- Extra Virgin Olive Oil
- Pecornio Romano Cheese
- 1 Lemon, juiced
- 1 Handful Fresh Flat Leaf Parsley, chopped
- 2 Teaspoon of Blackstone Chicken & Herb Seasoning Salt

Directions:
1. Bring a large pot or your Blackstone deep fryer filled with water to a boil.
2. Preheat your Blackstone griddle to medium heat, add a drizzle of extra virgin olive oil and add red onion, carrots and broccoli, tossing them around to coat evenly in a thin coating of olive oil. Place your Blackstone basting dome over it to cook 3-4 minutes, mixing halfway. During the last minute add a handful of salt (about 2-3 tbsp) to your pasta water. Add pasta, following the cook time on the box. Cook time for campanelle is 10 minutes, same amount of time as vegetables will take.
3. Remove dome and add zucchini, squash and bell peppers. Toss and cook 3-4 minutes, adding more oil if needed. Using the dome again will help steam the vegetables quickly and evenly.
4. Turn griddle to low. Add the fresh garlic and tomatoes, drizzle a little more olive oil and add the

Blackstone seasoning. Toss together for about 1-2 minutes.

5. Using a slotted spoon, remove pasta and place directly onto the griddle to combine with the vegetables. Do not let each scoop of pasta drain, you want the starchy pasta water in your dish! If you drain your pasta be sure to reserve 1 cup starchy pasta water to add to your pasta. Toss pasta and vegetables 30-60 seconds, then place into a large bowl.

6. Now is when you would mix the 1 cup pasta water into the pasta bowl if you used pasta you drained. Add the lemon juice. Drizzle olive oil. Mix together well.

7. Add as much freshly grated cheese and chopped parsley as you like to complete your pasta and enjoy!

Halloween Buffalo Chicken "pumpkins"

Servings:6
Cooking Time:20 Min

Ingredients:

- 1 lb ground chicken
- 1 egg, beaten
- 1 cup panko bread crumb
- 1/4 c carrots, grated or diced small
- 1/2 c celery, center leafy stalks, diced small
- 1/4 cup crumbled blue cheese
- 1/4 c green onions, chopped small
- 1 tbsp Blackstone Parmesan Ranch Seasoning
- 1 tbsp buffalo sauce
- olive oil
- 1/2 cup buffalo sauce
- 1 tbsp butter
- 1/4 c ranch dressing

Directions:

1. Mix ground chicken with the listed ingredients, except the oil. Form meatballs, about 16.
2. Turn Blackstone to medium - medium low heat.
3. Mix sauce ingredients in a small pot and place on Blackstone to heat.
4. Drizzle olive oil on Blackstone and add meatballs. allow meatballs to cook through, turning to cook on each side. Allow all sides to get golden brown, cover if needed. Meatballs should take about 8-10 minutes to cook through.
5. Plate meatballs. Drizzle with sauce. Garnish with green onions. For a Halloween theme, turn meatballs into pumpkins by topping with torn celery leaves and green onions!
6. Enjoy!

Easy Cinnamon Roll Bites

Servings:5
Cooking Time:x

Ingredients:

- 1 can fresh cinnamon rolls

Directions:

1. Pre-heat AirFryer to the low setting.
2. Remove cinnamon roll dough from can and separate.
3. Cut each individual cinnamon roll into 4 pieces. Lightly roll each piece into a ball (about 32 bites total)
4. Place in individual dough balls in the AirFryer baskets, leaving space for them to expand when baking.
5. Bake for 5 minutes or until cooked through.
6. Remove and cover with icing while still hot. Serve hot

Crispy Asian Broccoli

Servings:4
Cooking Time:x

Ingredients:

- 1/3 cup Soy Vay - Veri Veri Teriyaki Marinade & Sauce
- 1 tablespoon sesame oil
- 1 tablespoon Sriracha hot sauce (optional)
- 16 oz frozen broccoli florets
- Sesame seeds (for garnish)

Directions:

1. Preheat AirFryer to 425 degrees F for 10 minutes
2. Whisk together Teriyaki marinade with sesame oil and Sriracha.
3. Fold frozen broccoli florets into Asian marinade until well coated. Using tongs, place coated florets into the air fryer basket.

4. AirFry for 8-12 minutes, shaking basket and moving broccoli with tongs every four minutes. Air fry until broccoli is cooked through and slightly caramelized
5. Garnish with sesame seeds. Serve hot

Blackstone Airfryer Pork Egg Rolls

Servings:4
Cooking Time:20 Min

Ingredients:
- 8 Egg Roll Wraps
- 1/2 Lb. of 80/20 Ground Pork
- 1 1/2 Tablespoons of Minced Garlic
- 1 Tablespoons of Minced Ginger
- 1 Tablespoon of Sesame Oil
- 1/3 Cup of Sliced Green Onion
- 2 Cups of Shredded Cabbage (pre-shredded Cole Slaw mix is a great substitute)
- 2 Tablespoons of Soy Sauce
- Olive Oil
- Spray Vegetable Oil

Directions:
1. Pre-heat your Blackstone Airfryer to 400Â° and pre-heat your griddle to medium-high heat.
2. Add a drizzle of olive oil to the griddle and then the ground pork. Cook for 4-5 minutes, tossing often.
3. Add the garlic and ginger, toss and cook another 2-3 minutes.
4. Add sesame oil and cabbage and cook another 2 minutes, tossing often.
5. Add the green onions and soy sauce and toss to incorporate.
6. Lay out your egg roll wrappers and add a few tablespoons of the pork mix to the center of each. Using a touch of water, wet the border edges of the egg roll wrapper and fold one corner to the center. Wrap each side into the middle and roll the wrapper to meet the other end. These should look like little burritos. Repeat with remaining egg rolls.
7. Place the egg rolls into the Airfryer basket and evenly coat with spray oil. Place the basket back into the Airfryer and cook for 6-7 minutes. You can turn the egg rolls half way through for a more even color.
8. Serve hot with sweet Thai chili sauce.

Chocolate Greek Yogurt Pancakes

Servings:4
Cooking Time:10 Min

Ingredients:
- 1/2 Cup of Plain Greek Yogurt
- 1 Ripe Banana
- 1 1/4 Cup of Old-Fashioned Oats
- 2 Tablespoons of Cocoa Powder
- 2 Eggs
- 2-3 Tablespoons of Milk
- 1 Teaspoon of Baking Powder
- 1 Teaspoon of Vanilla Extract
- 1/4 Cup of Semi-Sweet Mini Chocolate Chips
- Optional Toppings: Fresh fruit, peanut butter, or your favorite syrup.

Directions:
1. In a blender, add all ingredients except for chocolate chips. Blend on high speed until the batter is smooth. Allow the batter to sit for 2-3 minutes before cooking to allow it to thicken.
2. Gently fold in chocolate chips.
3. Heat griddle to medium heat and coat with a thin layer of melted butter.
4. Pour batter onto griddle in 4-inch circles. Allow to cook on one side for about 2-3 minutes or until the edges have set. Flip pancake over and cook for an additional 2 minutes.
5. Repeat with remaining batter.

Sautéed Garlic Green Beans

Servings:6
Cooking Time:20 Min

Ingredients:
- 2 Lb. of Fresh Green Beans
- 1 Tablespoon of Extra Virgin Olive Oil
- 1 Teaspoon of Garlic Powder
- Salt and Pepper to taste

Directions:
1. In a large bowl, mix all ingredients until beans are well-coated.
2. Heat your griddle to medium-high heat and cover with a thin layer of olive oil.
3. Cook beans on griddle until they reach desired tenderness (about 12-15 minutes), turning occasionally. (You can also use our basting cover and a few tablespoons of water to steam this recipe)

Air Fryer Buffalo Cauliflower

Servings:6
Cooking Time:15 Min

Ingredients:
- 1 head of Cauliflower
- 1 cup Frank's Hot Sauce
- ½ stick Butter
- 2 tbs Vinegar
- 1 tbsp Worcestershire Sauce
- 1 tsp Garlic Powder

Directions:
1. Chop cauliflower into bite size pieces.
2. In a microwave safe bowl, melt butter. Whisk in the rest of the ingredients. Set aside.
3. Set Air Fryer to high heat.
4. Cook cauliflower for 5-7 minutes or until slightly browned.
5. Remove and put into an airtight container. Pour ½ of sauce over the cauliflower, seal lid, and give it a shake.
6. Put in the air fryer for 3 more minutes.
7. Remove tray from Air Fryer and spoon the cauliflower onto a serving plate. Pour remaining sauce over the cauliflower, add celery and blue cheese dressing for dipping.

Pita Bread / Flat Bread

Servings:1
Cooking Time:10 Min

Ingredients:
- 2 Teaspoons of Instant Dry Yeast
- 1 Teaspoon of Sugar
- 1 Teaspoon of Salt
- 1/2 Cup of Warm Milk
- 1/2 Cup of Warm Water
- 1 Tablespoon of Extra Virgin Olive Oil
- 2 and 1/2 Cups of Bread Flour

Directions:
1. In a large bowl, combine yeast, sugar, milk, water, salt, and olive oil.
2. Add 2 Â½ cups of flour to the liquid mixture. Mix with a large spoon or your hands until the flour is incorporated.
3. Transfer the dough to a lightly floured working surface and knead for 4-5 minutes until the dough becomes smooth.
4. Brush the bowl with some olive oil and put the dough back in it. Cover the bowl with a towel, place in a warm place, and let it rise for about 40 minutes.
5. Transfer the dough to your working surface. Divide the dough into 8 pieces and roll into balls. Drizzle a little olive oil on them and cover them with plastic wrap.
6. Let the dough balls rest for 10 more minutes.
7. Preheat your griddle to medium heat.
8. Lightly oil your working surface. Place a dough ball on your working surface and flatten it with the palm of your hand. Then use a rolling pin, roll it out to a circle 6" to 8" in diameter.
9. Carefully lay the pitas on the griddle and cook for 1-2 minutes on each side. Remove them from the griddle and wrap them in a towel to keep them warm.

Teriyaki Beef Kabobs

Servings:6
Cooking Time:18 Min

Ingredients:
- 2 Lb. of Beef Strip Steak (cubed)
- 1/2 Cup of Light Soy Sauce
- 4 Tablespoons of Brown Sugar
- 2 Tablespoons of Rice Vinegar
- 2 Garlic Cloves (minced)
- 1/2 Teaspoon of Onion Powder
- 1/2 Teaspoon of Ginger Powder

Directions:
1. Cut your strip steak into 1â cubes

2. In a sealable, gallon-sized plastic bag, add light soy sauce, brown sugar, rice vinegar, minced garlic, onion powder, and ginger powder. Knead to combine ingredients.

3. Add steak cubes to marinade and place in refrigerator 30 minutes - 8 hours (longer for better flavor).

4. Heat griddle to high heat and cover with a thin layer of olive oil.

5. Thread your beef onto skewers and place on hot griddle and cook for approximately 8 minutes, rotating every 2 minutes to cook evenly on all sides.

6. Cook to desired doneness (internal temp of 145 degrees for âmediumâ).

7. Remove from griddle and serve.

Sweet Spicy Bang Bang Shrimp

Servings:1
Cooking Time:10 Min

Ingredients:
- 1 Lb. of Peeled and De-veined Shrimp
- 1 Cup of Butter Milk
- 1 Cup of Corn Starch
- 1/2 Teaspoon of Garlic Powder
- 1/4 Cup of Sliced Green Onions
- 1-2 Tablespoon of Toasted Tuxedo Sesame Seeds
- 3/4 Cup of Mayo
- 1/2 Cup of Sweet Chili Sauce
- 1-2 Tablespoon of Sriracha Sauce

Directions:
1. Peel and de-vein shrimp, taking the tails off as well. Place shrimp and buttermilk in freezer bag and let sit in fridge for 30 min-2 hours.

2. Make your Bang Bang sauce by mixing mayo, sweet chili sauce, and sriracha sauce together. Adjust ingredients to your liking (adding more mayo and sweet chili for sweeter, more sriracha for spicier) and set aside. Slice your green onions and set aside. Toast your sesame seeds if not already bought toasted (toast a few minutes in a dry skillet)

3. Dump shrimp to drain in colander. Add corn starch and garlic powder to a new freezer bag and add shrimp, shake to coat evenly.

4. Turn Blackstone griddle on medium-high to high heat. Add a good amount of vegetable oil and add shrimp, shaking off excess cornstarch. Let cook til golden brown on one side, about 3-5 minutes. Flip and cook other side 3-5 min. Drizzle more oil on the backs right before flipping and add oil as needed under shrimp so they can fry up crispy!

5. Take off and set on a paper towel lined dish to drain extra oil. Toss carefully in Â½ -Â¾ of the Bang Bang Sauce to coat evenly, adding more if needed. Top with Sesame seeds and green onions and extra sauce.

6. Serve as is as an appetizer as is or great for Bang Bang Tacos & Shrimp Rice Bowls!

Jalapeno Cheese Crisps

Servings:10
Cooking Time:5 Min

Ingredients:
- Sharp White Cheddar, Shredded
- Sharp Orange Cheddar, Shredded
- Jalapenos (or jarred pickled jalapenos), Thinly Sliced
- Bacon Slices, Cooked and Crumbled
- Onion Powder

Directions:
1. Heat your Blackstone Griddle to medium heat, be sure surface is clean of excess oil.

2. Place about ¼ cup of shredded cheese onto the hot griddle.

3. After about a minute sprinkle a few pieces of bacon and 1-3 slices jalapeno on top and a light dusting of onion powder.

4. Once the cheese starts to get lacey, about 1-2 minutes, using a scraper or spatula lift the cheese carefully and flip.

5. Let cook 1 more minute. Set on paper towels to drain excess oil.

Chicken Enchiladas

Servings: 2
Cooking Time: 18 Min

Ingredients:
- 4 Corn Tortillas
- 1 Can of your favorite Enchilada Sauce
- 2.5 Oz. of Chunked Chicken Breast (In can)
- 4 Cheese Mexican Shredded Blend
- Shredded Iceberg Lettuce
- Freshly Chopped Cilantro
- Blackstone Taco & Fajita Seasoning
- Crema Mexicana

Directions:
1. Heat your Blackstone Griddle to high. Drizzle griddle top with olive oil.
2. Use Range Top Combo range burner or griddle top to heat enchilada sauce in a skillet or small stock pot.
3. When griddle top has reached high temperature, use tongs to submerge corn tortillas in enchilada sauce. Make sure both sides are coated in sauce. Place enchiladas on griddle top. Allow enchiladas to cook for at least a minute or two before continuing on to the following step.
4. Place chicken across center of each tortilla in a line.
5. Use spatula to gently fold both sides of the tortilla over the chicken (one side at a time). Use spatula to gently apply pressure to the top of the tortilla, causing the enchilada to conform to the classic enchilada shape.
6. Top with cheese to taste.
7. Squirt water on griddle top and immediately cover enchiladas with Basting Cover or close griddle hood. This will allow the cheese to melt and the tortillas to essentially bake.
8. Allow the tortillas to bake for 2.5-5 minutes, until cheese is melted and tortillas have reached the desired texture.
9. Remove enchiladas from griddle top, sprinkle with Blackstone taco and fajita seasoning, top with shredded iceburg lettuce, fresh chopped cilantro, and Crema Mexicana to taste.

Griddled Frozen Pina Colada

Servings: 4
Cooking Time: 25 Min

Ingredients:
- 1/2 Fresh Pineapple
- 4 Limes
- 8 Oz. of White Rum
- 4 Oz. of Dark Rum (Use for a Rum Runner as Well)
- 6 Oz. of Sweetened Cream of Coconut (Coco Lopez)
- 4 Oz. of Unsweetened Coconut Milk
- Unsweetened Coconut Shavings
- Heavy Whipping Cream (for Garnish)
- 2-3 Tablespoon of Powdered Sugar

Directions:
1. Peel the fresh pineapple and cut it into roughly 1 1/2 inch pieces. Place the pineapple pieces onto a few sheets of paper towel to dry the surface.
2. Cut 6 limes in half. Dry the halves with a paper towel.
3. Set your griddle to medium-high heat. Using a paper towel, spread a very thin layer of vegetable oil on the griddle top. When the griddle is hot, add your pineapple. Cook until you start to see a little carmelization (about one minute), then flip.
4. While the pineapples are caramelizing, add the limes to the other side of your griddle. Cook for about 3-4 minutes, or until the limes are caramelized and a toasty brown. Once the pineapple chunks and limes are done, pull them from the griddle and save for later.
5. Clean the griddle off to prepare to toast the coconut shavings. The griddle will need to be completely dry before toasting, as any moisture will make the coconut soft and soggy. Adjust the temperature of your griddle to medium.
6. Add the unsweetened coconut to the cleaned griddle top. Note: Make sure the coconut is unsweetened, as the sugars in sweetened coconut will burn.
7. Once you see the shavings start to brown slightly, toss the coconut shavings to prevent burning. Keep tossing the coconut every 10-15 seconds until they have

a golden color and crisp up. When they're done, remove them from the griddle set aside for later.

8. In a bowl, add a bit of heavy whipping cream and a 2-3 TBSP of powdered sugar. Whisk for 3-4 minutes, or until you have stiff peaks.

9. In a blender, add some ice. Add white rum, dark rum, sweetened cream of coconut, unsweetened coconut milk, your griddled pineapple, and squeeze 4 of your limes over the top. Blend everything until you've got a smooth and creamy creation. Pour the mix into a glass and then top it off with the whipped cream. For garnish, add the toasted coconut and finish with a cherry on top (optional).

Boston Cream Pie Pancakes

Servings:4
Cooking Time:20 Min

Ingredients:
- 1 cup yellow cake mix
- 1 cup pancake mix
- 1 cup milk
- 1 tsp vanilla
- 2 eggs
- 1 package instant vanilla pudding mix
- 3 cups cold milk
- 1 1/2 cups chocolate chips
- 1 tbs butter
- 3 tbs milk

Directions:
1. In a mixing bowl, pour pudding mix and milk. Whisk until slightly thickened.
2. Store in fridge while finishing pancakes.
3. Melt butter, milk, and chocolate in microwave for 30 seconds.
4. Mix together till smooth
5. Preheat griddle to medium-low.
6. In a mixing bowl, combine all of the pancake ingredients.
7. Melt some butter on your griddle top. Pour 1/4 cup of pancake batter onto griddle and cook 3-4 minutes or until you start to see some bubbles. Flip and cook another 2-3 minutes.
8. Once you have cooked all of the pancakes, remove the custard from the fridge and grab the ganache.
9. On a plate, begin creating layers by alternating pancakes with custard filling. Pour ganache over the top.

Parmesan Crisp Bruschetta

Servings:4
Cooking Time:10 Min

Ingredients:
- ½ cup Shredded Parmesan
- ½ cup Grana Padano
- 1 cup finely diced Tomato
- ¼ cup finely diced Red Onion
- 1 tablespoon minced Garlic
- 2 tablespoons chopped fresh Basil
- Balsamic Glaze
- Salt and Pepper
- Olive Oil

Directions:
1. In a large mixing bowl, add the tomatoes, onions, garlic, basil, and a pinch of parmesan. Add a drizzle of olive oil and a couple pinches of salt and pepper. Mix evenly and set aside for later.
2. Heat your griddle to medium-low heat. Mix both cheeses together then add about a tablespoon of cheese in a round 2-3 inch circle on the griddle. Cook for 2-3 minutes or until the cheese starts to crisp on the bottom. Flip and cook another 2 minutes or until the cheese is evenly golden and crisp. Remove from the griddle and let cool.
3. To plate, arrange the cheese crisps on a serving platter and top with a spoonful of the tomato mix. Garnish with a drizzle of balsamic glace and a few basil leaves.
4. Enjoy!

Greek Gyros (pork Or Chicken)

Servings:1
Cooking Time:10 Min

Ingredients:
- 2 Pork Tenderloins (or 4 Chicken Breasts)
- 1 Onion (1/2 shredded, 1/2 thinly sliced)

- 4 Garlic Cloves, finely minced
- 1 Tablespoon of Dried Marjoram
- 1 Tablespoon of Dried Ground Rosemary
- 2 tsp of Kosher Salt
- 3 Tablespoons of Extra Virgin Olive Oil
- 1/2 Teaspoon of Ground Black Pepper
- 1/4 Cup of White Wine
- 1 Tablespoon of Butter
- 2 Large Tomatoes, halved then sliced
- Tzatziki Sauce (Store bought or see recipe below)
- 8 Pieces Pita Bread
- 2 cups Greek yogurt
- 2 Cucumbers, peeled and seeded
- 1 Garlic clove, finely minced
- 2 TBSP white wine vinegar
- 1 Bunch Fresh Dill, finely chopped (or 3 tsp dry dill)
- 3 TBSP olive oil
- Salt & Pepper to taste

Directions:

1. Cut the onion in half. In a large bowl, shred 1/2 of the onion. Dice the other half of the onion and set aside for later. In the same large bowl combine the shredded onion, garlic, marjoram, rosemary, salt, olive oil, black pepper, and white wine Trim any of the white membrane from the tenderloins. Cut the tenderloins lengthwise and then slice into 1/4" pieces. Put the pork in the marinade, cover, and set in the fridge for up to 24 hours. Preheat griddle to medium high heat. Add all the pork to the griddle and cook until half done. Add the 2 Tablespoons of butter, and a few more Tablespoons of wine to the pork. Toss to melt butter and combine until finished cooking. Be careful not to overcook the pork. Remove from the heat and serve on Greek Pita Bread with sliced tomatoes, diced onions, and Tzatziki Sauce.
2. Cut the onion in half. In a large bowl, shred 1/2 of the onion. Dice the other half of the onion and set aside for later.
3. In the same large bowl combine the shredded onion, garlic, marjoram, rosemary, salt, olive oil, black pepper, and white wine
4. Trim any of the white membrane from the tenderloins. Cut the tenderloins lengthwise and then slice into 1/4" pieces.
5. Put the pork in the marinade, cover, and set in the fridge for up to 24 hours.
6. Preheat griddle to medium high heat.
7. Add all the pork to the griddle and cook until half done.
8. Add the 2 Tablespoons of butter, and a few more Tablespoons of wine to the pork. Toss to melt butter and combine until finished cooking. Be careful not to overcook the pork.
9. Remove from the heat and serve on Greek Pita Bread with sliced tomatoes, diced onions, and Tzatziki Sauce.
10. Peel the cucumbers cut them in half and spoon out the seeds from the middle. Grate with a cheese grater.
11. Combine the cucumber, yogurt, garlic (minced), 2 tablespoons white wine vinegar and 3 tablespoons of olive oil.
12. Mix until well combined
13. Add pepper and salt to taste.
14. Add the finely chopped fresh dill.
15. Refrigerate for at least an hour to let the flavors combine.

Ginger & Soy Glazed Salmon With Asian Green Beans

Servings:x
Cooking Time:x

Ingredients:
- Wild Alaskan Salmon Filets with skin on
- Raw Shrimp (deveined)
- 6 Tablespoons of Extra Virgin Olive Oil
- 3 Tablespoons of Bragg's Liquid Aminos or Low Sodium Soy Sauce
- 2 Tablespoons of Dijon Mustard
- 1 Tablespoon of Ginger Paste (or grated fresh ginger)
- 1 Clove Fresh Garlic, pressed or finely diced
- Avocado Oil or Coconut Oil
- Toasted Sesame Seeds
- Green Beans
- 1 Red Pepper or Several Small Multi-Color Peppers
- 1/2 Onion
- 1-2 Garlic Cloves, pressed or finely diced

- 2 Tablespoons of Butter
- 1/2 Teaspoon of Salt
- 3 Tablespoons of Liquid Aminos or Low-Sodium Soy Sauce
- 1 Green Onion, finely sliced for garnish
- 1 Teaspoon of Toasted Sesame Seeds for garnish

Directions:
1. If your fish is frozen, let thaw in the refrigerator overnight or run under cold water until thawed.
2. Turn on the Blackstone to high heat, then get pan of water boiling for the green beans.
3. To make the marinade, combine olive oil, liquid aminos or soy sauce, dijon mustard, ginger paste, and garlic clove. Stir well to combine.
4. Season the shrimp and salmon with salt and pepper to taste.
5. Turn heat down to medium and drizzle avocado oil on the griddle.
6. Put salmon on the griddle skin side down. You can wait a little bit to put the shrimp on because they will cook in under 3-4 minutes. Remove shrimp and cover when they are finished.
7. Pour marinade over the top of the shrimp and salmon. Toss shrimp in marinade to coat evenly. Add water by salmon and cover with a basting dome to cook all the way through.
8. While the salmon is cooking, add the green beans to the boiling water with a Tbsp. of salt.
9. Thinly slice the peppers and onion. Put oil on the griddle and saute the peppers and onions for several minutes until tender.
10. After the green beans have boiled for 1-2 minutes or until cooked, drain them and add to the peppers and onion. Cook for another minute or two. Add a clove of freshly pressed garlic, 2 Tbsp. butter, and a splash of aminos or soy sauce, and a little salt. Only cook for about 30 seconds to prevent burning the garlic. Remove from heat and serve hot.
11. Your shrimp should be done and removed from the griddle by now. Watch the salmon and cook until itâs flaky in the middle with no raw sections. Once itâs done, give it a quick splash of aminoâs and turn it over to sear for about 30 seconds to 1 minute. Remove from the heat. and garnish with toasted sesame seeds.
12. Serve the salmon and shrimp on top of the green beans and garnish with sesame seeds. Enjoy!

The Better Mac

Servings:1
Cooking Time:15 Min

Ingredients:
- 1/2 Lb. of 80/20 ground beef
- 2 Slices American Cheese
- 3 Tablespoons of Minced Onion
- 2 Tablespoons of Dill Pickle Relish
- 2 Tablespoons of Thousand Island Dressing
- Shredded Iceberg Lettuce, to Taste
- Two Burger Bun Heels and 1 Sesame Bun Brown
- Salt, Pepper, and Granulated Garlic to Taste
- Butter
- Recommended: Blackstone Press & Sear Burger Tool, Wax Paper, Olive Oil

Directions:
1. Blackstone Griddle on high heat. Cover griddle top with light coating of olive oil.
2. Weigh and roll two Â¼ lb ground beef meatballs.
3. Place meat balls on hot griddle top, cover each with wax paper, and use Press & Sear Burger Tool to smash each meatball. Hold pressure on Press & Sear Burger Tool for a few seconds to assure proper sear on patty.
4. Season patties to taste. We prefer a mix of salt, pepper, and granulated garlic.
5. Flip patties when bottoms are caramelized. This will take 4-5 minutes (should have black and brown accents).
6. Place a slice of American cheese on top of each patty.
7. Apply oil to an empty part of the griddle top. Drop minced onions into oil. Use spatula to mix onions as they caramelize.
8. Meanwhile, butter the insides of two burger heels and 1 burger crown. Place buns, butter side down, onto the hot griddle top.
9. Make the special sauce: Mix Dill pickle relish with Thousand Island Dressing.
10. Remove buns with they are toasted to perfection (golden brown).

11. Once cheese is completely melted, you can start to plate up your Better Mac.
12. Start with one heel. Cover it in the special sauce. Cover the sauce with shredded iceburg lettuce to taste. Place patty with cheese on top. Place the second bun heel on top of the bottom patty. Cover 2nd bun heel with Special Sauce. Place 2nd patty w/cheese on top of 2nd bun heel. Top with sautÃ¨ed onions to taste. Add crown.
13. Enjoy your Better MAC!

Lamb Lollipops With Mint Chimichurri

Servings:4
Cooking Time:15 Min

Ingredients:
- 12 Lamb Lollipops
- 2 tablespoons spicy brown Mustard
- 1 bunch Italian flat leaf Parsley
- ½ bunch fresh Mint Leaves
- 1 tablespoon minced Garlic
- The juice of 1 Lemon
- The juice of 2 Limes
- 2 tablespoon Red Wine Vinegar
- 2 teaspoons Red Pepper Flakes
- Olive oil
- Salt and pepper

Directions:
1. Pre-heat your griddle to high heat.
2. Finely chop the parsley and mint together and add to a mixing bowl. Add the garlic, lemon and lime juice, red wine vinegar, red pepper flakes and a pinch of salt and pepper. Add some olive oil and mix to evenly incorporate the ingredients. Reserve on the side for later.
3. Season the lamb lollipops with a bit olive oil, mustard and salt and pepper. Cook on high heat for 1-2 minutes per side or until caramelized and cooked to your liking.
4. To plate, arrange the cooked lamb lollipops on a large family style platter and pour the mint chimichurri over the top. Serve hot.

Bacon Fried Rice With Spicy Mayo

Servings:4
Cooking Time:10 Min

Ingredients:
- 4 Cups of Leftover Rice
- 1 Tablespoon of Japanese Mayonnaise
- 1 Cup of Bacon, diced
- 1 Cup of Onion, diced
- 1-2 Fresh Garlic Cloves, minced
- 1 Tablespoon of Wok Sauce or Oil
- 2 Tablespoons of Butter
- 3 Eggs
- 1/2 Cup of Green Scallions, sliced
- 1/2 Cup of Bean Sprouts
- 1 Tablespoon of Oyster Sauce
- 2 Tablespoons of Low Sodium Soy Sauce
- Salt & Pepper to taste
- Sesame Oil (about 2-3 tsp or to taste)
- 2 Tablespoons of Japanese Mayonnaise
- 1 Tablespoon of Sriracha
- 1/2 Teaspoon of Sesame Oil

Directions:
1. In a large mixing bowl combine rice and mayonnaise, coating the rice evenly and set aside.
2. Mix the soy sauce and oyster sauce and set aside.
3. Preheat Blackstone Griddle to medium-high heat and add the bacon. Quickly separate bacon, moving it around continuously to help it cook evenly. Do not let it cook completely, only about 1-2 minutes.
4. Add the onions to the bacon and bacon grease, keeping everything moving. Cook 1-2 minutes.
5. Add garlic, cook 30-60 seconds. Remove bacon, leaving grease on griddle and set aside. Scrape half of the grease off the griddle surface, keeping the rest to cook in.
6. Mix in seasoned wok oil and butter to the bacon grease. Quickly add the eggs, break the yolks, mix the eggs with the butter and oil while chopping the eggs into small pieces for about 30 seconds.
7. Add the rice. Combine rice and eggs, separating rice to cook evenly, keeping everything moving for 1-2

minutes. Season with salt and pepper. Add bean sprouts and let cook one minute.

8. Mix the bacon, onions, and garlic and add the green scallions, reserving some scallions for garnish.
9. Drizzle half of the soy sauce mixture and mix to coat evenly, adding more to taste if desired. Cook 1 minute. Keep everything moving through the cook time so that nothing burns. A light drizzle of sesame oil can be added and mixed through during the last 30 seconds of cook, or can be mixed in once rice is removed from heat.
10. Remove rice from griddle and garnish with more green scallions. Serve with spicy mayo.

Airfryer Strawberry Hand Pies

Servings:8
Cooking Time:20 Min

Ingredients:
- 1 Package of Pie Crust Dough
- 1 Small Jar of Strawberry Jam
- 1 Egg White
- ¼ cup of Sugar
- Cooking Spray

Directions:
1. On a clean dry surface, lay out a sheet of the pie dough. Using a cookie cutter cut out 8 shapes. Repeat with the second sheet of pie dough. If you desire more pies, ball up the discarded dough, roll out with a rolling pin, and cut out more shapes.
2. Place a tablespoon of jam in the center of the dough cutout. Place another piece of dough on top. Using a fork pinch the edges together. Brush the egg white over both sides and sprinkle with sugar.
3. Preheat air fryer to medium.
4. Spray cooking spray on air fryer trays, and place 4 hand pies in each tray.
5. Cook for 6-7 minutes or until golden brown, then flip and cook another 2-3 mins.
6. Remove from tray and enjoy!

3 Simple Burger Sauces

Servings:4
Cooking Time:5 Min

Ingredients:
- 1/4 Cup of Ketchup
- 1/4 Cup of Mustard
- 1/4 Cup of Mayonnaise
- 1 Tablespoon of Dill Relish
- 1/4 Cup of Mayonnaise
- 1/3 Cup of Sour Cream
- 2 Tablespoons of Lime Juice
- 1/2 Teaspoon of Garlic Powder
- 1/2 Teaspoon of Onion Powder
- 1 Tablespoon of Chipotle in Adobo
- 1 Tablespoon of Fresh Cilantro (chopped)
- Salt and Pepper
- 1 Teaspoon of Chopped Basil
- 1 Teaspoon of Chopped Chive
- 1 Teaspoon of Chopped Thyme
- 3/4 Cup of Mayonnaise
- 1 Teaspoon of Garlic Powder
- 2 Tablespoons of Lemon Juice
- Salt and Pepper

Directions:
1. Special Sauce Directions: In a small mixing bowl, add all the ingredients and mix evenly to combine. Chill and serve.
2. Chipotle Lime Sauce Directions: In a small mixing bowl, add all of the ingredients with a pinch of salt and pepper. Mix evenly to combine. Chill and serve.
3. Herby Mayo Directions: In a small mixing bowl, add all ingredients with a pinch of salt and pepper. Mix evenly to combine. Chill and serve.

Chicken Steak & Vegetable Hibachi

Servings:1
Cooking Time:10 Min

Ingredients:
- 5 Boneless Skinless Chicken Breasts
- Two 16 oz Packages of Sirloin Steaks
- 2 Large White Onions
- 4 Large Green Zucchini
- 16 Oz. of Sliced Mushrooms
- 2 Tablespoons of Canola or Vegetable Oil

- 8 Tablespoons of Low Sodium Soy Sauce
- 4 Tablespoons of Butter or Garlic Butter
- 1 Dash Iodized Salt
- 1 Dash Ground Pepper
- 1 Dash Lemon Juice
- 1/2 Cup of Grated Carrot
- 1/2 Cup of Peas
- 2-3 Scrambled Eggs
- 1/2 Cup of Diced Onion
- 2 Tablespoons of Unsalted butter
- 3 Tablespoons of Low Sodium Soy Sauce
- 2 Cups of Uncooked Parboiled Rice
- 2 1/2 Cups of Cups Water

Directions:
1. Slice the meat and vegetables into bite sized pieces.
2. Melt 2 Tbsp of butter, add the meat, then add 3 Tbsp of soy sauce.
3. Melt the other 2 Tbsp of butter, add the onions and zucchini, then add the last 5 Tbsp of soy sauce and a dash of salt and pepper.
4. Stir occasionally for 7- 8 minutes or to desired tenderness.
5. For the chicken, add lemon juice for the last minute of cooking and cook steak to desired temperature.
6. Add the mushrooms a few minutes before the meat is done because these cook fast!
7. Bring 2 Â½ cups water to rolling boil.
8. Add 2 cups rice and remove from heat, cover and simmer for 20 minutes.
9. Remove cover for 5 minutes so the rice absorbs the remaining water. Melt the butter on your flat top.
10. Once the rice has absorbed all the water, add the scrambled eggs, carrots, peas, and onions together on the griddle over medium heat.
11. Add the soy sauce, salt, and pepper and cook for about 8 minutes, stirring often.

Easy 5 Ingredient Air Fried Calzones

Servings:4
Cooking Time:x

Ingredients:

- Pizza dough
- 1 pound Italian sausage
- 1 cup pizza cheese blend
- 1 cup Ricotta cheese
- ½ cup sliced kalamata olives

Directions:
1. Crumble the sausage onto a pre-heated griddle over medium heat.
2. Using a spatula, break the sausage into small pieces while cooking.
3. Be sure to have the sausage broken down into very small and uniform bits. Cook the sausage until no pink remains and has rendered completely. Set aside to cool.
4. Divide the pizza dough into 2 pieces.
5. Roll the pizza dough out into a round shape resembling a medium pizza with no toppings.
6. Place the sausage crumbles on one side of the dough, leaving an inch margin on the side with no toppings.
7. Top with half of the ricotta, olives, and cheese blend. Distribute the toppings as evenly as possible so each bite contains diverse flavors and textures.
8. Repeat with the remaining ingredients to make a second calzone.
9. Transfer each calzone to a piece of parchment paper about the size of your air fry basket.
10. Preheat the air fry basket to 400F.
11. Place one calzone in each air fry basket and cook for 18 minutes until the crust is golden brown and the cheese is melty and delicious.

Loaded Bloody Marys

Servings:x
Cooking Time:x

Ingredients:

- 1.75 Liters Zing Zang Boody Marry Mix
- Titio's Vodka (or your preferred Vodka)
- 2 Tablespoons of Prepared Horseradish
- 1 Tablespoon of Worcestershire Sauce
- 1 Tablespoon of Celery Seed
- 1 Tablespoon of Old Bay
- 1 Lemon
- Tabasco hot sauce (or similar hot sauce) to taste
- Lump Crab Meat

- Shrimp butterflied with tails on
- Blue Cheese Olives
- Celery Stalks
- 1 Lemon

Directions:
1. In a large pitcher, mix all Bloody Mary ingredients. Note: this can stay refrigerated for up to 3 days.
2. Peel shrimp, leaving tails on. Butterfly by slicing along the top of the shrimp and remove veins and waste.
3. Toss shrimp in olive oil and old bay.
4. Cook shrimp for about 2 minutes per side, or until firm to touch. Note: let cool before serving on your Bloody Mary.
5. Wet the rim of your glass with a lemon wedge. Using a flat dish, pour old bay or the Blackstone Breakfast Blend seasoning to garnish the rim of your glass. Add ice and lump crab meat in layers.
6. Mix your Bloody Mary pitcher before pouring to ensure to incorporate any seasonings that fell to the bottom. Fill your glass.
7. Garnish with celery stalk, olives, shrimp, and more crab meat. Cheers!

Bacon Popcorn

Servings:4
Cooking Time:12 Min

Ingredients:
- 4 Bacon Strips (Thick Cut)
- ½ Cup of Corn Kernels
- ½ Tablespoon of Unsalted Butter
- 1 Teaspoon of Salt

Directions:
1. Heat your Blackstone griddle to medium-high heat and cook bacon until crisp. About 6-7 minutes.
2. Drain the bacon on a bit of paper towel and let cool, then chop small.
3. Add the corn kernels to the griddle and toss in the bacon fat. Group the kernels into a pile and cover. Cook for 5-6 minutes or until the "popping" sound stops. (Be sure to keep the cover on until the popping stops, otherwise, your corn will fly!)
4. Once the corn kernels are popped, add the butter and salt and toss to coat evenly.
5. Garnish the popcorn with the chopped bacon and serve hot.

Zucchini & Squash

Servings:x
Cooking Time:x

Ingredients:
- 2 Zucchini, Diced
- 2 Squash, Diced
- 1 Large Onion, Diced
- 2-3 Tomatoes on the Vine, Diced
- 5-6 Garlic Cloves, Roughly Chopped
- 1 Can Cannelloni Beans, Rinsed and Drained (optional)
- Extra Virgin Olive Oil
- Salt and Pepper to Taste

Directions:
1. Dice zucchini, squash, and onions and toss with extra virgin olive oil. You'll need about 1/4-1/2 cup to coat evenly. Season with salt and pepper to taste and set aside.
2. Dice the tomatoes and place them in a mixing bowl. Add a little salt and gently mix, then set aside. The salt will help the tomatoes release their juices, which creates better flavor for cooking.
3. Preheat your Blackstone to medium heat. Add the zucchini, squash and onions mixture. Toss frequently to cook until fork tender.
4. Add your garlic and tomatoes, then toss everything together. If you are using beans, add them as well. Cook for a few minutes.
5. Add a drizzle of oil if needed at any point throughout the cook, or you can plate it up and finish it off with a drizzle over the top.
6. Enjoy!

Marinated Cauliflower Steaks And Veggies

Servings:1
Cooking Time:10 Min

Ingredients:
- 1 Head of Cauliflower, Sliced 1 Inch Thick (saving any extra or broken pieces)
- 1/2 Cup of Vegetable Oil
- 1/4 Cup of Water
- 2 Tablespoons of Brazilian Steakhouse Seasoning
- 1/4 Teaspoon of Thyme
- 1/2 Teaspoon of Onion Powder
- Cracked Black Pepper to taste
- 1 Bunch Yellow Oyster Mushrooms
- 8 Oz. of Baby Bella (Crimini) Mushrooms, Sliced
- 3 Large Garlic Cloves, Smashed and Chopped
- 2 Tablespoons of Extra Virgin Olive Oil
- 1 Tablespoon of Curly Parsley, Chopped
- Dash of Red Pepper Flakes (optional)
- 2 Onions, Sliced 1/2" Thick
- 1 Bunch of Fresh Spinach
- 1 Handful of Melody Grape Tomatoes
- 3/4 Cup of Grated Parmesan Romano Blend Cheese
- 1/2 Stick of Butter

Directions:
1. Marinate the sliced and broken pieces of cauliflower in a freezer bag with all the ingredients in the Cauliflower Marinade Mix group. Gently knead the bag to combine, then let marinade for 20 minutes.
2. Marinate the mushrooms in a freezer bag with the ingredients in the Mushroom Marinade Mix for 20 minutes, carefully keeping the onions together. Leave a little parsley for garnishing.
3. Wash your spinach and set aside.
4. Turn your Blackstone griddle to medium high heat. Spread about a tbsp of butter on the hot griddle and add your cauliflower. Let cook 5 minutes. Flip and using a basting dome to steam for 3 minutes, then let cook uncovered for 4-5 more minutes or until cooked through. Use a toothpick to check for doneness to your liking. Set aside and top with cheese to melt.
5. Adding a little more butter in two spots, cook the onions and mushrooms separately in a little butter until done to your liking. I like mushrooms cooked no longer than 3 minutes and onions to have a nice char but still a little crunch, about 4 minutes on each side. Remove from griddle once cooked.
6. Throw the spinach on the griddle in the flavored oil and butter left on the grill to cook for 1-2 minutes.
7. Arrange your vegetables on top of the spinach and garnish with tomatoes, cheese, and chopped parsley.

Bananas Foster

Servings:1
Cooking Time:10 Min

Ingredients:
- 4 Tablespoons of Butter
- 1/4 Cup of Brown Sugar
- 1 Tablespoon of Ground Cinnamon
- 1 Sliced Banana
- 1/4 Cup of Brandy
- 3 Teaspoons of CrÃ¨me de Banana
- Vanilla Ice Cream

Directions:
1. Preheat the Blackstone griddle to Medium heat.
2. Put 4 Tbsp of butter on the griddle.
3. Add Â¼ Cup of Brown Sugar and 1 Tbsp of Ground Cinnamon to the butter.
4. Mix the ingredients together, then add one sliced banana.
5. Add Â¼ Cup Brandy and 3 Tbsp CrÃ¨me de Banana.
6. Immediately use a lighter to ignite the alcohol. Allow mixture to burn for at least 10 seconds, then mix until the flames are gone.
7. Use a spatula to transfer the syrup-like banana mixture onto scoops of ice cream.
8. Sprinkle a light dusting of Cinnamon on top of everything and enjoy.

Italian Sausage And Cheese

Servings:x
Cooking Time:x

Ingredients:
- 3 Long Italian Rolls or 4-6 flour toritillas
- 1 Lb. of Ground Italian Sausage, mild or hot
- 1 Green Bell Pepper, diced
- 1 Red Bell Pepper, diced
- 1 Onion, diced
- 1 Cup of Portobello Mushrooms, diced
- 2-3 Fresh Garlic Cloves, grated
- Italian Seasoning
- Garlic Powder
- Salt and Pepper
- 2 Tablespoons of Mayo (for toasting rolls)
- 1-2 Cups of Shredded Italian Blend Shredded Cheese
- 1-2 Cups of Marinara (Victoria marinara is a good choice)
- Extra Virgin Olive Oil

Directions:
1. Prepare all your ingredients by dicing red and green peppers, onions, mushrooms, and grate your garlic.
2. Preheat Blackstone to medium heat and drizzle olive oil. Add peppers and onions. Cook about 4 minutes, mixing throughout. Season with salt and pepper.
3. Add the mushrooms to the peppers and onions and cook 2-3 minutes longer. Move vegetables to the side on low to no heat.
4. Before starting your meat, place a small pot with a cup or two of marinara to the corner of your griddle on low to heat through.
5. Add the sausage to the griddle and cook through, chopping it up like taco meat. Season lightly with Italian seasoning and garlic powder.
6. Place tortillas on low heat for 30-60 seconds. Flip and add cheese and meat. Fold in half and allow tortilla to cook until golden brown, flipping to cook both sides. If using rolls instead of tortillas, while the meat is cooking spread a thin layer of mayonnaise on the inside of your rolls and place them mayo side down to lightly toast on low heat.
7. Turn Blackstone where meat is to low heat, add the grated garlic and mix into the meat well. Mix in the vegetables to the cooked sausage. Add half of the cheese and toss to mix through.
8. Divide meat into three portions and line up the meat mixture into three piles.
9. Add the rest of the cheese to top each pile of meat. Place roll or tortilla on top and allow to cook another minute or two.
10. Using your hand to hold the bread/tortilla and your spatula to slide under the sandwich, flip sandwiches over. Serve with marinara on top or on the side for dipping.

Scrapple And Eggs Breakfast Flatbread

Servings:4
Cooking Time:25 Min

Ingredients:
- 4 Scrapple Slices
- Salt and Black Pepper (to Taste)
- 1 Cup of Red, Yellow, and Green Pepper (Diced)
- 2 Vidalia Onions (Diced)
- 2 Tablespoons of Butter
- 8 Eggs
- Pizza Dough (Unit)
- 1 Cup of Cheddar Cheese (Shredded)
- 2 Tablespoons of Scallions (for Garnish)

Directions:
1. Preheat Griddle to Medium/High and coat with oil.
2. Place Peppers and Onions on griddle and cook until softened but still with a slight crunch.
3. Brown scrapple slices for 5 minutes, without turning. Once slices have browned on one side, turn and begin breaking into pieces using Blackstone spatula.
4. Add black pepper to taste and cook for an additional 5 minutes. Set aside.
5. In a bowl, whisk eggs and add salt. On a clean surface over medium heat, add eggs to griddle and scramble until cooked through.
6. Using a dash of flour, spread out pizza dough in a very thin rectangle (can make 2 out of one unit of dough).

Spread the scrambled eggs in an even layer over the crust and then add peppers, onions, and scrapple.

7. Finish with Cheddar Cheese and place on griddle over medium heat until crust is golden brown. To melt the cheese, place a basting dome or tin buffet pan over the pizza to steam. Top with scallions (optional).

Steakhouse Classic

Servings:2
Cooking Time:15 Min

Ingredients:
- 2 Ribeye or New York Strip Steaks
- 1 White or Yellow Onion
- 2 Garlic Cloves, minced
- Butter
- 2 Tablespoons of Balsamic Vinegar
- Chopped Parsley
- Kosher Salt
- Fresh Ground Black Pepper
- Canola Oil

Directions:
1. Set steaks out and let them get to room temperature.
2. Pat the steaks dry with a paper towel.
3. Season each side of the steaks generously with Kosher salt and pepper, then add a little canola oil to each side as well.
4. Preheat the griddle to medium-high heat.
5. Add some oil and a tablespoon of butter to the griddle.
6. Add the onion, garlic, and mushrooms to the griddle.
7. Cook until the onions and mushrooms start to soften, then add the balsamic vinegar. Turn the far right burner to low and move the onions and mushrooms over to the low heat.
8. Add your steaks to the griddle. Cook for a few minutes until you get a nice sear. Flip the steaks over and add a small pat of butter to the top of each steak.
9. Continue to cook until you reach the desired temperature.
10. Remove from heat and let the steaks rest for 5 minutes covered by tin foil (this step is very important).
11. Serve topped with the onions and mushrooms.

Salmon Tacos With Avocado & Corn Salsa

Servings:1
Cooking Time:10 Min

Ingredients:
- 3 Large Avocados, Peeled, Cored and Diced
- 1 Can Whole Kernel Corn (Drained)
- 1/3 Cup of Diced Red Onion
- 1 Bunch Cilantro, Chopped
- 1 Jalapeño (Diced)
- 2 Garlic Cloves, Minced
- 1 Lime, Juiced
- 2 Teaspoons of Olive Oil
- 2 Tablespoons of Apple Cider Vinegar
- 2 Lb. of Salmon, Skinned (Any Pin Bones Removed)
- 2 Tablespoons of Olive Oil
- 1 Lime
- 1 Teaspoon of Ground Cumin
- 1 Teaspoon of Chipotle Chili Powder
- 1 Teaspoon of Onion Powder
- 1 Teaspoon of Paprika
- 1 Teaspoon of Ground Coriander
- 1/2 Teaspoon of Salt
- 1/2 Teaspoon of Black Pepper
- 10 Corn Tortillas, Warmed
- 2 Cups of Red Cabbage, Thinly Sliced
- 1/2 Cup of Crumbled Cotija Cheese

Directions:
1. To assemble to Avocado and Corn Salsa, in a mixing bowl add ingredients from Avocado and Corn Salsa ingredient group. Season with salt and pepper to taste. Gently mix everything together, being careful to not mash avocado to much.
2. For the salmon, in a mixing bowl whisk together olive oil, juice from 1 lime, chipotle chili powder, cumin, onion powder, paprika, coriander, salt and freshly ground black pepper. Rub mixture over both sides of salmon.
3. Preheat the griddle to medium heat. Place salmon on griddle and cook about 3 minutes per side. Remove salmon from griddle and break into chunks.

4. Turn griddle to high heat. Put the corn tortillas on griddle to warm them up, about 30 second to 1 minute per side.

5. To assemble tacos, layer salmon in tortilla. Add sliced cabbage and avocado salsa. Top with cotija cheese and squeeze fresh lime juice over the top.

Maple Sausage Sweet Potato Hash

Servings:4
Cooking Time:20 Min

Ingredients:
- 1 Cup diced Sweet potatoes (peeled)
- 1 Cup diced Red potatoes
- 1/2 Cup yellow onion
- 1/2 Cup Celery
- 16 oz (1lb) Maple Sausage
- 1/3 cup of dried cranberries
- 1/2 Cup Chicken Broth or Stock
- Maple Syrup
- Salt
- Pepper
- Blackstone Chicken and Herb Seasoning
- 2 tbsp Unsalted Butter
- 1 tbsp olive oil

Directions:

1. Preheat your Blackstone griddle to med high. Place your Maple Sausage on griddle top, chop and cook. Be careful not burn. Also we're wanting to use the sausage fat after it's cooked to start cooking our other ingredients. So when your sausage is done slide it off to a cool zone of your griddle top.

2. Leaving your sausage on the griddle add your red potatoes, sweet potatoes, onions and celery. Depending on how much sausage fat you have remaining you'll also add 2 tbsp of unsalted butter, and roughly a tbs of olive oil. At this point we're going to also add a large pinch of kosher salt, pinch of coarse black pepper and your desired amount of your Blackstone chicken and herb seasoning. Toss to incorporate your butter, oil and seasonings. Once thoroughly incorporated you'll flatten out your ingredients to cover as much surface area so all ingredients are getting a chance to get a nice caramelization on the griddle top. This should take 3-4 minutes. Toss occasionally to get all sides caramelized.

3. Once you have a decent amount of color on your potatoes and you start to see your onions caramelizing we're going to cover the ingredients with a cooking dome or tin pan. Right before covering you'll add about a 1/3 of your Chicken stock to your ingredients and then cover. This will help steam the potatoes as well as adding a delicious flavor that your ingredients will soak up. Cover for 2-3 minutes. Occasionally toss the ingredients around and cover back up. You also might add a little stock as needed if you see that the potatoes are burning on the griddle top. This process should take about 8-10 minutes.

4. Once your potatoes are soft it's time to add our dried cranberries and a light drizzle of maple syrup. Be sure to not add too much syrup. You don't want your hash to be swimming in syrup. You just want a nice sheen. This will also start to reduce on the hot griddle top adding a glazed look and flavor.

5. Once you've incorporated the syrup and cranberries it's time to plate it up. Once plated I like to add a post dusting of the Blackstone Chicken and Herb Seasoning. Enjoy!

Steak, Arugula, Pear & Balsamic Flatbread

Servings:4
Cooking Time:10 Min

Ingredients:
- One 8-10 Oz. NY Strip Steak
- 2 Tablespoons of Blackstone Steakhouse Seasoning
- 1/3 Cup of Mayonnaise
- 2 Teaspoons of Fresh Rosemary, chopped
- 2 Teaspoons of Fresh Thyme, chopped
- 1 Lemon, juiced
- 1 Pear, sliced thin
- 2 Cups of Rocket Arugula
- 4 Pre-Made Flatbreads
- 1/2 Cup of Bleu Cheese Crumbles
- 1 Cup of Shredded Mozzarella Cheese
- 1/3 Cup of Balsamic Glaze

- Olive Oil

Directions:
1. Pre-heat your Blackstone Griddle to medium-high heat.
2. Add 1 tablespoon of olive oil over the steaks with 1 1/2 tablespoons of Blackstone Steakhouse Seasoning and rub to coat on all sides. Cook the steaks for 4 minutes per side or until cooked to desired doneness. Once they are finished, remove from the griddle and let rest.
3. In a small mixing bowl, add the mayonnaise, chopped herbs, lemon juice, and 1/2 tablespoon Blackstone Steakhouse Seasoning. Mix to evenly combine.
4. Set your griddle to medium-low heat and toast the flatbread on both sides for a couple of minutes.
5. Slice the steak into bite-sized pieces.
6. Remove the flatbread from the griddle and add some of the sauce to the tops of each. Add some of the steak and then a small handful of arugula. Add some bleu cheese crumbles and few slices of pear. Top the flatbread with some shredded mozzarella cheese and then place the flat bread back on the low heat side of your griddle. Cover with a basting dome to melt the cheese.
7. To plate, slice each flatbread into 4 pieces and drizzle the balsamic glaze over the top.

Pomegranate Soy Glazed Lamb Chops

Servings:6
Cooking Time:20 Min

Ingredients:
- 12 Lamb Chops
- 3 cups Pomegranate Juice
- 1 cup Soy Sauce
- 2 bunches of Green Onion, cleaned and trimmed
- ½ large Red Onion, thinly sliced
- 2 cups Arugula
- 2 cups Spring Mix Lettuce
- ¼ cup Pomegranate Arils
- 2 Oranges
- Salt & Pepper
- Olive Oil

Directions:
1. Preheat your griddle to medium-high heat.
2. Using a large sauté pan over an open burner, add the pomegranate juice, and soy. Turn to high heat and bring to a boil for 8-10 minutes. Reduce by 75% or until the consistency is close to maple syrup. Turn the heat off and let cool slightly. (it will thicken up a bit more as it cools)
3. Season the lamb chops with olive oil and salt & pepper on all sides.
4. Add a bit of olive oil to the griddle and cook the lamb chops for 2-3 minutes per side and finish fat side down for an additional 2 minutes.
5. For the last 4-5 minutes of cooking, add the green onions and lightly caramelize.
6. To a large mixing bowl, add the arugula, spring mix, red onion, pomegranate arils with a pinch of salt and pepper. Cut the peel and pith away from the oranges and cut into supremes and add to the bowl. Squeeze the remaining orange juice over the greens and discard the orange. Add a drizzle of olive oil and toss the salad to evenly coat.
7. To plate, Add some of the salad to you plate and then a few of the green onions. Add 3 lamb chops and drizzle with the pomegranate soy reduction sauce.
8. Enjoy!

Griddle Girl Air Fryer Cinnamon Apple Pie Cups

Servings:x
Cooking Time:x

Ingredients:
- 2 large green apples
- ¼ cup brown sugar
- 1 tbsp apple pie spice
- 2 tbsp melted butter
- 1/4 cup flour
- cooking spray
- vanilla ice cream
- caramel sauce

Directions:
1. Peel apples and chop into fine pieces.
2. In a bowl, mix apples, brown sugar, apple pie spice, and 1 tbsp butter. Set aside.
3. Flatten cinnamon rolls with a rolling pin. Spray silicone muffin cups with cooking spray. Fill each cup with 1 roll.
4. Set air fryer to medium and cook cinnamon rolls for 5 mins.
5. While the cinnamon rolls are cooking, melt 1 tbsp of butter on the griddle top, and cook apples on medium until softened.
6. Remove cinnamon rolls from air fryer and fill each cup with the apples. Cook for 3 more mins in the air fryer.
7. Remove apple pie cups from the silicone wrappers, top with ice-cream, and caramel drizzle.
8. Enjoy!

Pesto-ranch Chicken Artichoke Flatbread

Servings:4
Cooking Time:15 Min

Ingredients:
- 4 Boneless & Skinless Chicken Cutlets
- 2-3 Tablespoons of Blackstone Chicken & Herb Seasoning
- 1/4 Cup of Ranch Dressing
- 3 Tablespoons of Mayonnaise
- 3 Tablespoons of Pesto
- 1 1/2 Cups of Artichoke Hearts
- 1/2 Cup of Sliced Black Olives
- 1/3 Cup of Capers
- 3 Cups of Mozzarella Cheese
- 4 Flat-Bread Rounds

Directions:
1. Season your chicken breasts with a bit of olive oil and some of the Blackstone Chicken & Herb Seasoning on all sides, then cook on the griddle for 2-3 minutes per side or until the chicken is fully cooked.
2. Once the chicken is fully cooked, remove it from the griddle, dice, and place into a large mixing bowl.
3. Add the ranch, mayo, and pesto and stir to mix evenly.
4. Add the ¼ of the chicken to each of the flatbreads evenly over the surface. Add some of the artichoke hearts, olives, and capers evenly over each flatbread and then top with mozzarella cheese.
5. Turn your griddle down to medium-low heat and place each flatbread onto the griddle and cover with a basting dome to melt the cheese and toast the bottom. 4-5 minutes for a lightly toasted crust and a bit longer for a crispier texture.
6. Slice and serve hot.

Jambalaya

Servings:6-8
Cooking Time:35 Min

Ingredients:
- 4 8.8 oz packages Ready Rice
- 13-16 oz andouille sausage, diced
- 1-1.5 lb boneless chicken thighs, diced
- 1 lb shrimp, optional
- 1 large yellow onion, diced
- 1 c each red, green, yellow, poblano peppers, diced
- 2-3 celery stalks, diced
- 3 garlic cloves, chopped
- 1-2 tbsp creole seasoning or Blackstone cajun seasoning
- 1 bunch green onions, chopped divided in half
- 24 oz tomato sauce
- Olive oil
- Sour cream, optional

Directions:
1. Leftover cold white rice can be used, or if using ready rice packages, massage packages to loosen rice and place in a bowl. Set aside.
2. Preheat one side of the Blackstone to medium heat. Drizzle olive oil, about 1-2 tbsp, add celery and yellow onions to cook 3-4 minutes then add in the peppers to cook 2-3 minutes. On the other side preheat the Blackstone to medium high and drizzle with 1 tbsp olive oil and add chicken to cook 4 minutes. Add sausage and shrimp cook 3 minutes. Seasoning everything lightly with creole or cajun seasoning.

3. Turn all burners to medium or medium low and mix vegetables and meat together. Add rice and toss to incorporate.
4. Add tomato sauce and toss.
5. Add garlic and half of the green onions toss. Season with the rest of your seasoning. Salt and pepper if desired.
6. Plate and serve! Leftovers are even more delicious!

Zucchini Fritters

Servings:1
Cooking Time:10 Min

Ingredients:
- 4 Cups of Shredded Zucchini
- 2/3 Cup of All-Purpose Flour
- 2 Eggs, lightly beaten
- 1/3 Cup of Green Onion, sliced
- 1/2 Cup of Parmesan cheese, shredded
- Kosher salt
- Fresh Ground Black Pepper
- Sour Cream

Directions:
1. Grate the zucchini until you have 4 cups. Put it in a large bowl (or colander) and add 2 tsp of kosher salt and let it sit for a few minutes. The salt will draw the water out of the zucchini. Put all the shredded zucchini in a tea towel (or colander) and squeeze most of the liquid out.
2. In a large bowl, combine the shredded zucchini, eggs, flour, green onions, parmesan, a dash of salt and pepper.
3. Turn the griddle on to medium high heat.**
4. Add oil to the griddle, spread it around, and let it heat up.
5. Scoop 1/4 Cup of the Zucchini mixture onto the Griddle and flatten out to about 1/4" thick.
6. Cook on both sides until golden brown.
7. Serve topped with sour cream, green onions, and more parmesan cheese.

Pineapple And Pork French Toast

Servings:2
Cooking Time:32 Min

Ingredients:
- 4 Brioche Bread Slices (Thickly Cut)
- 4 Pork Slices
- 8 Oz. of Cream Cheese (Softened)
- 2 Cups of Crushed Pineapples (Drained)
- 1 Cup of Whole Milk
- 3 Eggs
- 2 Teaspoons of Vanilla
- 2 Tablespoons of Brown Sugar
- 5 Tablespoons of Butter
- 2 Tablespoons of Powdered Sugar
- 3 Cups of Pineapple Chunks
- 1 Cup of Sugar
- 3/4 Cup of Pineapple Juice
- 1 Tablespoon of Cornstarch
- 1/4 Cup of Water

Directions:
1. Starting with the compote, preheat griddle to medium/ high heat.
2. In a saucepan combine pineapple chunks with sugar and juice. Stir to dissolve.
3. Whisk together cornstarch and water.
4. Cook Pineapples for 5-10 minutes or until pineapples soften.
5. Stir in cornstarch mixture and simmer 5-10 minutes until thickened.
6. For the french toast, in a bowl, combine cream cheese and crushed pineapple.
7. Heat griddle to Medium/Low Heat.
8. Cook 4 slices of Pork Roll about 2 minutes each side.
9. In a shallow dish whisk together milk, eggs, vanilla, and brown sugar.
10. Lay out 4 slices of Brioche Bread and Spoon Cream Cheese Mixture and slice of Pork Roll on each.
11. Fold together the pieces as a sandwich.
12. Soak both sides of each sandwich in the egg mixture and set aside.

13. Melt butter on the griddle and place each stuffed French Toast on griddle and cook until each side is golden brown and cooked through.
14. Remove from heat and top with Pineapple Compote (powdered sugar optional).

Onion Mushroom Bbq Swiss Burger

Servings: 4
Cooking Time: 15 Min

Ingredients:
- 2 cups julienned yellow onion
- 2 cups sliced mushrooms
- 1-2 pounds 80/20 ground beef (more or less depending on how big you like your burgers)
- Blackstone Whiskey Burger Seasoning
- BBQ Sauce
- 8 slices swiss cheese
- 4 jumbo hamburger buns
- Salt and pepper
- Olive oil

Directions:
1. Heat your griddle to medium heat. Add a bit of olive and then the onions and mushrooms. Season with a pinch of salt and pepper and cook for 10 minutes, tossing often. Once the onions and mushrooms have caramelized slightly, move them over to the cooler side of the griddle.
2. Form the ground beef into 4 equal hamburger patties. Season evenly with Blackstone Whiskey Burger Seasoning on both sides. Cook for 3 minutes per side. Once cooked the way you like, add some of the onions and mushrooms over the tops of each burger.
3. Add some BBQ sauce over the veggies and then 2 slices of swiss. Cover to melt.
4. Lightly toast the buns on both sides and then add some BBQ Sauce to the bottom buns. Add the burger over the top and serve hot.

Air Fried Beef Tacos

Servings: 4
Cooking Time: x

Ingredients:
- 1 pound ground beef
- 12 corn hard taco shells
- 1 taco-seasoning packet or 2TBSP of Blackstone Taco and Fajita seasoning
- 1 cup water
- 2 cups shredded taco cheese blend (Monterey jack and cheddar)
- Diced tomato
- Shredded Lettuce
- Sliced olives
- Sour Cream
- Guacamole

Directions:
1. Pre-heat the griddle to medium.
2. Using a spatula, chop ground beef on the griddle top while cooking, breaking meat up into very small granular pieces.
3. While the meat is cooking, fats will render and oil is often released from the beef. These oils add little or no benefit to the tacos and can be scraped into the grease catch and eventually discarded.
4. Sprinkle taco seasoning as evenly as possible over cooked ground beef. Combine seasoning and beef with a spatula to incorporate. Add water to the seasoned beef. Using a squirt bottle with water makes directing the water to the meat much simpler.
5. Stir the beef and spices with the water and allow it to reduce until the water has been evaporated and the meat is well coated. Remove from griddle and set aside.
6. Preheat the AirFryer to the lowest setting.
7. If you have a metal taco holder place the taco shells in the holder.
8. Partially cook the hard corn taco shells inside the air fryer for two minutes and remove.
9. Stuff each taco shell with about two tablespoons of the seasoned taco meat and top with an additional two tablespoons of shredded cheese.
10. Return the stuffed taco shells in the optional holder to the air fryer to melt for 3-4 minutes. Top with your preferred additional toppings and serve immediately.

Thai Chicken Quesadillas

Servings: 1
Cooking Time: 10 Min

Ingredients:
- 1 Lb. of Boneless Skinless Chicken Breast
- 4 Cups of Shredded Monterrey Jack Cheese
- 2 Cups of Sweet Chili Sauce
- 1/2 Cup of Green Onions, Sliced
- 1/4 Cup of Cilantro, Chopped
- Granulated Garlic to Taste
- Sea Salt to Taste
- 4 Large 10-12" Flour Tortillas

Directions:
1. Preheat the Blackstone griddle to high heat and coat the griddle top with oil.
2. Dice chicken breast into very small cubes. Cook chicken on griddle, seasoning to taste with granulated garlic and sea salt.
3. Turn burners down half way to the medium-low heat.
4. Make sure griddle top is well oiled. Lay two tortillas on griddle top. Cover one tortilla with 1 cup of shredded Monterrey Jack, making sure cheese is evenly distributed and tortilla is covered. Spread desired amount of chicken evenly over cheese.
5. Spoon or pour 1/4 cup of Sweet Chili Sauce over cheese. Immediately cover with 1/4 cup sliced green onions and 2 TBSP of cilantro. Then cover all ingredients with a another cup of cheese. Place another tortilla on top. Repeat process on second tortilla.
6. If necessary, use the Blackstone Bacon Press (available in the Blackstone Breakfast Kit) or a spatula to flatten quesadilla as the cheese melts and ingredients combine within tortillas.
7. Frequently use spatula to check underneath tortilla ensuring it turns golden brown. Carefully turn each quesadilla and repeat cooking process on other side. Quesadillas are ready when both sides are golden brown and cheese is completely melted within tortillas.
8. Slice quesadillas in the same manner as a pizza using a chef's knife. Each quesadilla makes 4 or 8 individual pieces, depending on the desired size of servings.

Shiitake And Asparagus Risotto With Seared Salmon

Servings: 2
Cooking Time: 45 Min

Ingredients:
- 4 6-8 oz. salmon fillets
- 1 cup Arborio rice
- 3 cups chicken stock
- 2 cups sliced shiitake mushrooms
- 1 cup chopped asparagus
- 2 tablespoons unsalted butter
- 2 teaspoons garlic powder
- 1 cup shredded parmesan cheese
- The juice of 1 lemon
- ½ cup white wine (I like Pinot Grigio)
- Salt and pepper
- Olive oil

Directions:
1. In a large sauté pan, add a few tablespoons of olive oil and the Arborio rice. Stir to coat the rice in the oil. Cook over medium-high heat for 5-7 minutes stirring often. Add ½ cup of the chicken stock stirring constantly. Once the liquid has absorbed, add another half cup. Repeat the process for the remaining chicken stock. (Keep stirring so that the Arborio doesn't stick and burn on the bottom of the pan.)
2. Heat your griddle to medium-high heat and add a drizzle of olive oil and the mushrooms. Add the butter with a pinch of salt & pepper and toss to incorporate. Cook for 4-5 minutes then add the asparagus and garlic powder. Toss to incorporate and cook another 3-4 minutes.
3. Add the mushrooms and asparagus to the risotto pan with the shredded parmesan, lemon juice and white wine. Stir to incorporate evenly and reduce the heat to low. Cover with a lid and cook for an additional 5-7 minutes.
4. While the risotto finishes cooking, season the salmon fillets with salt & pepper and a bit garlic powder. Add a drizzle of olive oil to the griddle over high heat. Cook the salmon presentation side down first for 2-3 minutes per side.

5. For the garnish, make to 1 tablespoon piles of shredded parmesan cheese on the griddle top. Cook for 30-45 seconds or until golden brown and then flip and cook another 30-45 seconds. This little cheese chip is delicious and gives texture to the finished dish.

6. To plate, add some of the risotto to the center of the plate and then the seared salmon fillet draped over the top. Add the cheese chips to the risotto, add a pinch of chopped parsley, a lemon wedge and a few shaves of parmesan.

Sweetbabytots

Servings:8-10
Cooking Time:20 Min

Ingredients:
- 20 Frozen Tator-Tots
- 10 slices bacon, thin cut
- 20 slices pickled jalapeno
- 1/4 c Sweet Baby Rays BBQ Sauce
- 20 toothpick

Directions:
1. Preheat Blackstone Airfryers to high heat or 425 degrees.
2. Place frozen tator-tots on a dish on the counter to slightly thaw for 5 minutes, just enough to help toothpick slide throw them.
3. Slice bacon strips in half.
4. Lay bacon flat, top with a jalapeno slice, then a tator top, and wrap with bacon. Securing bacon with a toothpick.
5. Brush bacon with your favorite Sweet Baby Rays BBQ sauce.
6. Place tator-tots in preheated Blackstone Airfryer drawer evenly spaced out. Cook 8-10 minutes. Checking tots halfway, gently shaking, or flipping tots for even cooking.
7. Serve with extra bbq sauce for dipping.
8. Enjoy!

Airfryer Blackberry Scones

Servings:6
Cooking Time:30 Min

Ingredients:
- 2 cups all-purpose flour
- 1/3 cup sugar
- 1 tsp baking powder
- 1/4 tsp baking soda
- 1/2 tsp salt
- 1/2 cup butter frozen
- 1/2 cup plain Greek yogurt
- 1 egg large
- 1 Tbs vanilla extract
- 1 cup blackberries washed and patted dry
- 1 1/4 cup powdered sugar
- 2 Tbs melted butter
- 1/2 tsp vanilla
- 1 tbs milk
- 1 tbs fresh lemon juice

Directions:
1. Shred the frozen butter using a cheese grater into a bowl. Add the flour, sugar, baking soda, baking powder, salt, and mix with hands attempting to keep the butter cold.
2. Add yogurt, egg, and vanilla to the mixture; mix together with hands. Add Blackberries, and gently mix together until berries are coated.
3. Place a piece of parchment paper on the counter. Pour dough onto parchment and form into a circle pressing until 1" high then cut into 8 triangles.
4. Preheat Air Fryer to medium; spray cooking spray on the tray. Place scones in each air fryer tray.
5. Cook 7-8 minutes, or until a nice golden brown. Remove and let cool while making the glaze.
6. In a bowl, mix powdered sugar, vanilla, lemon juice, and milk. drizzle over scones, and enjoy!

Enchiladas

Servings:4-6
Cooking Time:20 Min

Ingredients:
- Flour or Corn tortillas (full size)
- 1 LB. Ground beef (80/20)
- Red sauce (Old El Paso)
- Cheese (block of sharp cheddar)
- Half Yellow onion

- Romaine lettuce
- Tomato (on the vine)
- Tortilla Chips (garnish)
- Blackstone taco seasoning
- Red Chile Sauce
- Green Chile Sauce
- Salsa

Directions:
1. Preheat Griddle to Medium-High.
2. Take the beef and place it on the griddle and season with salt and pepper.
3. When the beef is halfway cooked, add about diced yellow onion and continue to cook beef until onions are caramelized and beef is browned.
4. Lightly season with Blackstone Taco Seasoning. And slide off to indirect heat.
5. Turn your heat to low or off altogether. Add a light amount of olive oil to the griddle, place your tortillas on the griddle to warm up.
6. On your warmed-up tortilla, add a light amount of shredded cheddar cheese, beef and onions, and 2-3 tablespoons or red chile sauce. Fold both ends of the tortilla with a spatula and tongs overlapping to roll to create the enchilada. The cheese inside should act as a glue to help keep the tortilla rolled. Place aside.
7. Now on to our cheese enchiladas. Follow the same steps as the beef, but only use shredded cheddar cheese and green chiles inside. Roll as many as you would like and set aside.
8. Turn one burner on your griddle to high heat. Using your Blackstone cast iron serving platter, place one cheese and one beef enchilada in the serving tray. Cover both with shredded cheddar and pre-shredded Mexican blend cheese. Cover the beef enchilada with more red chile sauce and your cheese enchilada with more green chiles.
9. Place the cast iron serving tray on the hot side of the griddle, spray water around the tray and cover with your basting dome. Allow 2-3 minutes to heat the enchiladas up and melt all your cheese. Remove the basting dome, pull serving platter of the griddle, add shredded lettuce, tomato, and onions for garnish and enjoy!

Buffalo-sriracha Ranch Chicken Sandwich

Servings:4
Cooking Time:10 Min

Ingredients:
- 4-6 Thick Cut Bacon Slices
- 4 Chicken Cutlets
- 1 Tablespoon of Unsalted Butter
- 1 Tablespoon of Hot Sauce
- 1 Tablespoon of Sriracha
- 1/3 Cup of Ranch Dressing
- 1 Cup of Shredded Lettuce
- 4 Tomato Slices
- 4 Potato Buns
- Salt & Pepper

Directions:
1. Heat your Blackstone to medium and cook the bacon. Once cooked, drain on paper towel.
2. Season the chicken cutlets with salt and pepper and cook in the bacon fat over medium heat. Cook for 2-3 minutes and then flip. Cook another 2-3 minutes or until fully cooked.
3. Place a small sauce pot on the griddle and add the butter, hot sauce and sriracha. Stir until the butter is melted and the ingredients are evenly combined.
4. To a small mixing bowl, add the ranch dressing and the buffalo-sriracha sauce. Stir to evenly combine.
5. Toast the buns on the griddle top until golden.
6. To build, add some shredded lettuce to the bottom bun, then add some sauce. Add bacon, tomato and then the chicken cutlet. Add more sauce over the top and then the top bun. Serve hot.

Margherita Grilled Cheese

Servings:1
Cooking Time:10 Min

Ingredients:
- 8 Slices of Sourdough Bread
- Mozzarella Cheese
- 8-12 Tomato Slices
- Fresh Basil Leaves
- Garlic Pepper Seasoning

- Olive Oil

Directions:
1. Put two pieces of bread on your work surface.
2. On one piece of bread layer cheese, tomato slices, basil, then cheese again.
3. Sprinkle with garlic pepper and top with other piece of bread.
4. Brush the outside of bread with olive oil (could also use butter). Put a little olive oil on the griddle as well. The Olive oil will give you an even crispier crust on the outside of the bread.
5. Turn your griddle on medium low heat and toast each side of your sandwich until golden brown.

Betty's Upside Down Pizza

Servings: 3-6
Cooking Time: 30 Min

Ingredients:
- Stonefire thin artisan pizza crust, 2 pack
- ½ lb provolone, Boar's head
- Fresh mozzarella, ball, log or pearls
- Fresh Basil
- Boars Head sopressata, pepperoni cups, salami, Italian sausage
- 1 can San Marzano tomatoes (San Marzano tomato of Agro Sarnese-Nocerino D.O.P. Preferred) or substitute good quality crushed tomatoes
- 2 tbsp Extra Virgin olive oil
- 3 garlic cloves, smashed & chopped
- 1 tsp oregano
- 4 basil leaves, torn
- Salt
- 4 tbsp extra virgin olive oil
- 2-3 large cloves fresh garlic, minced
- ½ tsp dried basil
- ½ tsp dried oregano
- ½ tsp dried parsley
- 1 tsp crushed red pepper (optional)

Directions:
1. In a mixing bowl add tomatoes and spoon off a few spoonfuls of extra liquid. Using your hands, crush tomatoes slightly. Mix in oil, torn basil, oregano, garlic and salt to taste. Sauce is ready for use. Since pizza is being griddled sauce can be heated in a small pot directly on the Blackstone griddle for even cooking a few minutes before starting pizza. Heating the sauce will also help cheeses to melt since this is a griddle top pizza and not a pizza oven cooked pizza.
2. On medium low heat add pizza crust upside down to heat and slightly crisp top of pizza crust. Depending on how well done or soft you like your crust. Flip and turn heat to low to begin to cook and crisp up the bottom giving you time to add ingredients.
3. Drizzle 1 tbsp garlic oil and spread around pizza. Add provolone cheese evenly around pizza.
4. Add pizza sauce, using a spoon to spread out sauce.
5. Add fresh mozzarella spread out around pizza. Raise the griddle heat to medium and cook until desired crispness checking the bottom occasionally. Mozzarella should melt quickly once placed on top of the heated pizza sauce however a dome may be used if needed.
6. Remove pizza and garnish with fresh basil. Drizzle with garlic oil, optional.

Bruschetta Crostini

Servings: 6
Cooking Time: 75 Min

Ingredients:
- 4 tomatoes on the vine
- 3 garlic cloves smashed and chopped
- ½ red onion diced small
- 10-12 large basil leaves
- ¼ - ½ cup pecorino romano cheese
- ½ cup extra virgin olive oil
- salt to taste
- balsamic glaze
- 1 loaf bread, french baguette
- 1 log sliced mozzarella
- 1 large garlic clove
- ¼ c extra virgin olive oil

Directions:
1. Dice tomatoes and place in a bowl. Season with salt. Add chopped garlic and diced onions.
2. Chiffonade the basil by stacking the leaves, rolling the stack of leaves lengthwise and slicing to create strips or ribbons of basil. Add them to the tomatoes.

3. Drizzle tomatoes with extra virgin olive oil and gently mix ingredients to combine. Add desired amount of grated cheese.
4. Cover mixture with plastic wrap and place bowl on top of a larger container filled with ice and let sit out on the counter 30-60 minutes before preparing crostini.
5. Turn Blackstone to medium heat.
6. Slice the baguette into 1 inch pieces.
7. Slice garlic clove in half and rub the curbside of the garlic clove on the bread.
8. Brush olive oil onto one side of the sliced bread and place oiled side down onto the Blackstone. Remove after 2-3 minutes or until toasted
9. Place one piece of fresh mozzarella on toasted slices of bread. Spoon over the Bruschetta and drizzle with Balsamic glaze.

Pineapple Chicken And Adobo Crunchwraps

Servings:4
Cooking Time:20 Min

Ingredients:
- 4-6 boneless, skinless Chicken Thighs
- 3 slices of Pineapple
- 2 thick slices of Red Onion
- 2 Jalapeno Peppers, sliced in half lengthwise
- 2 Limes
- ½ cup Sour Cream
- 1 tablespoon Adobo
- 2 tablespoons Beer
- ½ bunch of Fresh Cilantro
- 4 extra-large Flour Tortillas
- 2 cups shredded Cheese
- 4 street taco size Corn Tortillas
- Blackstone Tequila Lime Seasoning
- Olive Oil
- Salt and Pepper

Directions:
1. Heat your griddle to medium-high heat, add a bit of olive oil and the chicken. Season generously with the Blackstone Tequila Lime Seasoning. Toss to evenly coat and cook for 4-5 minutes.
2. To the other side of your griddle, preheated to medium-high heat, add a drizzle of olive oil, the pineapple, red onion, jalapeno and lime (cut side down). Cook for 3-4 minutes or until the vegetables are caramelized. Flip and cook another 2 minutes.
3. Add a squeeze of lime over the chicken and toss to evenly coat. Once the chicken is fully cooked, remove from the griddle and chop small.
4. Remove the vegetables and pineapple from the griddle and chop everything together with a squeeze of lime juice.
5. In a small mixing bowl, add the sour cream, adobo, beer and a bit of the Tequila Lime Seasoning and mix evenly.
6. Clean the griddle where the veggies were cooked and add a bit of oil and the corn tortilla. Cook for 2-3 minutes per side or until the corn tortilla is crisp.
7. To assemble, spread some of the cheese into the center of the flour tortilla. Add some of the chicken, pineapple salsa, fresh cilantro, about a tablespoon of the sauce, a bit more cheese and then the crisp corn tortilla over the top. Add a bit more cheese on top of the corn tortilla and then wrap the flour tortilla up and over the corn tortilla.
8. Place the wrap folded side down onto the griddle and cook for 3-4 minutes or until golden and toasted, flip and repeat.
9. Slice and serve hot.
10. Enjoy!

Peach Bourbon Cocktail

Servings:4
Cooking Time:15 Min

Ingredients:
- 2 Peaches, Sliced
- 8 Oz. of Thyme Simple Syrup
- 8 Oz. of Bourbon
- Ginger Ale

Directions:
1. In a plastic container, add equal parts water and sugar, as well as a sprig of fresh thyme. Seal the container and shake well until sugar is dissolved.

2. Set griddle to high heat. Slice two peaches into wedges and dry off with a paper towel, then place on the griddle. Cook for about 90 seconds, or until they are caramelized and golden.

3. In a cocktail shaker, add two peach wedges. Using a muddle, push and turn 5-6 times to break up the peach. Add ice, 2 ounces of thyme simple syrup, and 2 ounces of bourbon and shake well.

4. In a high ball glass, add some ice and strain the cocktail. Top it off with some ginger ale and garnish with a fresh peach wedge and fresh thyme.

Crispy Sweet Potato Cubes With Cinnamon

Servings:4
Cooking Time:x

Ingredients:

- 2 medium sweet potatoes
- 3 tablespoons vegetable oil
- 1 tablespoon cinnamon
- 1 teaspoon garlic salt
- ½ teaspoon pepper

Directions:

1. Preheat Air Fryer to medium high heat for 10 minutes.
2. Peel the sweet potatoes and cube into ¾ inch square pieces. Add remaining ingredients to a large mixing bowl and stir to combine.
3. Add the sweet potato cubes to the oil and seasoning mixture. Fold the mixture until the oil and spices completely coat the sweet potato cubes.
4. Pour into the air fryer basket and cook for 6 minutes.
5. Shake and stir the sweet potato cubes and return to the air fryer. Cook for an additional 6 minutes or until the outside is golden brown and the inside is well cooked, with an almost creamy consistency.
6. Serve immediately.

Chili-mojo Steak Kebabs

Servings:4
Cooking Time:10 Min

Ingredients:

- 2 Lb. of New York Strip Steak, cut into 2" cubes
- 2 Tablespoons of Blackstone All-Purpose Seasoning
- 1 Cup of Orange Juice
- 1/4 Cup of Tequila
- 2 Tablespoons of Garlic Powder
- 2 Teaspoons of Chili Powder
- 1/4 Cup of Lime Juice
- Wooden Skewers
- 1/4 Cup of Orange Juice
- 3 Tablespoons of Lime Juice
- 1/4 Cup of Olive Oil
- 2 Tablespoons of Garlic Powder
- 2 Tablespoons of Fresh Oregano Leaves
- 2 Teaspoons of Chili Flakes
- Salt & Pepper

Directions:

1. In a large bowl, add the steak, Blackstone All Purpose Seasoning, orange juice, lime juice, a bit of olive oil, garlic powder and chili powder. Mix evenly and refrigerate for 30-45 minutes.
2. Using the wooden skewers, skewer the steak with as many cubes as you like.
3. In a small mixing bowl, add all the Mojo Ingredients and mix to evenly combine.
4. Get your coals on the Blackstone Griddle Charcoal Grill Combo as hot as you can. Cook the skewers for 2 minutes, drizzle a bit of Mojo over the top and turn. Repeat until the steak is cooked to your desired temp.
5. To plate, add all the skewers to a large platter and drizzle some of the Mojo over the top.

Griddle Girl Breakfast Pancake Tacos

Servings:x
Cooking Time:x

Ingredients:

- 1 cup pancake mix
- 2/3 cup water
- ½ cup strawberries
- ½ cup blackberries
- ½ cup blueberries

- A few sprigs fresh mint
- 8 oz softened cream cheese
- 2 tbsp heavy whipping cream
- ½ cup powdered sugar
- 1 tbsp butter
- maple syrup

Directions:
1. In a bowl, pour pancake mix and water, stir to combine, and set aside.
2. Cut berries into bite size pieces, and roughly chop mint.
3. Mash cream cheese, add heavy cream, and powdered sugar. Stir to combine and set aside.
4. Heat griddle top to medium. Melt 1 tbsp butter and cook pancakes.
5. Remove the pancakes, and put them in a taco tray.
6. Fill each pancake taco with 1-2 tbsp of cream cheese, top with berries, and drizzle with syrup.
7. Enjoy!

Sesame Seared Ahi Tuna

Servings:6
Cooking Time:1 Hour Min

Ingredients:
- Sushi grade Ahi Tuna
- Sesame Seeds
- Sesame Oil
- ¼ cup Soy Sauce
- 2 tbs Rice Vinegar
- 1 tbsp minced Garlic
- 1 tsp Sesame Oil
- 1 tbsp Brown Sugar
- 1 tsp Ground Ginger
- 2 tbsp Green Onion
- Juice from 1 Lime
- 1 tbsp Brown Sugar
- 1 tbsp minced Garlic
- 1 tbsp Soy Sauce
- 1 tbsp Rice Vinegar
- 1 tsp Sesame Oil
- 1 tbsp Green Onions
- Spiralize 2 Carrots and 1 Cucumber
- 1 tbsp Hoisin Sauce
- ¼ cup Orange Juice
- 1 tbsp Soy Sauce
- 1 tsp Sesame Oil
- 1 tsp Ground Ginger
- 1 tsp Sesame Seeds

Directions:
1. Mix all the ingredients together for the marinade. Place tuna steaks into the marinade, cover, and put in the refrigerator for 1 hour.
2. Spiralize cucumbers and carrots and pour dressing over it. Put into the refrigerator for an hour.
3. Mix all the dipping sauce ingredients together and set aside.
4. Heat griddle to high heat. Let get very hot and drizzle some sesame oil.
5. Pour ½ cup sesame seeds onto a plate. Dip ahi tuna onto the seeds coating it evenly.
6. Place on a scalding hot griddle and cook each side for 4 minutes.
7. Remove from the griddle and slice thinly.
8. Put slaw onto a serving plate, top with seared tuna, and add dipping sauce to the side.

Mini Ham And Cheddar Quiche Cups

Servings:4
Cooking Time:x

Ingredients:
- 6 eggs
- 4 tablespoons cream cheese, softened
- 2 tablespoons half and half or milk
- ½ cup shredded cheddar cheese
- 1 tablespoon butter
- 3/4 cup diced ham

Directions:
1. Melt butter on the griddle preheated to medium. Sauté ham for five minutes or until begins to slightly brown. Set aside.
2. Whisk eggs with cream cheese and half and half until very smooth. Add a pinch of salt and pepper if desired.
3. Pre-heat AirFryer to 375°F for 10 minutes.

4. Stir ham and cheddar into the egg mixture.
5. Using a non-stick food spray or butter, grease four medium sized ramekins. Ladle the egg mixture equally into the four ramekins and cook in the AirFryer for 15-20 minutes or until the egg mixture has set and completely cooked.

Elotte

Servings:x
Cooking Time:x

Ingredients:
- 2 Tablespoon of Butter
- 3 Cups of Corn (4 ears)
- 1/2 Jalapeno, No Seeds
- 3 Tablespoons of Mayo
- 1 Clove Garlic
- 2 Green Onions
- 1/2 Bunch of Cilantro
- 1 Lime
- 1/4 Cup of Cotija or Feta Cheese
- Tajin Seasoning (optional)

Directions:
1. Remove corn from the cob if using fresh corn.
2. Heat Blackstone griddle to a medium heat. Melt the butter and add the corn. Toss until cooked and well charred. This takes about 5-10 minutes.
3. Seed jalapeno and mince. Chop cilantro.
4. Mix mayo, jalapeno, garlic, green onions, cilantro, lime and cheese together in a bowl. Add the charred corn and toss together until well mixed. Top with Tajin seasoning for extra flavor if desired.
5. Serve warm or at room temp with whole grain tortilla chips.

Cheese Steak Egg Rolls

Servings:1
Cooking Time:10 Min

Ingredients:
- 1 Lb. of Chopped Steak (Thin Sliced Sirloin or Ribeye or Ground Beef)
- 4-5 Slices White American Cheese
- 1/4 Cup of Green Pepper, Diced Small
- 1/4 Cup of White Onion, Diced Small
- 1 Tablespoon of Worcestershire Sauce
- 8 Wonton Wrappers
- Garlic Powder
- Salt and Pepper
- Vegetable Oil
- Sriracha Ketchup

Directions:
1. Turn Blackstone griddle on medium heat and drizzle lightly with vegetable oil. Cook the onions and peppers, season with salt and pepper, for about 3 minutes. Set aside and turn griddle to high heat. Add chopped steak or ground beef.
2. Use your Blackstone spatula and scraper, chop your meat up into small pieces. Turn heat to medium-low, add the worcestershire, season to taste with salt, pepper, garlic powder and mix in the peppers and onions.
3. Lay the cheese on top of the meat and cover with a dome to steam melt the cheese. Take meat off the griddle and place in a large bowl and mix the cheese to coat evenly. Cover and let meat mixture cool slightly so you can handle it when preparing your eggrolls.
4. Follow the instructions on the back of the wonton wrapper, placing wrappers in a diamond shape spoon on a oval shaped layer of meat in the center. Fold the bottom up and around the mixture, fold the sides in and then roll upwards. Seal by rubbing warm water along seams. Place on parchment paper until ready to fry.
5. Turn Blackstone griddle back on to high heat and add a generous amount of vegetable oil towards the opposite side of your griddle as your grease spout. It helps to slightly angle griddle so that oil runs to where you want by placing a ¼ inch wedge under both the wheels so that the oil does not run right to the wrong side and off the griddle since you need a good amount of oil to fry the eggrolls in. Place eggrolls in the hot oil, turning to cook all sides of the wonton wrappers until golden brown.
6. Serve with Sriracha Ketchup.

Pineapple Chicken Quesadillas

Servings: 4
Cooking Time: 30 Min

Ingredients:
- 1 lb chicken tenders
- 2 tbsp mayonnaise, Dukes preferred
- 1 tbsp Blackstone All Purpose Seasoning
- 2 cups BBQ sauce
- 20 oz can crushed pineapple, drained
- 1 red onion, sliced thin
- 1 bunch cilantro, chopped
- 8 10 inch flour tortillas
- 1 16 oz block of cheddar cheese, shredded
- 1 cup sour cream
- 1 lime
- 1 tbsp cumin
- zest of lime

Directions:
1. Dice tenders into bite sized pieces. Place in a storage bag with mayonnaise and All Purpose seasoning (or your favorite dry bbq seasoning) massage bag to coat chicken evenly and refrigerate 20 minutes to overnight.
2. Mix Sour cream, zest of one lime and juice of one lime along with 1 tbsp of cumin. Refrigerate until ready to use.
3. Preheat Blackstone to medium heat, add chicken to cook. 4-6 minutes total. Set chicken aside.
4. Turn Blackstone to low heat, remove anything left behind from cooking the chicken and add a light spray or drizzle of oil.
5. Add tortillas and begin to layer cheese, chicken, pineapple, cilantro, red onion, and a drizzle of bbq sauce.
6. Turn heat to medium and fold tortillas in half. When golden brown and crisp on both sides. Remove and serve with sour cream mixture. Enjoy!

Hot Honey Tequila Lime Slaw

Servings: x
Cooking Time: x

Ingredients:
- 1 Head Purple Cabbage Shredded
- 5-6 Bulbs Green Onion whites and greens chopped
- 1/2 Bunch Cilantro chopped stems included
- 1/5 - 3/4 Cup of Olive Oil
- 1 Large Lime juiced
- 1 Tablespoon of Blackstone Tequila Lime Seasoning
- 1 Tablespoon of Honey
- 1/2 Jalapeno chopped small, use more or less depending on heat
- 1/2 Teaspoon of Garlic Powder
- Pinch of pink sea salt optional

Directions:
1. Slice/shred cabbage and mix with green onions and cilantro.
2. Mix dressing ingredients.
3. Pour over cabbage mixture and mix well to coat evenly.
4. Refrigerate at least one hour before using.

Sweet Potato & Black Bean Burritos

Servings: x
Cooking Time: x

Ingredients:
- 2 Sweet Potatoes, petite diced
- 1 Red Bell Pepper, petite diced
- 1 Purple Onion, petite diced
- 1 Jalapeno, diced (leave in seeds for extra heat)
- 1 1/2 Teaspoon of Cumin
- 1 1/2 Teaspoon of Chili Powder
- 1 Teaspoon of Salt
- 1/4 Teaspoon of Black Pepper
- Avocado Oil
- 1 Small Bunch of Cilantro
- 1 Lime to juice
- 1 Can of Black Beans, rinsed
- 12 Tortillas
- Colby & Monterey Jack Cheese
- Guacamole, Salsa & Chips (optional side)

Directions:
1. Turn on Blackstone to medium heat. Drizzle with avocado oil.

2. Add the chopped sweet potato, red bell pepper, purple onion and jalapeno. Sprinkle with cumin & chili powder, salt, and pepper. Toss to combine. Pour some water over the mix and cover with a large basting dome. These will take about 10 minutes to cook. Check every couple minutes and give them a toss to prevent burning.

3. Meanwhile, chop the cilantro and add to a bowl. Squeeze the lime in, then add the black beans (drained and rinsed). Stir together.

4. Add sweet potato mixture to the bean bowl and toss.

5. Heat tortillas on a clean portion of the griddle on low until soft.

6. To assemble burritos, fill tortillas with the mixture, add a layer of cheese, and wrap it. Note: If you want to put some in the freezer, wrap them in aluminum foil.

7. Before serving, put burritos on the griddle to make them crispy. Cook with a little oil if you want a more fried crispy taste. Cook for about 1 minute on each side until they are golden brown.

Seared Ahi Tuna

Servings:4
Cooking Time:36 Min

Ingredients:
- One 5-6 Oz. of Ahi Tuna Steak, sushi grade
- 3 Tablespoons of Ponzu Sauce
- 1/4 Cup of Toasted Sesame Seeds (or enough to coat filet completely)
- 2 1/2 Tablespoons of Sesame Oil

Directions:
1. Marinate ahi tuna in ponzu sauce for 30 minutes in refrigerator, turning fish over every 5 minutes.
2. Preheat Blackstone to High Heat.
3. Fill a small dish with sesame seeds and coat the tuna steak on all sides with sesame seeds.
4. Add 1 tbsp sesame oil to preheated griddle and quickly place tuna in the oil to sear 1-1.5 minutes, depending, for rare.
5. Add 1 tbsp sesame oil to griddle, flipping tuna into oil and sear 1-1.5 minutes.
6. Using tongs, sear edges for 20-30 seconds all around the steak in remaining 1/2 tbsp sesame oil.
7. Remove tuna and place on the Blackstone cutting board and slice into thin strips.

Croque Monsieur

Servings:4
Cooking Time:20 Min

Ingredients:
- ½ stick Unsalted Butter
- 2 tablespoons Bacon fat
- ¼ cup All-purpose Flour
- 1 ½ cup Whole Milk
- 2 cups shredded Gruyere
- 8 slices crusty White Bread
- 16 thin slices sweet Ham
- ¼ cup spicy brown Mustard
- 2 tablespoons chopped flat leaf Parsley
- Olive oil
- Salt and pepper

Directions:
1. Using a small sauce pot over medium heat, add the butter and bacon fat and melt. Add the flour and stir to combine. Cook for 3-4 minutes then add 1/3 of the milk. Whisk to evenly combine and then add the remaining milk and whisk to incorporate. Cook for an additional 5-7 minutes over low heat. Add salt and pepper to taste and 1/3 of the shredded gruyere and stir to evenly melt.
2. Toast the bread on both side with a bit of olive oil.
3. Add a thin spread of mustard to each slice of toast and then add some shredded gruyere over the tops of 4. Add 2 slices of ham over the cheese and then a bit of the creamy sauce. Add 2 more pieces of ham and then a bit more shredded gruyere over the top. Add the top piece of bread to build the sandwich and then place on the griddle over low heat to melt the cheese.
4. Garnish with chopped parsley (if desired, torch the cheese to get a bit of color) slice and serve hot.

Cheesechicken Sandwiches

Servings:4
Cooking Time:10 Min

Ingredients:
- 4 chicken cutlets
- 1 sweet yellow onion, julienne
- ½ red bell pepper, julienne
- ½ green bell pepper, Julienne
- 1 cup sliced mushrooms
- 1/3 cup ranch dressing
- ¼ cup buffalo sauce
- 8 slices pepper jack cheese
- Blackstone Cheesesteak Seasoning
- 4 hoagie rolls
- Salt and pepper
- Olive oil

Directions:
1. Pre-heat your griddle to medium-high heat.
2. Season the chicken cutlets with salt, pepper, and a good bit of Blackstone Cheesesteak Seasoning on both sides.
3. Add 2 tablespoons of olive oil to the hot griddle and cook the chicken for 3 minutes per side.
4. Add a bit more olive oil next to the chicken and add the onions, bell peppers, and mushrooms with a bit more Blackstone Cheesesteak Seasoning. Toss to evenly coat and cook for 3-5 minutes.
5. Once the chicken is nearly finished, using your spatulas or a knife and cut the chicken into bite-sized pieces. Make 4 even piles of chicken and add some of the veggies over the tops of each. Add a couple of pieces of pepper jack cheese over each stack and cover to melt.
6. In a small bowl, mix the ranch and buffalo sauce evenly and add to the bottom of each hoagie roll. Add the chicken stacks to the hoagie rolls, slice, and serve hot.

Healthy Pineapple Chicken

Servings:6
Cooking Time:80 Min

Ingredients:
- 2 Lb. of Chicken Tenderloins
- 6 Oz. of Pineapple Juice
- 1/4 Cup of Honey
- 1/4 Cup of Brown Sugar
- 1/4 Cup of Soy Sauce
- 2 Tablespoons of Ketchup
- 1 Tablespoon of Dijon Mustard
- 1 Garlic Clove, minced
- 1 Tablespoon of Onion Powder
- 1 Fresh Pineapple (Optional), cut into chunks (canned pineapple tidbits also work well)

Directions:
1. In a gallon-sized sealable plastic bag, combine pineapple juice, honey, brown sugar, soy sauce, ketchup, mustard, garlic, and onion powder. Knead bag until well-combined.
2. Add chicken tenderloins to marinade and knead bag to coat evenly.
3. Place in fridge 1-6 hours to marinade.
4. Heat griddle to medium-high heat and coat the surface with a thin layer of olive oil.
5. Place chicken on griddle and cook for approximately 8-10 minutes (until internal temperature reaches 165 degrees), turning chicken every two minutes.
6. (Optional) Add fresh pineapple to a different part of griddle and cook for 5 minutes, turning occasionally. Serve pineapple with chicken.

Lamb Tacos

Servings:x
Cooking Time:x

Ingredients:
- 1 Lb. of Ground Lamb
- 1 Teaspoon of Dried Mint
- 1/4 Teaspoon of Garlic Powder
- 1/4 Teaspoon of Dried Parsley
- Salt and Pepper to taste
- 4 Large Tortilla Shells
- 1 Cucumber, diced
- 1 Tomato, diced
- 1/4 Cup of Red Onion, sliced thin
- 1 Cup of Feta Cheese, crumbled
- Tzatziki Sauce or Sour Cream

Directions:

1. Turn Blackstone on medium heat and add the ground lamb.
2. Using the Blackstone scraper or spatula, chop up the ground meat and cook for 4-5 minutes or until the meat starts to brown up a bit.
3. Push the ground meat to one side of the griddle and drain some, not all, of the fat scraping the excess fat liquid off. Lamb tends to have a higher fat content than beef, so be careful of the splatter.
4. Add the dry seasonings and mix together well.
5. Lightly toast the tortillas on the Blackstone Griddle and serve with lettuce, tomato, cucumber, red onion and tzatziki or sour cream.

Marinated Lamb Chops

Servings:x
Cooking Time:x

Ingredients:
- 1 Package Lamb Chops
- 1/2 Cup of Extra Virgin Olive Oil
- 1/2 Cup of Red Wine Vinegar
- 6-8 Fresh Garlic Cloves, one per lamb chop
- 2 Teaspoons of Dried Oregano
- Salt and Pepper to Taste
- Butter for the Griddle

Directions:
1. Peel, press, and roughly chop garlic cloves.
2. Drizzle oil and vinegar over lamb chops.
3. Add garlic, oregano, salt, and pepper. Rub over chops evenly.
4. Allow meat to sit in marinade at least 15-20 minutes on kitchen counter before cooking.
5. Set griddle to med-high/high heat. Spread a tbsp or two of butter over griddle and place lamb chops in butter to sear. Cook time will vary on griddle temp, thickness of chops and meat temperature preference. I like medium to medium well lamb.
6. Flip chops to sear other side, adding butter if needed. Turn griddle to medium low to finish cooking. I cook my one inch chops from room temperature for about 3-4 minutes per side.
7. Allow lamb chops to rest on a dish with a tbsp or two of butter spread out on the dish before eating. This will give you lots of delicious dipping juices to enjoy each slice with!

Seared Garlic Ribeye With Carrots, Asparagus, And Gremolata

Servings:4
Cooking Time:15 Min

Ingredients:
- 4, 8-10 oz. Ribeye steaks
- 5-6 carrots, cut in half lengthwise
- A handful of asparagus, cleaned and trimmed
- 6-8 large garlic cloves
- Olive oil
- Salt and Peppers
- ½ cup chopped parsley
- 2 teaspoons lemon zest
- 1 teaspoon grated garlic
- 3 tablespoons lemon juice
- 3 tablespoons Olive oil
- Salt and pepper

Directions:
1. Heat your griddle to medium-high heat. Add 1-2 tablespoons olive oil and then the carrots, cut side down, and cook for 3-4 minutes.
2. Season the steaks on both sides with salt and pepper then add to the griddle. Cook for 3-4 minutes per side depending on preferred doneness. After your first flip, add the garlic cloves and asparagus with a bit of salt and pepper and cook for 4-5 minutes, tossing often.
3. Mix all of the Gremolata ingredients in a bowl evenly and reserve for plating.
4. Once the steaks are cooked to the desired doneness, remove from the griddle and let rest for 4-5 minutes.
5. To plate, add a few pieces of carrot and asparagus to the plate and then top with the steak. Garnish with a few spoons of the Gremolata over the top and finally the caramelized garlic.

Arugula And Prosciutto Pizza With Balsamic Reduction

Servings:x
Cooking Time:x

Ingredients:
- 1 Crust of Pizza Dough
- 8 Oz. of Fresh Mozzarella Cheese (cut into 1/4" slices)
- 4 Slices Prosciutto (torn or cut into 1/2" pieces)
- 1 Cup of Baby Arugula
- 2-3 Tablespoons of Balsamic reduction
- 1/2 Cup of Fresh Crushed tomatoes (optional)
- 2 Tablespoons of Extra Virgin Olive Oil

Directions:
1. Turn Pizza Oven on to medium high heat.
2. Stretch out your dough.
3. The base of your pizza can either be the crushed tomatoes or just drizzled with extra virgin olive oil. Either one works great for this pizza.
4. Place fresh mozzarella on next and cook in the Pizza Oven until crust is golden brown.
5. Remove pizza from oven and top with prosciutto, arugula, and drizzle with balsamic reduction.

Bacon Jalapeño Corn Fritters

Servings:4
Cooking Time:15 Min

Ingredients:
- 4 strips thick cut bacon
- ¾ cup all purpose flour
- ¾ cup cornmeal
- 1 ½ teaspoons baking powder
- ½ tablespoon smoked paprika
- 1 red jalapeno pepper, minced
- The juice of 1 lime
- 1 cup whole milk
- 2 fresh ears of corn, kernels removed
- Sauce Ingredients:
- 1/3 cup mayonnaise
- 1/3 cup sour cream
- The juice of 1 lime
- 2 teaspoons smoked paprika
- 2 tablespoons chopped cilantro
- Salt and pepper

Directions:
1. Cook the bacon well done on your griddle at medium heat.
2. In a large mixing bowl, add the flour, cornmeal, baking powder, smoked paprika, jalapeno, lime juice, milk, and corn with a pinch of salt and pepper. Mix evenly to incorporate all ingredients.
3. Once the bacon is finished, chop it small and add it to the batter. Mix evenly to incorporate everything evenly.
4. Using a spoon, make small rounds or ovals with the batter and cook in the bacon fat for 3 minutes per side or until the fritters are crisp and golden.
5. In a small mixing bowl, add all of the sauce ingredients and mix evenly.
6. To plate, slice the fritters and serve with the sauce.

Pastrami Cheese Burger With Smack Sauce

Servings:4
Cooking Time:10 Min

Ingredients:
- 1.5 Lb. of 80/20 Ground Beef, formed into 4 burger patties
- 1 Tablespoon of Finely Chopped Jalapeno Pepper
- 1 Tablespoon of Finely Chopped Red Onion
- 2 Teaspoons of Blackstone Crazy Cajun Seasoning
- 1 Tablespoon of Lemon Juice
- 1/3 Cup of Thousand Island Dressing
- 1/4 Cup of Mayonnaise
- 1 Tablespoon of Unsalted Butter
- 1/2 Lb. of Thinly Sliced Pastrami
- 4 Slices Colby Jack Cheese
- 2 Cups of Shredded Romaine Lettuce
- Salt and Pepper
- Olive Oil

Directions:
1. In a small mixing bowl, add the jalapeno, red onion, Blackstone Crazy Cajun Seasoning, lemon juice,

thousand island dressing, and mayonnaise. This is the smack sauce. Mix evenly to combine and reserve for later.
2. With your Blackstone set to medium-high heat, add a bit of olive oil. Season your burger patties with salt and pepper on both sides and cook in the olive oil for 3-4 minutes per side.
3. On the other side of your griddle, add the butter and pastrami. Cook for 3-4 minutes, tossing often.
4. Add some of the cooked pastrami over each burger patty and then add a slice of cheese. Cover with a basting dome to melt the cheese.
5. Toast the buns and then add some of the smack sauce to the bottoms of each. Add some shredded lettuce and then a burger, add the top buns and serve hot.

Garlicky Sesame Teriyaki Yaki Soba Noodles

Servings:4
Cooking Time:20 Min

Ingredients:
- 1 lb Ground Beef
- 1 17.75 oz pack refrigerated Yaki Soba Noodles
- ½-1 c Blackstone Sesame Teriyaki Sear & Serve
- 1 bunch or 1 c Green Onions, sliced and divided
- 5 Garlic Cloves, chopped
- 2 tbsp + 1 tsp seasoned Wok Oil or Stir Fry Oil
- 2 tbsp Sesame Seeds

Directions:
1. Slice green onions dividing onions using the whites and some green for cooking and reserving some for garnishing.
2. Prepare yaki soba noodles per instructions on package by either microwaving to warm and separate or run under warm water and toss in a light drizzle or 1 tsp of wok oil, set aside.
3. On medium high to high heat drizzle 1 tbsp wok oil and add ground beef to cook. Using a spatula or scraper to chop the meat until cooked through.
4. Form an open space in the center of your pile of ground beef and add 1 tbsp wok oil adding the garlic and green onions including the whites of the onions mixing to coat with oil and allow to cook 30-60 seconds. Toss garlic and onions into the ground beef.
5. Add prepared yaki soba noodles and toss together using two spatulas.
6. Lower heat to medium or medium low and mix in the desired amount of Blackstone Sesame Teriyaki Sear and Serve sauce to evenly coat.
7. Remove, plate and garnish with sesame seeds and green onions.
8. Enjoy!

Bacon Cheeseburger Quesadillas

Servings:4
Cooking Time:15 Min

Ingredients:
- 4-6 Strips Thick cut Bacon
- 1 Lb. of 80/20 Ground beef
- 2 Tablespoons of Blackstone All Purpose Seasoning
- 3 Tablespoons of Dill relish
- 2 Cups of Shredded cheddar cheese
- 4 Large Tortillas
- 1/4 Cup of Mayonnaise
- 1/4 Cup of Ketchup
- 2 Tablespoons of Worcestershire sauce
- 2 Tablespoons of Yellow mustard
- 1 Teaspoon of Garlic powder
- 1 Teaspoon of Blackstone All Purpose Seasoning

Directions:
1. Heat your Blackstone Griddle to medium-high heat and cook the bacon well done. Remove the bacon from the griddle and chop small.
2. Add the ground beef and Blackstone All Purpose seasoning to the griddle and chop the meat. Be sure to mix in some of the remaining bacon fat into the beef as it cooks. Cook for 3-4 minutes.
3. Add the chopped bacon and relish and toss to mix everything together. Cook for another 3 minutes.
4. Move the beef mix to the side of the griddle and add your tortillas. Add a handful of cheese evenly over the tortillas and then some of the beef mix to one side. Cook for 2 minutes and then fold in half. You can use a bacon press or weight to hold the quesadilla in place.

5. In a small bowl, add the mayonnaise, ketchup, Worcestershire sauce, mustard, garlic powder and Blackstone All Purpose Seasoning. Mix evenly to incorporate all ingredients.

6. Once the cheese is all melted, remove the quesadilla from the griddle and cut into quarters. Serve hot with the Comeback Sauce.

Crispy Buffalo Cauliflower

Servings:4
Cooking Time:x

Ingredients:

- 1 package frozen cauliflower florets
- 1 cup flour
- 1 tablespoon salt
- 1 tablespoon pepper
- ¼ tablespoon cayenne pepper
- 1 egg
- 1 cup milk
- 3 cups panko breadcrumbs

Directions:

1. Allow the cauliflower to thaw at room temperature for 30 minutes.
2. Mix together the flour, salt, pepper, and cayenne for dredging.
3. Pat the cauliflower florets dry with a paper towel.
4. Whisk together the egg and milk. Using a hand blender or hand mixer is preferable, as you want the egg and milk to be very smooth.
5. Individually dredge the florets first in the dredge flour, making sure they are well coated but in a thin layer.
6. Knock off any additional clumping, then dunk them into the egg-milk to coat, followed by the panko breadcrumbs.
7. The florets should be well coated on all exposed nooks with the panko breadcrumbs.
8. Keep the florets cool in the refrigerator while you preheat the air fryer to 375F.
9. Working in batches, place the florets in a single layer to cook in the air fry basket on a piece of parchment paper. Cook for 15 minutes turning at least twice until the breading is golden brown and the cauliflower is piping hot. I enjoy dipping them in ranch dressing but they are delicious on their own.

Salmon Potato And Brussel Sprout Boats

Servings:2
Cooking Time:x

Ingredients:

- 2-4 Oz. of Wild Caught Salmon Filets
- 1 Can Diced Potatoes, Drained and Rinsed
- 6 Oz. of Brussel Sprouts
- 2 Tablespoons of Salted Butter
- 1/4 Cup of Extra Virgin Olive Oil
- 2 Tablespoons of Dijon Mustard
- 2-3 Garlic Cloves, Chopped
- 1 Tablespoon of Lemon Juice, Freshly Squeezed
- 1/2 Tablespoon of Curly Parsley
- Pink Sea Salt to Taste
- Black Pepper, Fresh Cracked

Directions:

1. Whisk together the sauce ingredients and set aside. Rinse and let potatoes drain well. Slice brussel sprouts into quarters.
2. Make two round tin foil boats just a tad smaller than your Blackstone Basting Cover using double layers of tin foil
3. Add the brussel sprouts and potatoes divided evenly into the foil, leaving room in the center for the fish.
4. Toss half of the sauce, about two spoonfuls, with the vegetables. Rinse and pat dry salmon well. Dry fish is key!
5. Place Â½ tbsp of butter in foil and place salmon filet on top of butter. Spread remaining sauce evenly over fish, about 1 spoonful per filet and top each filet with Â½ tbsp of butter.
6. Set your Blackstone to medium to medium-high heat and place foil on the griddle.
7. Cover with your Basting Cover, checking ever 2-3 minutes and mixing vegetables around. Cook time total is around 10-12 minutes, carefully flipping fish over for the last couple minutes
8. Serve with lemon wedge, garnish with parsley.

Marinated Caprese Chicken

Servings: 6
Cooking Time: 20 Min

Ingredients:
- 6 Boneless, Skinless Chicken Breasts (each breast should be about 6 ounces and trimmed of excess fat.)
- 1 Cup of Italian Dressing
- 8 Oz. of Fresh Mozzarella Cheese Ball (sliced)
- 2 Ripe Tomatoes (sliced)
- 1/2 Cup of Basil (chopped)
- 1/3 Cup of Balsamic Glaze

Directions:
1. Place chicken breasts in a sealable plastic bag and add Italian dressing. Knead to coat evenly and leave in fridge 1-12 hours to marinate.
2. Heat griddle to medium-high heat and cover with a thin coat of olive oil.
3. Remove chicken from marinade and cook on griddle for approximately 5 minutes each side (internal temperature should reach 165 degrees).
4. During the last 3 minutes of cooking, top chicken with fresh sliced mozzarella cheese and cook until done.
5. Remove chicken from griddle and top with tomato slices and garnish with chopped basil and balsamic glaze to taste.

Country Western Burger

Servings: 1
Cooking Time: 10 Min

Ingredients:
- 4 Lb. of Ground Beef
- 1/4 Cup of Liquid Smoke
- Granulated Garlic to taste
- Salt and Pepper to taste
- 1 Package Thick Sliced Black Pepper Bacon
- 1 Bag Breaded Onion Rings
- 10-12 Slices Monterrey Jack Cheese Slices
- Country Bob's All Purpose Sauce (Available at Walmart and other Grocery Stores)
- Texas Toast Bread

Directions:
1. Preheat the Blackstone griddle to high heat. When heated, lightly coat the griddle top with oil.
2. Mix 4 lbs. Ground beef with 1/4 cup Liquid smoke.
3. Place frozen battered Onion rings on griddle top. Flip onion rings when first side is crispy and slightly blackened.
4. Place Bacon strips on griddle. Use Blackstone Bacon Press (available in the Blackstone Breakfast Kit) to keep bacon flat.
5. Drop Burger patties onto hot griddle top. Season with garlic, salt, and pepper to taste, or use your favorite burger or western-style seasoning.
6. When onion rings are ready, move them to one end of the griddle. Turn heat zone off and allow onion rings to stay warm while patties continue cooking.
7. Flip patties when first side is seared and slightly blackened. Season second side of burger patty.
8. Add a slice of Monterrey Jack cheese to burger patty as it nears completion.
9. Add two strips of cooked bacon to to burger patty and top it with one or two onion rings. Use the Blackstone 12" Round Basting Cover to quickly melt the cheese.
10. Lay slices of Texas Toast on griddle top. Toast until golden brown, flip, and toast the other side.
11. Plate it up and top the burger with Country Bob's all Purpose Sauce.

Jalapeño Popper Quesadilla

Servings: 2
Cooking Time: 15 Min

Ingredients:
- Flour tortilla
- Mexican blend cheese
- Cream Cheese
- Jalapeños
- Bacon
- Salt
- Pepper
- Ancho Chile
- Chili Powder
- Garlic powder
- Onion Powder

Directions:
1. Preheat your griddle on medium high and add your bacon. 4 strips should be plenty for 2-3 quesadillas.
2. While your bacon is cooking rough chop your jalapeños. Feel free to leave the seeds in them for a little extra heat. Once you have your jalapeños chopped up you can add them to griddle and cook them in the bacon fat. You don't have to do this, but this really elevates the flavor of the jalapeño and bacon. That should only take about 2-3 minutes.
3. While that's cooking you can add about 2/3 cup of cream cheese to a mixing bowl. Roughly 1-2 cups of your Mexican blend pre shredded cheese, a pinch of garlic powder, onion powder, chili powder and ancho chili powder and a pinch of salt and pepper.
4. Your bacon and jalapeños should be done by this time. Pull off your bacon to drain on a paper towel and add your jalapeños directly to your bowl. Give your bacon a rough chop and add that to the mixing bowl with your other ingredients and mix well.
5. Once that is mixed well turn your griddle to medium low and place two tortillas down. You can use your bacon fat to help toast your quesadillas. Once those are down and toasting add your ingredients to one side of each of your tortillas. This can be a little hard to spread out with a spoon so I recommend using your griddle spatula to spread over one side of each of your tortillas and then fold your tortilla over to keep your ingredients inside to cook. Once one side it toasted to your liking flip over and toast the other side. Your ingredients should be melted and ready to go. Pull off when each side is toasted and the ingredients are melted. Slice up and enjoy!

Crabby Melts

Servings:4
Cooking Time:x

Ingredients:
- 1/2 Cup of Mayonnaise
- 1/2 Teaspoon of Sugar
- 1/2 Teaspoon of Mustard Powder
- 1/2 Teaspoon of Lemon Juice
- 1 Teaspoon of Parsley, Dry
- 1 Teaspoon of Old Bay Seasoning
- 1 Teaspoon of Worcestershire Sauce
- 2 Tablespoons of Butter, Melted
- 1 Lb. of Crabmeat
- 1 Green Pepper, Diced
- 1 Tablespoon of Extra Virgin Olive Oil
- 8 Rye Bread Slices
- Mayonnaise to Spread
- 8 Provolone Cheese Slices

Directions:
1. Whisk together all of the sauce ingredients and fold in the crab meat without breaking apart the lumps.
2. Set Blackstone Griddle to medium-high heat and cook peppers in olive oil until soft. Use the Blackstone Basting Cover to help steam the peppers soft. Set peppers aside on no heat or in a bowl.
3. Turn Blackstone to medium heat.
4. Spread a thin layer of mayonnaise on the outside of the bread and place on the griddle. Add the provolone cheese, crab meat mixture and green peppers.
5. Let them cook slowly until golden brown and melted. The Blackstone Basting Cover with a squirt of water around the sandwich will help melt everything together!

Hot Italian Sausage Rigatoni In Red Sauce

Servings:4
Cooking Time:25 Min

Ingredients:
- 4-6 Johnsonville Hot Italian Sausages
- ¾ cup diced Sweet Onion
- 2 tablespoons minced Garlic
- 1, 24 oz jar of Rao's Bolognese Sauce
- 2 tablespoons fresh Oregano leaves, rough chop
- 1 tablespoon fresh Basil, rough chop
- 1 cup diced Tomato
- 1 box of Rigatoni Noodles, cooked to al dente (mostly cooked)
- 1 cup fresh Spinach Leaves
- 1 cup shredded Mozzarella Cheese
- 1/3 cup fresh shredded Parmesan

- 1 large aluminum pan
- Salt and pepper
- Olive oil

Directions:
1. Heat your griddle to medium-high heat and add a bit of olive oil. Cook the sausages for 4-6 minutes turning often.
2. Place the aluminum pan on the griddle over medium heat. Add a bit of olive oil and the onions. Cook for 3 minutes then add the garlic. Cook for another 2 minutes stirring often.
3. Add the Rao's tomato sauce over the onions and garlic and bring to a simmer. Then add the sausage, oregano, and basil with a bit of salt and pepper. Let the sausage cook for 5 minutes, turning often.
4. Once the sausage is cooked, remove it from the sauce, slice into bite sized pieces and add it back to the sauce pan. Then, add the spinach and the noodles and stir to evenly combine.
5. Top with the mozzarella cheese and cover with a dome for another 5 minutes.
6. Serve hot and garnish with the shredded parmesan and fresh basil.
7. Enjoy!

Cheese Sausage Stuffing Balls

Servings:1
Cooking Time:10 Min

Ingredients:
- 1 Lb. of Sage Flavored Breakfast Sausage
- 2-3 Celery Stalks, Diced Small
- 1 Onion, Diced Small
- 3 Tablespoons of Salted Butter
- 2 Cloves Garlic, Grated
- 1 Teaspoon of Poultry Seasoning
- 1 14oz Bag Herb Seasoned Stuffing, like Pepperidge Farm Herb Seasoned Classic Stuffing
- 1 Cup of Chicken Stock
- 1 Cup of Cheddar Cheese
- 1/2 Cup of Parmesan Cheese
- 3 Eggs, Beaten
- 1/4 Cup of Curly Parsley, chopped
- Salt and Pepper to Taste
- Vegetable Oil and 1-2 TBSP butter for cooking

Directions:
1. Cook and crumble the sausage in a pan or on the Blackstone and set aside.
2. In the same pan or on the Blackstone cook onions and celery in 3 tbsp butter on medium heat until soft. Add the garlic and poultry seasoning and cook 1 additional minute.
3. Add the mixture to the sausage and let cool 5 minutes.
4. Add the dry stuffing mixture (you can replace cut up bread for for the store bought stuffing if you want) to the sausage mixture, add the chicken broth and gently mix to coat.
5. Season with salt and/or pepper to your liking.
6. Add the cheese, eggs and parsley and gently mix. Refrigerate mixture for at least 20 minutes, this will make forming the balls easier.
7. With your hands, form balls to your size liking. I suggest small for a great appetizer or large (about ¼ cup) for dinner serving size.
8. Turn your Blackstone to medium heat, about 350 degrees.
9. Drizzle vegetable oil and 1-2 tbsp of real butter on the griddle and mix.
10. Place your sausage balls on, turning to cook evenly on all sides, about 1-2 minutes on each side.
11. Serve with gravy or cranberry sauce for dipping!

Bacon Fried Corn 2.0

Servings:7
Cooking Time:17 Min

Ingredients:
- 1 Lb. of Thick Sliced Hickory Smoked Bacon
- 2 Tablespoons of Pureed Garlic
- 2 Lb. of Bag of Frozen Corn
- 1 Teaspoon of Crushed Red Pepper
- 1/4 Cup of Fresh Chopped Cilantro
- 1 Tablespoon of Blackstone Taco & Fajita Seasoning

Directions:
1. Set the Blackstone griddle to medium heat.

2. Dice bacon into small pieces and pour onto hot griddle top. Use spatulas to frequently mix bacon. We recommend cooking the bacon until it's slightly crispy but not burned. Bacon should still be pliable. Cooking times will vary but this step, but it will take 7-10 minutes minimum.
3. Once the bacon has cooked, add garlic and thoroughly mix with bacon.
4. Add corn to the bacon and continue mixing, making sure all ingredients are combined evenly.
5. Allow corn to cook for 5 minutes. After 5 minutes, use a spoon to test the corn. If it's hot, proceed to the next step. If the corn is still cold or lukewarm, allow it to cook for a few more minutes.
6. Add crushed red pepper, cilantro, and Blackstone Taco and Fajita Seasoning. Mix evenly and serve immediately.

Bbq Chicken Cheesesteaks

Servings:2
Cooking Time:20 Min

Ingredients:
- 2- 12 inch Italian Rolls
- 1.5 lbs chicken breast
- 6 strips bacon, thick cut
- 1 tbsp Blackstone All Purpose Seasoning
- 1 cup monterary jack, shredded (sub american or cheddar)
- 1/2 cup BBQ Sauce, Duke's
- 2 tbsp red onion, diced
- 1/2 tsp parsely, garnish optional

Directions:
1. Dice up chicken breast, as small or big as you'd like, set aside.
2. Cut bacon into small pieces and set aside.
3. Turn Blackstone on and set to medium heat, add the bacon and cook slowly keeping the bacon grease from draining off, this is what you'll cook the chicken in.
4. When bacon is about 3/4 through cooking, add the chicken to the bacon and bacon grease. Add the Blackstone All Purpose Seasoning and mix to coat chicken completely and allow to cook 3-5 minutes.
5. Add a drizzle of bbq sauce and mix into the chicken and bacon mixture.
6. Turn Blackstone to low and seperate the meat mixture into two piles, add cheese and mix through to melt.
7. Form two piles of meat the same shape as each roll, add a drizzle of BBQ sauce to each and place rolls ontop of the meat let sit about one minute.
8. Holding the roll with one hand, slide a spatula under the meat and flip. Plate and garnish with fresh chopped red onions and parsely.

Lo-country Broil

Servings:4
Cooking Time:x

Ingredients:
- 16-20 large shrimp, peeled and deveined
- 1.5 pounds smoked sausage links
- 4 corn ears
- 1 10-12 oz. bag roasted frozen red potato quarters
- 1 medium sweet onion
- ½ cup Old Bay Seasoning or Lo-Country Style Shrimp Boil seasoning
- 3-tablespoons oil

Directions:
1. Preheat your griddle to medium-high and the air fryer to high.
2. Cut and remove the top and bottom stems from the onion. Clean all exterior onionskin and discard. Cut the onion in half and then quarter each half. Peel apart the petals and set aside.
3. Slice the smoked sausage into silver dollar rounds about the thickness of a pencil.
4. Sauté the sausage and onion on the griddle in some butter until the sausage begins to develop some color and the onions begin to wilt.
5. In a large bowl, mix shrimp, corn, and potato quarters with oil until well coated. Once coated, sprinkle with seasoning and toss until even.
6. Place the corn and potato in one of the AirFryer baskets and begin cooking.
7. After five minutes, add the sausage and onion from the griddle and the shrimp to the other AirFryer basket.

8. Cook for an additional 5 minutes or until the shrimp is fully cooked.
9. Combine the contents of both AirFryer baskets by pouring them onto a platter and serve immediately.

Taco Salad

Servings:4-6
Cooking Time:20 Min

Ingredients:
- 1 lb 80/20 ground beef
- Blackstone Tequila Lime Seasoning
- The juice of 2 limes
- ¼ cup beer (lager is best)
- 2 cups Nacho Cheese Doritos
- 2 cups shredded romaine lettuce
- 14 cup diced red onion
- ¼ cup diced tomato
- 1-2 jalapenos, thinly sliced
- ¼ cup pineapple juice
- 1 tablespoon red wine vinegar
- ½ cup corn
- ½ cup black beans, drained and rinsed
- 1/3 cup shredded Colby jack cheese
- 1/3 cup Zesty Italian Salad Dressing
- salt

Directions:
1. Add the jalapeno peppers to a small mixing bowl with the pineapple juice, red wine vinegar, a bit of olive oil and a pinch of salt. Stir to combine and let marinate for the rest of the cook.
2. Heat your griddle to medium heat and add the ground beef. Season generously with Blackstone Tequila Lime Seasoning and toss to evenly incorporate. Cook for 4-5 minutes, tossing often.
3. Add lime juice and beer and toss to evenly incorporate. Cook for another 3-4 minutes then move the beef over to the cooler side of the griddle.
4. Add the corn and beans to the hot side of the griddle and toss in the remaining beef fat and seasoning. Cook for 3-4 minutes, tossing often.
5. To plate, using a large serving bowl, add some Doritos to the bottom and then the shredded lettuce. Add the beef over the top and then the corn and beans. Add the tomato, red onion, cheese and pickled jalapeno peppers. Finish by adding the Zesty Italian Salad Dressing and serve family style.

Funfetti Pancakes

Servings:4
Cooking Time:15 Min

Ingredients:
- 1 Cup Funfetti Cake Mix
- 1 Cup Pancake Mix
- 1 Cup Milk
- 2 Eggs
- 2 tbsp Sprinkles
- 1 tsp Vanilla
- 1 Cup Powdered Sugar
- 2 tbsp Cream
- 1 tsp Vanilla
- Whipped Cream
- Cherries
- Sprinkles

Directions:
1. In a mixing bowl, combine all of the ingredients to make the pancake batter.
2. Heat griddle to medium.
3. Make pancakes by pouring 1/4 cup of batter on the griddle top. Once you begin to see bubbles, flip the pancakes and cook another 2-3 minutes.
4. Stack 5-6 pancakes on a plate, and drizzle with icing, top with whipped cream, cherry, and more sprinkles.
5. Enjoy!

Marinated Steak Tips

Servings:6
Cooking Time:17 Min

Ingredients:
- 1/2 Cup of Lite Soy Sauce
- 1/3 Cup of Extra Virgin Olive Oil
- 1/4 Cup of Worcestershire Sauce
- 1 Teaspoon of Minced Garlic
- 2 Tablespoons of Dried Basil
- 1 Tablespoon of Dried Parsley
- 1 Teaspoon of Black Pepper

- 2 Lb. of Flat Iron or Top Sirloin Steak (Cut in 1-inch Cubes)

Directions:
1. Combine soy sauce, olive oil, Worcestershire sauce, garlic, parsley, and pepper in sealable gallon-sized plastic bag. Knead well to combine all ingredients.
2. Add steak cubes into marinade bag and knead well to coat evenly.
3. Place in refrigerator 2-24 hours.
4. Heat griddle to high heat and coat evenly with olive oil.
5. Add steak bites to griddle and cook to desired doneness (approximately 5 minutes or 145 degrees internal temperature for âmediumâ steak bites)
6. *Pro Tip* using a colander to strain excess marinade from your steak bites makes griddle clean up even easier.

Grilled Corn Salad

Servings:6
Cooking Time:25 Min

Ingredients:
- 6 Ears of Corn, Shucked
- 1 Green Pepper, Diced
- 2 Roma Tomatoes, Diced
- 1/4 Cup of Red Onion, Diced
- 1/2 Bunch Fresh Cilantro, Finely Chopped
- 2 Tablespoons of Olive Oil
- Salt & Pepper (to taste)
- Grated Parmesan Cheese (Optional)

Directions:
1. Heat your griddle to medium-high heat and cover with a thin layer of olive oil.
2. Place the ears of corn on your griddle and and cook until corn is tender (about 10 minutes), rotating occasionally, until some blackness starts to appear.
3. Remove the corn from the griddle and let it rest until cool enough to handle.
4. With a sharp knife slice the corn off the cobs into a large bowl and combine with all other ingredients. Toss until well-mixed.
5. Season with salt and pepper to taste. Top with grated parmesan cheese. (optional)

Mozzarella En Carrozza

Servings:1
Cooking Time:20 Min

Ingredients:
- 3 slices white bread
- 4-5 thick slices fresh mozzarella
- 1 egg, beaten
- 1 tbsp milk
- 1 cup Italian bread crumbs with pecorino romano
- 1 cup marinara sauce, Rao preferred
- fresh basil

Directions:
1. Stack three slices of bread with fresh mozzarella like you would a club sandwich. slice crust off all four sides. set aside.
2. In two separate shallow bowls or dishes, beat together egg and milk in one and pour breadcrumbs into another. (add some fresh grated pecorino cheese if desired or if you have breadcrumbs without cheese added)
3. Set Blackstone to preheat to medium low.
4. Carefully and quickly dredge, without soaking, each side of your stacked sandwich into the egg mixture and then into the breadcrumbs to coat completely.
5. Drizzle enough olive oil to place sandwich into and let cook low and slow (as to not burn and allow time for the cheese inside to melt through) until golden brown. lower heat if needed.
6. Using tongs turn sandwich onto each side to cook adding a drizzle of oil under as needed to fry until each side is done.
7. Place sandwich cut in half or in fours on a bed of warm marinara sauce and garnish with basil.
8. Enjoy!

Bourbon Berry Lemonade

Servings:4
Cooking Time:15 Min

Ingredients:
- 2 Cups of Fresh Blackberries
- 2 Cups of Fresh Raspberries
- 1/3 Cup of Brown Sugar

- 3 Tablespoons of Honey
- 2 Cups of Bourbon for Syrup
- 8 Oz. of Bourbon for Cocktail
- 12 Lemons, Cut in Half
- Tonic Water or OR Club Soda
- 1 Teaspoon of Vegetable Oil

Directions:
1. Set your griddle to high heat. Using a sauté pan, add the berries, brown sugar, honey and bourbon and bring to a boil. Let the liquid reduce by 2/3rds, or until it looks like syrup. About 10 minutes.
2. To the other side of the griddle, add a very thin layer of vegetable oil and place the lemons cut side down and cook for 5-6 minutes, or until the lemons are caramelized and golden.
3. Once the lemons and berries are finished, strain them into separate containers for later. (Pro-Tip: The syrup and caramelized lemon juice can be used for lots of different applications and will hold in the refrigerator for 3-4 days.)
4. To make your cocktail, add some ice to a high-ball glass and 2 ounces of bourbon. Add 2-3 ounces of caramelized lemon juice and then a splash of tonic water or club soda. To finish, add 1-2 ounces of the bourbon berry syrup and garnish with a couple of fresh berries and a lemon wedge.

Bacon Jalapeño Popper Burger

Servings:1
Cooking Time:10 Min

Ingredients:
- 2 Lb. of 80/20 Ground Beef
- 1 Lb. of Bacon
- 8 Oz. of Cream Cheese
- 8 Oz. of Shredded Cheddar Cheese
- 2 Fresh Jalapeños, Diced
- 1 Tapatío Hot Sauce (Extra for Bacon)
- 2 Teaspoons of Horseradish
- 1 Red Onion, Sliced
- 2 Large Tomatoes, Sliced
- 6-8 Hamburger Buns

Directions:
1. Preheat your griddle to medium high
2. Form your hamburger into 6-8 patties
3. Put all of the bacon on the griddle. Lightly season bacon with pepper and drizzle with Tapatío Hot Sauce to taste.
4. When the bacon is done, pull from griddle and chop into small pieces
5. Dice the Jalapeños and sauté on griddle (use some of the bacon grease).
6. In a large bowl mix cream cheese, shredded cheddar, cooked Jalapeños, diced bacon, 1 tablespoon Tapatío, and 2 tsp horseradish.
7. Put your burgers on the griddle and season with salt and pepper.
8. Flip your burger when one side is browned. Then top each burger with the cheese mixture.
9. Cover burgers with a basting cover until the cheese mixture is melted.
10. Toast hamburger buns on the griddle.
11. Serve your burgers with tomato and onion slices (lettuce optional).

Family-style Mussels With Red Sauce

Servings:x
Cooking Time:x

Ingredients:
- 1-2 Lb. of Mussels, Cleaned and debarred
- 2 24 Oz. of Jars Marinara; Victoria or Rao are good quality sauces
- 1 Lb. of Ground Italian Sausage, hot or sweet
- 4-5 Garlic Cloves, smashed and chopped
- 1 Handful Roughly Chopped Flat Leaf Parsley, plus 1-2 tbsp chopped for garnish
- Extra Virgin Olive Oil
- Crushed Red Pepper Flakes, optional
- Loaf crusty bread, sliced
- *Recommended--disposable rectangular tin tray

Directions:
1. Preheat Blackstone to medium high heat. Add sausage to cook completely. Use you Blackstone scraper or spatula to chop meat as you would taco meat.

2. Place tin tray directly on clean side of the Blackstone, add a drizzle of extra virgin olive oil. About 2 tablespoons.
3. Add garlic, crushed red pepper and a few whole pieces of parsley roughly chopped to the oil, including the stems. Shake tin or stir around to cook garlic 1-2 minutes or just until fragrant. Be sure not to burn garlic.
4. Add the cooked sausage and marinara sauce to the tin and mix everything together. Let cook a few minutes, or until the sauce starts to bubble.
5. Add the mussels into the sauce and mix well, spreading the mussels out evenly. Cover with foil and let cook 3-4 minutes, gently shaking pan a couple times during to help make room for mussels to open.
6. Remove foil, mix mussels and allow them to cook 30 more seconds. This will help any mussels that need more room to open. Remove tin tray from heat, garnish with fresh chopped parsley and enjoy!

Zesty Chicken Caesar Sticks

Servings:20
Cooking Time:25 Min

Ingredients:
- 3 Lb. of Ground Chicken
- 2 Cups of Panko
- 3 Garlic Cloves (grated or minced)
- 3 Tablespoons of Caesar Dressing
- 3 Tablespoons of Curly Parsley (chopped)
- 1 Cup of Pecorino Cheese (grated)
- 1 Tablespoon of Worcestershire Sauce
- 1 Tablespoon of Dijon Mustard
- Lemon, Juiced and zested
- 1 Teaspoon of Black Pepper
- Salt to Taste
- Extra Virgin Olive Oil
- Kabob Sticks

Directions:
1. Soak kabob sticks in water and set aside.
2. Combine all ingredients by hand, cover and refrigerate mixture for 20 minutes.
3. Rinse and pat sticks dry.
4. Scoop out meat mixture about Â¼ cup or the size to fit your palm, and form a oval shape to slide kabob stick into.
5. Heat your Blackstone Griddle to medium heat and drizzle a little extra virgin olive oil and place kabobs on the griddle.
6. Cook on both sides about 5 minutes or until golden brown.
7. Use the Basting Cover midway, adding a drizzle of water to help chicken cook through for about 1 minute.
8. Serve with lemon wedges, caesar dressing and shaved pecorino cheese.

Grilled Chicken And Roasted Red Pepper Sandwiches With Fontina Cheese

Servings:4
Cooking Time:x

Ingredients:
- 1 Lb. of Skinless, Boneless Chicken Breast halves or tenderloins
- 1 Tablespoon of Fresh Lemon Juice
- 1 Tablespoon of Dijon Mustard
- 2 Teaspoon of Extra Virgin Olive Oil
- 1/4 Teaspoon of Dried Marjoram
- 1/4 Teaspoon of Dried Thyme
- 7 Oz. of Bottle Roasted Red Bell Peppers, drained and sliced
- 1 Tablespoon of Red Wine Vinegar
- 1/8 Teaspoons of Freshly Ground Black Pepper
- 1 Cup of Vertically Sliced Onion
- 1 Teaspoon of Sugar
- 3/4 Teaspoon of Fennel Seeds, Crushed
- 1/4 Teaspoon of Crushed Red Pepper
- 1/2 Teaspoon of Salt
- 5 Garlic Cloves
- 3 Oz. of Fontina Cheese, Sliced
- 12 Oz. of Loaf Rosemary Focaccia, Cut in Half Horizontally
- 4 Teaspoon of Low-Fat Mayonnaise
- Avocado Oil

Directions:

1. Pound chicken to ¾-inch thickness, or use tenderloins.
2. Combine lemon juice, mustard, oil, marjoram, thyme, 1 garlic clove, and chicken in a large zip-lock plastic bag. Seal the bag and let marinate in refrigerator 2 hours or more, turning occasionally.
3. Heat Blackstone over medium-high heat, then turn down to medium once it's warmed up.
4. Pour avocado oil on the blackstone to start sauteing the chicken on one half and the red pepper and onion mix on the other half.
5. Put the raw chicken on the griddle and start cooking.
6. Put the onions on the other half of the griddle. Once the onions are starting to get tender, add the remaining ingredients (4-garlic cloves, onion, sugar, fennel, crushed red pepper, and salt) and sauté 1 minute. Cook until the onions are tender, stirring frequently. Add red bell peppers and sauté for another five minutes. Stir in vinegar and black pepper.
7. Once chicken is done, cool slightly, cut chicken into slices.
8. Prepare a space on the griddle to toast the bread. Put the cut bread with the cut side down on the Blackstone for a minute to warm up the inside of the bread. Spread cut sides of bread evenly with mayonnaise. Arrange cheese on bottom half of bread. Arrange chicken and pepper mixture over cheese. Top with top half of bread, press lightly. (You can use a griddle press if desired.)
9. Griddle for 3 minutes on each side, or until cheese melts. Cut into quarters Yield 4 servings (serving size: 1 sandwich quarter)

Garlic Parmesan Potatoes

Servings:6
Cooking Time:25 Min

Ingredients:
- 8 Red Potatoes With Skins on, Scrubbed and Diced
- 3 Tablespoons of Olive Oil
- 1 1/2 Tablespoons of Paprika
- 3/4 Tablespoon of Garlic powder
- 1/2 Tablespoon of Salt
- 1/4 Tablespoon of Pepper
- 1/4 Cup of Grated Parmesan Cheese

Directions:
1. Heat your griddle to high heat and cover the surface evenly with olive oil.
2. In a large bowl, combine diced potatoes, olive oil, paprika, garlic powder, salt, and pepper. Stir to coat potatoes evenly.
3. Cook over high heat, stirring occasionally, for about 10 minutes.
4. Add parmesan cheese and continue cooking another 5 minutes or until desired doneness (the longer you cook them the crispier the outside of the potatoes becomes).

Caribbean Jerk Chicken

Servings:6
Cooking Time:20 Min

Ingredients:
- 1 Yellow Onion, chopped into quarters
- 2 Green Onions, chopped
- 1 Habanero Chili Pepper, seeded and chopped
- 2 Garlic Cloves
- 1 Tablespoon of Five-Spice Powder
- 1 Teaspoon of Allspice
- 1 Teaspoon of Dried Thyme
- 1/2 Teaspoon of Ground Nutmeg
- 1 Teaspoon of Salt
- 1 Teaspoon of Ground Black Pepper
- 1/2 Cup of Soy Sauce
- 1 Tablespoon of Vegetable Oil
- 3 Lb. of Chicken Pieces (breasts, thighs, or drumsticks)

Directions:
1. To make the marinade, combine all ingredients except for the chicken in a food processor or blender. Blend until everything is mostly smooth (it will resemble a course and gritty paste).
2. Place chicken pieces in a gallon-sized resealable bag and pour the marinade over the chicken. Seal the bag tightly and then knead the bag to cover chicken completely.
3. Let chicken marinate for 6-8 hours in the fridge.

4. Remove chicken from fridge, preheat griddle to medium-high heat, and cover with a thin coat of olive oil.
5. Place chicken on griddle and cook for approximately 8-10 minutes (until internal temperature reaches 165 degrees), turning chicken every two minutes.

Pesto Ranch Chicken Sandwich

Servings:4
Cooking Time:15 Min

Ingredients:
- 4-6 Chicken Cutlets
- 4 Tablespoons of Blackstone Chicken & Herb Seasoning
- 1/4 Cup of Pesto
- 1/4 Cup of Ranch Dressing
- 1/4 Cup of Mayonnaise
- 2 Tablespoons of Sun-Dried Tomato Puree/Spread
- The Juice of 1 Lemon
- 12 Large Fresh Basil Leaves
- 8 Slices Provolone Cheese
- 4 Hoagie or Sub Rolls Cut in Half
- Olive Oil

Directions:
1. In a small mixing bowl, add the mayonnaise, sun-dried tomato puree, and lemon juice. Mix evenly and reserve for later.
2. Heat your Blackstone Griddle to medium-high heat.
3. Season each of the chicken cutlets with a bit of olive oil and Blackstone Chicken & Herb Seasoning on both sides. Cook for 3-4 minute per side or until fully cooked.
4. Toast the cut side of each hoagie or sub roll.
5. To the bottom side of each roll, add some pesto and then some of the ranch dressing. Slice the chicken cutlets in half and add over the top. Add a few fresh basil leaves and then 2 pieces of provolone cheese. To the top buns, add some of the sun-dried tomato mayonnaise and then place on top of the sandwich.
6. Turn your Blackstone Griddle to Low heat and add the sandwiches. Cover and cook for 5 minutes or until the cheese is melted. Slice and serve hot.

Shiitake Cranberry Green Beans

Servings:4
Cooking Time:15 Min

Ingredients:
- 1 cup diced Pancetta
- 3 cup sliced Shiitake Mushrooms
- 1 pound Green Beans, cleaned and trimmed
- 3 cloves Garlic, thinly sliced
- 2 tablespoon Unsalted Butter
- 1/3 cup Dried Cranberries
- 1 teaspoon Lemon Juice
- Salt and Pepper

Directions:
1. Heat your griddle to medium heat and cook the pancetta for 5-6 minutes, tossing often. Once the pancetta is fully cooked and crisp, remove from the griddle and reserve for later.
2. Add the mushrooms to the left over pancetta fat and cook for 2-3 minutes. Add the green beans, butter and bit of salt and pepper. Toss to combine and cook for 3-4 minutes.
3. Add the garlic, dried cranberries, and the pancetta. Toss to evenly combine. Add some water and steam for 3-5 minutes or until the beans are tender.
4. Serve in a platter family style.
5. Enjoy!

Hawaiian Mac Salad

Servings:x
Cooking Time:x

Ingredients:
- 1 Lb. of Elbow Macaroni
- 2-3 Carrots, shredded (amount varies dependent on size)
- 1/4 Cup of Yellow Onion, shredded
- 2.5 Tablespoons of Apple Cider Vinegar
- 2.5 Cups of Hellman's Mayonnaise (no substitutes)
- 1/2 Cup of Milk
- 2 Teaspoons of Sugar
- Salt & Pepper to taste

Directions:
1. Boil pasta and drain well.

2. While still hot, put macaroni in storage container and add vinegar. Mix well.
3. Add shredded carrots and onions while still warm and mix. Let sit 10 minutes, gently mixing every couple of minutes.
4. Whisk together mayonnaise, milk, and sugar in mixing bowl while you wait for your pasta to slightly cool in step 3.
5. Add salt and pepper to taste. Refrigerate 5 hours or overnight.

New Mexico Breakfast Quesadillas

Servings:1
Cooking Time:10 Min

Ingredients:
- 6 Eggs
- 2 Cups of Diced Russet Potatoes
- 1 Lb. of Thick Sliced Bacon
- 6 Cups of Shredded Fiesta Blend Cheese (Monterey Jack, Cheddar, Queso Quesadillas & Asadero), Divided
- 1 Fresh Minced Garlic Clove
- 1/2 Cup of Diced Red Onion
- Salt & Pepper to Taste
- Freshly Chopped Cilantro
- 505 Southwestern Hatch Valley Flame Roasted Green Chile
- 8 Large 10"-12" Flour Tortillas

Directions:
1. Preheat the Blackstone griddle to high heat.
2. Cook bacon on griddle. No need to use oil. Bacon will create its own grease for use throughout the entire recipe. Use the Blackstone Bacon Press (available in the Blackstone Breakfast Kit) if you wish to keep your bacon flat.
3. Peel and dice enough Russet Potatoes to make 2 full cups. By now there should be enough bacon grease on the griddle top to cook your potatoes. Drop 1 Tbsp Fresh minced garlic and 1/2 cup Diced red onion onto bacon grease. Use spatula to flip onions and garlic. Drop all diced Russet Potatoes onto onions and garlic.
4. Meanwhile, your bacon should be almost fully cooked. If using the 36" griddle, turn the far right burner off. Move cooked bacon to the end of the griddle. Allow bacon to sit and stay warm in the zone that is turned off. Otherwise, remove cooked bacon from griddle and wrap in aluminum foil to keep warm.
5. Continue to flip and mix potatoes, onions, and garlic, incorporating flavors as they cook.
6. Beat eggs. Drop egg mix onto oiled griddle. Season to taste with salt and pepper. Scrambled eggs will cook very fast on the griddle. Use spatula to flip and break up eggs as they cook. When they are finished cooking, move them to the end of the griddle alongside cooked bacon. If using smaller griddle, set eggs aside with cooked bacon until potatoes are finished cooking.
7. Cook potatoes until they have a slight crust on them. Dice bacon. Combine bacon, potatoes, and eggs using spatulas.
8. Lay four tortillas on griddle top. Cover each tortilla evenly with 3/4 cup of Shredded Fiesta Blend Cheese, 1/4 cup potatoes, 1/4 of the available bacon, 2 Tbsp hatch green chile (more or less to personal taste), and 1 Tbsp cilantro. Top with 3/4 cup cheese. Add top tortilla.
9. If necessary, use the Blackstone Bacon Press or a spatula to flatten quesadilla as the cheese melts and ingredients combine within tortillas. Frequently use spatula to check underneath tortilla ensuring it turns golden brown. Carefully turn each quesadilla and repeat cooking process on other side. Quesadillas are ready when both sides are golden brown and cheese is completely melted inside tortillas.
10. Slice quesadillas in the same manner as a pizza using a chef's knife. Each quesadilla makes 4 or 8 individual pieces, depending on the desired size of servings.

Pretzel Sliders

Servings:1
Cooking Time:10 Min

Ingredients:
- 1 Lb. of Ground Beef
- 1 Envelope Onion Soup Mix (Lipton or Comparable)
- 1 Package Bacon

- 6 Slices Cheddar Cheese
- 6 Slices Sliced Provolone Cheese
- 6 Slices Sliced Baby Swiss Cheese
- Granulated Garlic to taste
- Cracked Black Pepper to taste
- Sea Salt to taste
- Classic Yellow Mustard to taste
- 6 Pretzel Slider Rolls (Labriola brand can be found in Costco's bakery)

Directions:

1. Preheat the Blackstone griddle to medium or high heat. Cook enough strips of bacon on the griddle to garnish all of the sliders. Use the Blackstone Bacon Press (available in the Blackstone Breakfast Kit) to keep the bacon from curling up. When the bacon is cooked, turn one of the end burners off and slide bacon to that side of the griddle to keep it warm.

2. Mix 1 lb. ground beef with 1 envelope of onion soup mix. Make small slider-sized patties the same circumference as the pretzel slider rolls.

3. Place slider patties on the griddle. Season to taste with granulated garlic, cracked black pepper, and sea salt. Flip the patties once there is a good blackened sear on one side. Season the second side of the patty.

4. When the patties are almost done cooking, it's time to add cheese. Use an upside down drinking glass or a biscuit/cookie cutter to cut large sandwich-sized slices down to slider-sized cheese slices. To each patty, add one slice of cheddar, one slice of provolone, one slice of baby Swiss, and top with one final slice of cheddar.

5. Add two crossed strips of bacon. Use the Blackstone 12" Round Basting Cover to quickly melt the cheese.

6. Slice pretzel slider rolls in two. Place rolls (both crowns and heels) upside down on the griddle top. Check rolls frequently to assure they get toasted golden brown.

7. Top the burger with classic yellow mustard, serve, and enjoy!

RECIPE INDEX

3 Simple Burger Sauces 107

A
Air Fried Beef Tacos 117
Air Fryer Buffalo Cauliflower 100
Air Fryer Homemade Sweet And Savory Tortilla Chips 34
Air Fryer Spinach, Feta, And Sun-dried Tomato Stuffed Chicken 60
Air Fryer Stuffed French Toast 95
Airfryer Biscuits And Maple Sausage Gravy 76
Airfryer Blackberry Scones 119
Airfryer Mini Spinach And Cheese Quiche 59
Airfryer Oreos 16
Airfryer Sausage Pancake Muffins 27
Airfryer Strawberry Hand Pies 107
Airy Fryer Breakfast Biscuit Bombs 62
Amaretto Brioche French Toast With Chocolate Syrup 52
Amish Onion Patties 74
Apple Stuffed French Toast With Bourbon Caramel Sauce 68
Arugula And Prosciutto Pizza With Balsamic Reduction 130

B
Bacon Blue Cherry Brussels 57
Bacon Cheese Burger Dogs 30
Bacon Cheese Burger With Coriander Pickled Red Onions & Smoky Mayo 30
Bacon Cheeseburger Quesadillas 131
Bacon Chicken Party Dip 90
Bacon Fried Corn 2.0 135
Bacon Fried Corn 3.0 45
Bacon Fried Rice With Spicy Mayo 106
Bacon Jalapeño Corn Fritters 130
Bacon Jalapeño Popper Burger 139
Bacon Pancakes With Strawberry Whiskey Syrup And Whipped Cream 89
Bacon Popcorn 109
Bacon Wrapped Beer Battered Deep Fried Pickles 74
Bacon, Egg, And Cheese Pancake Sliders 44
Bananas Foster 110
Bbq Chicken Bacon Pizza 46
Bbq Chicken Cheesesteaks 136
Bbq Chicken Stir-fry 63
Bbq Reuben Pork Sandwich 56
Beer Battered Fish & Chips 54
Beer Braised Bratwurst 18
Betty Springs Chicken 21
Betty's Bite Sized Chinese Meatballs 66
Betty's Italian Cutlets 64
Betty's Shrimp Fried Rice 34
Betty's Thyme Wings 25
Betty's Upside Down Pizza 121
Betty's Bigger Better Crab Bahms 25
Bettys Buffalo Chicken Cheesesteaks 22
Betty's Burrata Sandwiches 94
Betty's Ricotta Doughnuts 92
Black Bean Triangle Bites 16
Blackstone Airfryer Pork Egg Rolls 99
Blackstone Betty's Blackstone Airfryer Cannolis 71
Blt Hot Dogs With The Blackstone Air Fryer Combo 83
Blue Cheese Burgers 23
Bonzai Pipeline Tacos 40
Boston Cream Pie Pancakes 103
Bourbon Berry Lemonade 138
Breakfast Sausage & Egg Baskets 85
Bruschetta Crostini 121
Brussels Sprouts With Dried Cranberries 42
Buffalo Blue Cheese Chicken Balls 82
Buffalo Chicken Fritters 53
Buffalo Ranch Chicken Flatbread 37
Buffalo-sriracha Ranch Chicken Sandwich 120
Butte Montana Style Beef & Pork Pasty 38
Butter Bathed Filet And Lobster Surf & Turf 33
Buttermilk Bathed Rosemary Chicken Thighs 92
Buttermilk Pancakes 72
Buttermilk Syrup 59

C
California-style Salmon Tacos 69
Caramelized Grilled Pineapple 47
Caribbean Jerk Chicken 141
Caribbean Jerk Vegetables 89
Carne Asada Fajitas 18

Cashew Chicken Stir Fry 36
Cheese Chicken Sandwiches 52
Cheese Sausage Stuffing Balls 135
Cheese Steak Egg Rolls 125
Cheesechicken Sandwiches 128
Cheesesteak Pasta 17
Cherries Jubilee 84
Chicken Bruschetta 48
Chicken Caesar Salad 20
Chicken Cordon Bleu 27
Chicken Enchiladas 102
Chicken Parmesan Ranch Sandwich 52
Chicken Piccata Pasta 78
Chicken Sausage & Vegetable Stir Fry 35
Chicken Steak & Vegetable Hibachi 107
Chicken Stir Fry Noodles 39
Chili Lime Chicken Fajitas 72
Chili-mojo Steak Kebabs 123
Chocolate Greek Yogurt Pancakes 99
Chorizo Breakfast Hash 79
Cinnamon Apple 91
Cj's Rooty Tooty Fresh And Fruity Breakfast 66
Classic Margherita Pizza 60
Corn Bread Thanksgiving Stuffing 95
Corn Crab & Cheddar Fritters 37
Corn Fritters 75
Country Western Burger 133
Crab Cakes With Grapefruit Salad 50
Crabby Melts 134
Cranberry Brussel Sprouts With Pistachios & Parmesan 29
Cranberry Jalapeño Sausage Stuffing 54
Cream Filling For Crepes 16
Crepes 36
Crispy Asian Broccoli 98
Crispy Buffalo Cauliflower 132
Crispy Cod 82
Crispy Salmon Belly Salad With Honey Soy Glazed Shiitakes And Arugula 97
Crispy Smashed Potatoes With Bacon And Cilantro 77
Crispy Steak Bites 58
Crispy Sweet Potato Cubes With Cinnamon 123
Croque Madame 86
Croque Monsieur 127
Crunchy Crab Melts 58

E
Easy 5 Ingredient Air Fried Calzones 108
Easy Cinnamon Roll Bites 98
Elevated Avocado Toast 32
Elotte 125
Enchiladas 119

F
Fajitas 41
Fall Harvest French Toast 87
Family-style Mussels With Red Sauce 139
Flank Steak With Chimichurri Sauce 73
Fluffy Protein Pancakes 91
Fried Green Tomatoes 44
Frito Bandito 46
Funfetti Pancakes 137
Funnel Cake Swirls 37

G
Garlic Parmesan Potatoes 141
Garlic Parmesan Zucchini 94
Garlic Shrimp With Ponzu Rice 24
Garlic Soy Pork Chops 83
Garlicky Sesame Teriyaki Yaki Soba Noodles 131
Ginger & Soy Glazed Salmon With Asian Green Beans 104
Gochujang Sticky Steak Bites 41
Gouda Ale Sliders 81
Greek Gyros (pork Or Chicken) 103
Greek Turkey Burger 87
Greek Tzatziki Sauce 76
Green Chile Chicken Quesadilla 90
Griddle Chili Dogs 79
Griddle Girl Air Fryer Apple Fries 78
Griddle Girl Air Fryer Cinnamon Apple Pie Cups 114
Griddle Girl Breakfast Pancake Tacos 123
Griddled Banana Bread With Cream Cheese Glaze And Candied Bacon 39
Griddled Chicken Street Tacos 65
Griddled Frozen Pina Colada 102
Griddled Grapefruit Shandy 70
Griddled Peaches 23
Griddled Pineapple And Ice Cream 44
Grilled Chicken And Roasted Red Pepper Sandwiches With Fontina Cheese 140
Grilled Corn Salad 138
Grilled Shrimp & Arugula Salad 51

Grilled Vegetable Italian Quinoa Bowl 42
Ground Turkey Taco Stir Fry 82

H
Halloween Buffalo Chicken "pumpkins" 98
Ham Fried Rice 29
Hawaiian Chicken Skewers 28
Hawaiian Mac Salad 142
Hawaiian Meat Marinade And Sauce For Chicken Or Pork 91
Healthy Pineapple Chicken 128
Honey Garlic Chicken Skewers 33
Hot Honey Tequila Lime Slaw 126
Hot Italian Sausage Rigatoni In Red Sauce 134
How To Make Crepes 48
Huckleberry Pancakes 68

I
Italian Sausage And Cheese 111

J
Jalapeno Cheese Crisps 101
Jalapeño Popper Quesadilla 133
Jamaican Jerk Seasoning 65
Jambalaya 115
Johnny Cakes With Bourbon Salted Caramel Sauce 96
Juicy Lucy Bacon Burger 24

K
Korean Fire Chicken Lettuce Wraps 47

L
Lamb Lollipops With Mint Chimichurri 106
Lamb Tacos 128
Lemon Blueberry Pancakes 22
Loaded Bloody Marys 108
Loaded Italian Pork Sandwiches 70
Lo-country Broil 136

M
Mango Tango Turkey Burger 49
Maple Glazed Green Beans 48
Maple Sausage Sweet Potato Hash 113
Margarita 31
Margherita Grilled Cheese 120
Marinated Balsamic Pork Chops 69
Marinated Caprese Chicken 133
Marinated Cauliflower Steaks And Veggies 110
Marinated Flat Iron Steak 59
Marinated Lamb Chops 129
Marinated Steak Tips 137
Mediterranean Pork Kabobs 40
Mexican Breakfast Molletes 80
Mini Beef Wellingtons 35
Mini Chicken Pot Pies 60
Mini Ham And Cheddar Quiche Cups 124
Mongolian Chicken Lettuce Wraps 95
Mozzarella En Carrozza 138
Muffuletta Panini 21

N
Nate's Favorite Breakfast Sammich 45
New Mexico Breakfast Quesadillas 143
New York Style Pizza Dough (cold Rise) 76
New York Style Pizza Dough (fast Rise) 27

O
Octopus 47
Oklahoma Fried Onion Burgers 31
Olive Oil Flatbread 77
Onchos 68
Onion Mushroom Bbq Swiss Burger 117

P
Pancake Kabobs 81
Pancetta Green Beans With Shitakes And Cranberries 40
Parmesan Crisp Bruschetta 103
Pasta Primavera 97
Pastrami Cheese Burger With Smack Sauce 130
Patty Melt 19
Peach Bourbon Cocktail 122
Peanut Butter & Banana Crepes 92
Pepperoni Pizza 77
Pesto Ranch Chicken Sandwich 142
Pesto-ranch Chicken Artichoke Flatbread 115
Philly Cheesesteak 56
Pickle Brined Chicken Sandwich 26
Pickle Chic Sandwiches 88
Pineapple And Pork French Toast 116
Pineapple Chicken And Adobo Crunchwraps 122
Pineapple Chicken Quesadillas 126
Pita Bread / Flat Bread 100
Pizza Cheesesteak 28
Pomegranate Soy Glazed Lamb Chops 114
Pork Cutlets 80

Portobello Mushrooms 55
Pretzel Sliders 143
Pulled Pork Breakfast Tacos 66

Q
Quick Collards 64

R
Ramen Burger 55
Reversed Sear Ribeye With Smoked Garlic, Zucchini, And Squash 93
Ricotta Lemon Griddle Cakes 54
Rosemary Garlic Potatoes 61

S
S'mores Mini Pies 41
Salmon Potato And Brussel Sprout Boats 132
Salmon Street Taco 70
Salmon Tacos With Avocado & Corn Salsa 112
Salmon With Honey Soy Glaze 53
Sausage And Sage Thanksgiving Stuffing 43
Sausage Gravy Breakfast Totchos 26
Sautéed Garlic Green Beans 99
Savory Candied Sweet Potatoes 85
Scrapple And Eggs Breakfast Flatbread 111
Seared Ahi Tuna 127
Seared Garlic Ribeye With Carrots, Asparagus, And Gremolata 129
Sesame Seared Ahi Tuna 124
Shiitake And Asparagus Risotto With Seared Salmon 118
Shiitake Cranberry Green Beans 142
Shrimp Lejon With Thousand Island Dressing 46
Shrimp Scampi 84
Slammin' Cajun Salmon 62
S'mores Pancakes 88
Spicy Griddle Pineapple Margarita 49
Spinach Omelette 51
Steak Frites 2-ways 23
Steak, Arugula, Pear & Balsamic Flatbread 113
Steakhouse Classic 112
Steamed Ranch Carrots 61
Strawberries And Cream Pancakes 57
Street Tacos With Pineapple Pickled Jalapeno Peppers 43

Stuffed French Toast 32
Sweet & Spicy Parmesan Pickle Chips 72
Sweet And Spicy Mexican Chicken 30
Sweet Dessert Sandwich 61
Sweet Potato & Black Bean Burritos 126
Sweet Potato Pizza 93
Sweet Spicy Bang Bang Shrimp 101
Sweetbabytots 119

T
Taco Salad 137
Tacos Borrachos 17
Tamari Ponzu Salmon With Sweet Chili Broccoli And Potato Crisps 75
Tequila Chicken Skewers 20
Tequila Party Cake 71
Teriyaki Beef Kabobs 100
Thai Chicken Quesadillas 118
Thai Kai Chicken Sliders 19
Thai Style Beef Souvlaki With Peanut Sauce 19
Thai Sweet Chili Chicken Pizza 78
Thanksgiving Leftovers Grilled Cheese Sandwich 67
Thanksgiving Turkey Breast 63
The Better Mac 105
The Lippy Spritz Cocktail 92
Tomatillos Avocado Salsa Fresca 27
Tomato Salad 87
Tumeric Cauliflower 50
Turkey Party Pita Pockets 32
Twice Cooked Griddle Baked Potatoes 73

U
Ultimate Breakfast Platter 55

W
Whiskey-honey Salmon With Cajun Stir Fried Rice 96
Wild Caught Jumbo Scallops With Shredded Sprouts & Prosciutto 86

Z
Zesty Chicken Caesar Sticks 140
Zucchini & Squash 109
Zucchini Fritters 116
Zucchini Pizza Bites 23

www.ingramcontent.com/pod-product-compliance
Lightning Source LLC
Chambersburg PA
CBHW081414080526
44589CB00016B/2534